GARLAND STUDIES ON

INDUSTRIAL PRODUCTIVITY

edited by

STUART BRUCHEY
ALLAN NEVINS PROFESSOR EMERITUS
COLUMBIA UNIVERSITY

A GARLAND SERIES

LABOR'S POWER AND INDUSTRIAL PERFORMANCE

AUTOMOBILE PRODUCTION REGIMES IN THE U.S., GERMANY, AND JAPAN

STAVROS P. GAVROGLOU

GARLAND PUBLISHING, INC.
A MEMBER OF THE TAYLOR & FRANCIS GROUP
NEW YORK & LONDON / 1998

Library of Congress Cataloging-in-Publication Data

Gavroglou, Stavros P., 1959–
Labor's power and industrial performance : automobile
production regimes in the U.S., Germany, and Japan / Stavros
Gavroglou.
       p.   cm. — (Garland studies on industrial productivity)
Includes bibliographical references and index.
ISBN 0-8153-3244-0 (alk. paper)
1. Trade-unions—Automobile industry workers—United
States. 2. Trade-unions—Automobile industry workers—Ger-
many. 3. Trade-unions—Automobile industry workers—Japan.
4. Automobile industry and trade—Labor productivity—United
States. 5. Automobile industry and trade—Labor productivity—
Germany. 6. Automobile industry and trade—Labor productiv-
ity—Japan. I. Title. II. Series.
HD6515.A8G38 1998
331.88'1292—dc21

                                                      98-37453

Printed on acid-free, 250-year-life paper
Manufactured in the United States of America

Contents

Acknowledgments

I dedicate this work to the memory of my father, Paris, and to that remarkable pillar of strength and inspiration, my mother, Sophia.

I thank Mark Kesselman of Columbia University for his intellectual leadership, and the C.U.N.Y. Center for Labor-Management Policy Studies for backing my research during its difficult initial stages. Special thanks are due to Mata, George, and to all those in New York and in Athens who enlivened my Spartan life during the long years of this project.

Labor's Power and Industrial Performance

CHAPTER 1

Introduction

Labor's Power and Industrial Performance in Comparative Perspective

THE PROBLEM

Why were American unions unable to prevent the erosion of wages and the loss of hundreds of thousands of good jobs in the 1980s?

Is industrial competitiveness in a global economy compatible with strong unions?

What led American industrial companies, long the envy of the rest of the world, to emulate many of the production methods of their foreign rivals? Has labor been similarly hurt by international competition and technological change elsewhere? Is the competitive success of foreign companies based on low-wage production or on "smarter," more participatory methods of organizing production? Are Japanese and German industrial relations so different from each other, or is there a common basis for their competitive success? Do the recent changes in labor-management relations in the US auto industry represent a promising new departure for labor or the certification of its demise?

The analytic framework of production politics developed here is an effort to answer the above questions, by illuminating the relationship between labor's power in production and industrial performance. Narrowing the field of analysis to the automobile production regimes of the US, Germany, and Japan, from the 1950s to the early-1990s,[1] it will be argued that important variations in labor's fortunes and competitive success among these regimes can be explained by the **distinct patterns**

of labor inclusion in corporate decision making that define each regime. The thesis of this book is that the integration of labor's interests in corporate decision making is an important determinant of the production regime's performance and of labor's fortunes therein. The (relative) integration of capital's and labor's interests around production facilitates the integration of their functions in production, and results in more equitable and efficient production regimes.

THE THEORETICAL CONTEXT

Given our concern with American labor's fortunes in a global economy, focussing our inquiry on the relationship between industrial relations and industrial performance is quite appropriate. Certainly, labor's fortunes are not determined solely by industrial relations. State policy, for example, may even shape the framework of industrial relations itself, by altering the content, interpretation, or enforcement of labor law—how labor and capital are organized, the scope of bargaining, role of arbitration and courts, regulation of strikes, property and citizenship/workplace rights.[2] State policy may also affect industrial relations by shaping the environment in which the social actors operate—capital markets,[3] and labor's degree of dependence on capital for survival.[4]

While we remain aware of such influences on industrial relations, we believe that the conceptual loss involved in narrowing the scope of our inquiry to labor's power in corporate governance is small. Well-researched influences on labor's fortunes that originate outside industrial relations are not likely to be lost in the confines of our analysis, even if they are not addressed directly. We focus on industrial relations as a proximate determinant of labor's fortunes, not as the only one.

Moreover, industrial relations offers a unique domain where labor, simultaneously, is constituted as such, creates value, and (potentially) re-constitutes itself. In other words, industrial relations allows us to examine what it actually means to be a worker (the obligations and rights pertaining to labor in production), how effective such a worker is in production (performance), and how human beings occasionally change the conditions that define them (human agency in history).

It is widely accepted that being a world-class producer requires continuous adaptation to changing market conditions. Appropriate industrial relations is a critical component of such adaptability. Thus, while industrial, fiscal, and trade policy may also facilitate such adaptability and competitiveness, they do so largely through their effects on production. Thus industrial relations, while not insulated from such influences, is a critical testing ground for the viability of diverse forms of social organization and political orientation.

Comparative industrial relations has gained a heightened significance for political economy in recent years, as globalization has put various national configurations of organizing production in direct interaction with each other. The intensification of international competition has rendered developments in each national production regime more consequential for the others than ever before. While the social actors shaping a country's production regime continue to be national, the proving ground of a production regime is becoming increasingly international. Success or failure is no longer established on the basis of a regime's past performance, but relative to the performance of other regimes competing in a global economy.

At the outset of our inquiry into the link between industrial relations and industrial performance in a cross-national and cross-cultural setting, we are alerted to the need to reexamine the assumptions and definitions of key categories of analysis, such as labor's power and industrial performance. Without such re-conceptualization, the accumulated knowledge and intellectual instruments developed in a specific historical/cultural context might prove to have limited "travelling power" across others, and thus prevent us from appreciating the true bases of strength and weakness of less familiar industrial relations systems. We develop our analytic framework of production politics by drawing critically from the following three perspectives on the relationship between industrial relations and industrial performance: control/regulation of labor, organizational efficiency, flexibility. These perspectives are presented more fully in Chapter 2.

Control/Regulation of Labor

These closely related approaches view industrial relations as power relations that stem from and maintain capitalist class relations.[5] Accordingly, the capitalist imperative to control labor during the labor process, or, more broadly, to regulate industrial relations according to the needs of a phase/type of accumulation, is a more fundamental motive force behind a capitalist industrial relations regime than maximizing production efficiency.[6] Transformations in capitalist production regimes, even when they appear to entail advances for labor, are likely to mask deeper structures of capitalist domination of labor: wage increases are accompanied by deskilling, the further separation of conception and execution, and alienation; while collective bargaining rights flourish only as long as they serve capital's need for demand stimulation.[7]

The undisputable contribution of this perspective to our understanding of labor-capital relations in production notwithstanding, we find its functionalist mode of reasoning problematic. Its conceptual map makes it nearly impossible to identify instances of genuine advances in labor's power that fall outside the "needs" of the "phase of accumulation." As a consequence, the perspective tends to underestimate the extent and significance of actual reversals in deskilling and in the separation of conception and execution during the labor process. Moreover, its emphasis on capital's needs to control labor leads it to underestimate the significance of genuine performance-maximization concerns in the organization of modern capitalist production.

Organizational Efficiency

This approach's focus on the performance considerations behind industrial-relations or work-organization changes is particularly welcome, given today's intensely competitive context.[8] Comparing the competitive performance of different methods of production adopted by different capitalists is instructive of the range of possible ways of organizing production and labor-management relations. Unfortunately, however, authors in this approach ignore the insights of the control/regulation approach. Capital's methods in production are not adopted in a vacuum but in a social context and respective class formations. Writings in this approach do not sufficiency isolate the effects of certain "successful" production methods from the particular industrial relations context in which they are adopted.

Flexibility

Here we can distinguish three subdivisions, according to the meaning given to flexibility by different authors.

    (A) Flexible Specialization. One of the biggest contributions of this perspective is its formidable attack on notions of technological determinism in the study of industrial relations and performance.[9] In this

approach, a certain production system prevails in a certain historical period not because it is the "one best method" of organizing production given the level of technological development, but because of its "fit" with conjunctural circumstances as well as with tactical choices (and hedges) made by historical actors. Even within the limits of capitalism, the domination of the mass production paradigm in the 20th century was not technologically predicated—nor is it now.

However, formulations in this perspective of alternatives to mass production tend to be excessively ambiguous. "Flexible specialization," becomes a "catch-all concept—open, indeterminate, and unspecified, [often changing its] meaning to fit new situations"[10] Moreover, despite the stated intentions of some of its authors, the flexibility perspective limits the role of selecting/constructing a production paradigm to the considerations/choices of capitalists, the state, to markets, and to historical accident—while largely ignoring labor as a social and historical agent.

(B) Flexible Democratic Centralism. Most welcome is these authors' attention to labor's contribution in the making of production regimes, particularly that of postwar Germany.[11] Most original is their identification of labor's power as an ingredient of equity as well as of efficacy, albeit only under conditions of social-democracy or, in some formulations, of neo-corporatist articulation of capital and labor (and the state).[12]

Unfortunately, however, they see the compatibility of labor's power and industrial performance as necessarily embedded in a social-democratic or corporatist context. While this is plausible in comparisons among many Western production regimes, it becomes less pertinent when we consider the case of Japan, or even of the post-1984 US auto industry. The approach is ill-at-ease to explain how, despite the complete absence of social-democratic or neo-corporatist arrangements in these two cases, labor there has fared better than in some more social-democratic/neo-corporatist contexts (such as the pre-Thatcher United Kingdom and France).

Thus, Wolfgang Streeck's impressive argument that German labor's strength, far from impeding, has contributed to the German auto industry's remarkable recovery from the crisis of the mid-1970s, ends up with a disappointing theorization of a "functional equivalence" between strong-labor and weak-labor possibilities of industrial success. Left unexplored is the functional equivalence between different **forms** of labor's power and industrial success. Lowell Turner's otherwise most welcome effort to link industrial democracy with industrial performance through a US-German comparison is also not entirely satisfactory. It is thwarted by its lack of consideration of the industrial performance of the two regimes. Turner also seems to underestimate the gains of American labor through Jointness, as he fails to identify what distinguishes this regime from the traditional American regime it replaced. Moreover, he orients his effort in testing an unexciting (if not tautological) central hypothesis: that (corporatist) industrial relations in Germany display more inter-plant uniformity than (pluralist) industrial relations in the US.

(C) Flexible Integration. What is most refreshing in this perspective is the allocation of more than a passive role to labor in the making of a production regime, particularly that of Japan. In contrast to the views of the control/regulation and of the social-democratic perspectives, Japanese industrial success is seen as closely related to the integration of employment stability and continuous training/reskilling into corporate decision making. Analyses in this perspective range from historical ones, such as Lazonick's and Kenney and Florida's, to game-theoretic ones, such as Aoki's.[13]

Through different methodologies, authors in this perspective argue that horizontal coordination of production units, traditionally considered an impediment to effective managerial control and corporate performance, offers the requisite flexibility to compete in world markets. The integration, as opposed to segmentation/compartmentalisation, of conception and execution, of coordination and operative functions, and, ultimately, of labor and management personnel, is not only more equitable but also leads to higher levels of industrial performance, in large measure by enabling a more flexible allocation of corporate resources. Higher levels of training, broader worker skills, and higher levels of mutual commitment between labor and management are among the key factors identified as contributing to said levels of flexibility and industrial success.

Authors in this perspective, however, are too hesitant to apply their insights to a better understanding of Western production regimes, and when they do they are not altogether convincing. Kenney and Florida, for example, fail to consider the relationship between labor's power and industrial performance in Germany, in part because they compare Japan to an amalgam of "European" production regimes—lumping together regimes as disparate as those of Germany, France, and Britain.

Lazonick and Aoki, for their part, refrain from exploring forms of flexible integration that diverge from the Japanese model, such as that of German codetermination.

Production Politics: Framework and Hypotheses

Building on the insights and steering away from the limitations of the above perspectives, we have developed a framework of analysis of industrial relations which we call **production politics**. It is a framework for cross-national analysis of industrial relations that focusses on the relationship between relations **of** production and relations **in** production.[14] It is an analytic framework that allows us to identify distinct modes of labor inclusion in the production regime and distinct patterns of industrial performance, as well as to develop hypotheses about the relationship between labor inclusion and regime performance.

While the framework of production politics is developed fully in the next chapter, it would be useful here to define its main components (see Table 1).

By **relations** of and in production we refer to the pattern of association, relative segregation or integration, between the owners of the means of production (capital, management) and the operators of the means of production (labor, unions). By relations **of** production we refer to the organization of the fundamental **interests** of capital and labor concerning production.

By relations **in** production we refer to the organization of **functions** which capital (management) and labor perform during production.

Labor's fundamental interests are distinguishable into two broad areas, redistributive and productivist interests, which correspond to redistributive and productivist decisions confronting producers. The former are decisions pertaining to how the produced wealth is to be redistributed among those involved in its production, while productivist decisions pertain to how the wealth is to be produced in the first place (choice of product, process, workforce). Labor's redistributive interests denote primarily wages; redistributive interests may also refer to administrative rationality (as opposed to capriciousness or nepotism) in

Table 1: Production Regimes of Labor Inclusion

Organization of interests of labor and capital	Segregation	Integration / \	
		Representative	Incorporative
—basis of labor's inclusion	exit	exit voice	exit fusion
—scope of labor's inclusion (issues)	redistributive	redistributive productivist	redistributive productivist
Organization of functions of labor and capital			
—labor's functions in production	execution	execution conception	execution conception
—contribution of labor to performance	indirect	direct	direct
Cases	pre-1984 USA	Germany	Japan

discipline and promotions. Labor's productivist interests denote primarily employment stability; productivist interests may also refer to industrial performance and reskilling (which contribute to employment stability).[15] It must be added that job classifications, work rules, and seniority-based layoff procedures, often referred to as an expression of workers' control, do not represent labor's ability to secure its productivist interests. Rather, as with disciplinary regulations, they must be seen as mechanisms for defending labor's redistributive interests by stabilizing the effort-reward ratio and preventing indirect ways of punishing union activists.

While the division of labor under capitalism inevitably differentiates the functions of labor from management's, there can be distinct types of differentiation. Labor-management segregation in production refers to the traditional American type of functional differentiation, whereby labor's functions are narrowly defined and strictly isolated from managerial functions—wherein the conception-execution divide is wide and deep. Labor-management integration in production refers to less familiar types, whereby labor's functions are broader, often approximating supervisory or coordinating functions— wherein the conception-execution divide, while there, is somehow bridged.

Labor's inclusion in corporate decision making can be distinguished into two distinct types, segregated inclusion and integrated inclusion. **Segregated inclusion** refers to production regimes where, labor is included only as an actor *a priori* different from and subordinate to capital ("hired help"), and where only labor's redistributive interests, in isolation from productivist ones, are reflected in corporate decision making. Segregated inclusion regimes result from the institutionalization only of labor's exit-power. In **integrated inclusion** regimes, labor is considered part of the firm itself and thus given relatively ample access in and influence over redistributive as well as productivist decisions. Integrated inclusion regimes result from the institutionalization of labor's exit-power, but also its voice-power (where labor is considered a "junior partner," as in Germany) or its fusion power (where labor is considered a "tenured member," as in Japan).

As the various formulations of the flexibility perspective indicate, functional integration of management and labor, in contrast to the fordist view, is quite possible in advanced capitalism—despite the risks it involves for capital in control over the labor process. It is becoming evident that functional integration is a critically important element of world-class industrial production. In previous periods, capital could avoid functional integration in favor of a less efficient but more profitable process of functional segregation. However, if efficiency could be sacrificed in favor of control within a national setting of a previous period, that is much less feasible in a contemporary context of intense competition with foreign producers that have adopted functional integration. But, it must also be stressed, switching from functional segregation to functional integration does not only involve a change in mindset, an overcoming of the taboo of endowing workers with more initiative and discretion during production. Functional integration is unlikely to take root unless it is accompanied by interest integration. Relations in production are anchored on relations of production.

The affinity of interest and functional integration stems from two sets of considerations. First, from the perspective of capitalists habituated to operate in a context of interest and functional segregation, a shift to functional integration does not appear to be absolutely necessary. Profits can be maintained or increased in face of intensified competition without having to grant labor more skills and authority to improve industrial performance. Instead, capital can adopt production methods whose costs are "externalized" to, and borne by labor, most famously through variants of the hire-and-fire method (de-industrializing, downsizing, outsourcing, part-time employment). Capital can do this inasmuch as, in segregation regimes, labor's interests are not included in productivist decisions. By contrast, in integrated inclusion regimes, such wasteful practices are less likely, inasmuch as labor's interests are included in productivist decision making.

As a corollary, capital in integrated inclusion regimes (i.e. in a context of interest integration), bereft of the option of (socially) wasteful profit-maintenance or profit-enhancement methods, must rely exclusively on enhancing industrial performance by genuinely reducing production costs, not only to itself but to the regime as a whole. Thus under more pressure form labor for genuine improvements in industrial performance, capital in a context of interest integration is more likely to adopt genuinely innovative methods that improve industrial performance, including the solicitation of labor's active cooperation in improving industrial performance through functional integration. In such regimes, capital is in fact likely to solicit labor's active cooperation in improving production, despite the fact that such an upgraded role for labor involves training costs for capital and the loss of some control over the labor process to labor: unable to simply "shed redundant labor" during cyclical or seasonal downturns, capital finds that investing in the reskilling of and the solicitation of the active support by such workforce is ultimately well worth it cost.

Second, in integrated inclusion regimes, the integration of labor's redistributive and productivist interests with the firm's constitutes a direct inducement for labor to actively cooperate with capital to enhance industrial performance. By contrast, in segregated inclusion labor has little if any stake in actively cooperating in efforts to enhance productivity, as the latter may even prove directly inimical to labor's productivist interests (layoffs). In fact, in the absence of interest integration, attempts at functional integration are likely to flounder, because labor is likely to try to use any degree of discretion it has on the shop floor not in order to enhance productivity (in which it has no stake) but in order to minimize the work effort. This point is aptly illustrated in the following account from an earlier period, which is worth quoting at some length:

> A Mexican in a large [U.S.] automobile factory was giving the final tightening to the nuts on automobile-engine cylinder heads. There are a dozen or more nuts around this part. The engines passed the Mexican rapidly on a conveyor. His instructions were to test all the nuts and if he found *one* or *two* loose to tighten them, but if three or more were loose he was not expected to have time to tighten that many. In such cases he marked the engine with chalk and it was later set aside from the conveyor and given special attention. The superintendent found that the number of engines so set aside reached an annoying total in the day's work. He made several unsuccessful attempts to locate the trouble. Finally, by carefully watching all the men on the conveyor line, he discovered that the Mexican was unscrewing a *third* tight nut whenever he found two already loose. It was easier to loosen *one* nut than to tighten *two*.[16]

Labor's power refers to labor's ability to secure its interests. I am using "power" in Weber's sense, as

> the probability that one actor within a social relationship will be in a position to carry out his own will despite resistance.[17]

To the extent to which the satisfaction of labor's interests depends on more or less labor-friendly corporate decisions, labor's power is directly related to labor's ability to secure the inclusion of its interests in the decision making calculus of the firm. Thus, depending on which type of labor's interests are at stake, labor's power is distinguished into redistributive power and productivist power. Further, labor's power is differentiated according to the way in which (or the resource on the basis on which) labor influences corporate decision making. Exit-power refers to labor's ability to affect corporate decision making by (the threat of) bringing production to a halt (against capital's wishes) by striking; it is usually applied to secure the inclusion of labor's redistributive interests. Voice-power refers to labor's ability to include its redistributive as well as productivist interests by gaining formal representation and voting power in the decision making forums of the firm. Fusion-power also refers to the ability to defend redistributive as well as productivist decisions, by incorporating labor into, or making it inseparable from, the body of the firm.[18]

This book examines three central hypotheses derived from the above typology of production regimes, exploring the relationship bewteen labor's power and to industrial performance in the automobile industries of the U.S., Germany and Japan. The direction of causation between the mode of labor inclusion in the production regime, on the one hand, and labor's power and the regime's performance will not be tested directly, but will be inferred form the findings of the three hypotheses.

Hypothesis I: In regimes of integrated inclusion labor has more power than in regimes of segregated inclusion.

Hypothesis II: In regimes of integrated inclusion industrial performance is stronger than in regimes of segregated inclusion.

Hypothesis III: The transformation of production regimes of segregated inclusion into regimes of integrated inclusion is accompanied by an increase in labor's (productivist) power, as well as an improvement in industrial performance.

RESEARCH STRATEGY AND DESIGN

The three hypotheses above can be tested by comparing the evolution of industrial relations and industrial performance of the automobile industry in the US, Germany and Japan, from the mid-1970s to the mid-1990s.

An obvious limitation of this strategy is the small number of the cases (three countries). Elementary statistical knowledge suggests that even if the relationship between the variables examined is shown to be consistent with what we hypothesized, a causal argument is harder to make the fewer the number of cases examined. Given the impracticality of including more cases, however, this is a limitation we must live with. We expect this weakness to be somewhat mitigated, by showing that the relationship observed among the variables holds over a large number of years. Moreover, the cases of the auto industries of the U.S., Germany, and Japan, were not selected randomly, nor because they confirmed they hypotheses. Rather, they were selected as the three largest auto industries of the world, embedded in the largest national economies of the world, that can be viewed as Weberian ideal types of the distinct regimes they represent.

The main purpose of focussing on **a single industry** is to control for the significant, "independent" effects of the nature of the product or of capital intensity on the labor process and thus on industrial relations and performance.

We have decided on a **cross-national** analysis, because we expect that intra-national differences in labor's power in corporate decision making and in levels of industrial performance (within the same industry but across firms) to be possibly too small to discern. Cross-plant or cross-firm differences, even if they are discernable, are still hard to ascribe, given the plethora of structural, conjunctural, and even personal influences that are of consequence at such lower level of abstraction.

Several considerations guide our **choice of industry**. First, because the auto industry is among the oldest industries in each country under consideration, its industrial relations are highly institutionalized and well-enough defined. This makes it easier to discern patterns of industrial relations and industrial performance and identify similarities and differences among the three countries. Second, the similarly high degree of unionization in the auto industry of each country, allows us to control for union density as a dimension of labor's power, and thus to focus on less studied, more subtle determinants/dimensions of labor's power. Third, the auto industry is of the highest importance for each national economy and has been a pace-setter for its national industrial relations. Thus, while each country's auto industry is hardly representative of the other industries in the nation, it can be argued that it is at least a very consequential and indicative case of the dynamics of labor-management relations in the respective economy.

Our focus on **aggregate** industry measures and characteristics is certainly not cost-free. Cross-national comparisons of whole industries are likely to obscure intra-industry variations (across firms and/or across sectors). We expect, however, based on our preliminary research, that the magnitude of intra-industry variations to be small compared to cross-national variations.

Similarly, our focus on aggregate data, particularly in reference to labor's contribution to industrial performance and to labor's fortunes, may abstract too much from concrete workers. There is certainly a price to be paid for our aggregate approach. We expect this price to entail loss in detail, nuance, and narrative vitality. We adopt it, however, in an effort to generalize from concrete workers' and unions' orientations towards, and experiences from their production regime, not in order to ignore them. Far from denying the contribution of human agency in institutional structures and outcomes, our research strategy is aimed at assessing workers' collective impact on the production regime, as well as the production regime's impact on workers's lives.

The **choice of countries**, given a cross-national comparison of auto industries, is easy to justify. By any account, the US, Germany, and Japan are the three top auto producers in the world, and the three largest national economies in the world; thus the conclusions of our analysis would be highly relevant for advanced capitalist production. Moreover, the vast geo-political and historical differences among them are likely to have resulted in large and consequential variations in patterns of labor's power and of industrial performance. We treat the case of US autos more extensively than those of Germany and Japan for two reasons. The US case is at the center of our interest and the point of reference of our comparative analysis; and, unlike the other two cases, the American auto industry has experienced a significant transformation in the mid-1980s which requires further documentation and analysis.

The **time frame** is the period from the late-1960s to the early-1990s. More recent data, when available, are provided only indicatively. The Reunification of Germany strains the comparability of post-1991 data. It has put the German production regime under tremendous stress, altering key parameters such as labor supply, location of production, skill formation, work culture, etc. The focus of the analysis will be the decade of the 1980s, when international competition and technological diffusion intensified, while the hypothesized American regime transformation took place. case of Germany, data for the post-reunification period, when available, are not suitable for our comparative analysis. The Reunification of Germany puts its production regime under tremendous stress, altering key parameters such as labor supply, size of market, skill formation, work practices. The focus of the analysis will be the decade of the 1980s, when international competition and technological diffusion intensified, while the hypothesized American regime transformation took place.

Given the controversial nature of the concept of **labor's power** in corporate decision making, we assess it in each regime through two complementary types of evidence.

First, we analyze the institutional arrangements through which labor's redistributive and productivist power in corporate decision making is exercised in each regime. In this regard we examine the scope of corporate governance issues that are subject to labor's influence, and the mechanisms through which labor exercises such influence.

Secondly, in order to ascertain that our conceptualization of labor's power in each production regime is grounded in reality and not a mere abstraction, we analyze the substantive outcomes of each regime for labor's fundamental interests. Specifically, we distinguish between labor's redistributive and productivist interests, corresponding to parallel distinctions in the scope of labor influence in corporate decisions (redistributive and productivist power). We further stipulate, plausibly, that labor's redistributive and productivist interests are epitomized by total hourly compensation and annual employment stability, respectively; and thus we appropriately operationalize them as such.[19]

We propose to compare the **industrial performance** of the three production regimes through two complementary indicators, the annual balance of trade in automobiles and automobile reliability ratings. These indicators express consumer evaluations of the value and quality of the products of each regime. We arrive at these indicators because we find other, more widely used indicators of industrial performance, such as productivity and profitability, very misleading. The latter tell us more about how efficient the regime seems to capital than how efficient the production regime, which includes labor, actually is.[20] Thus, according to the widely used definitions of productivity as output per hour worked or per employee, the productivity of a regime would double if employment is cut in half, while the social costs of unemployment are left out of the calculation since they are not borne by the employer. Also a wage reduction or an incease in the rate of exploitation would also inflate the measure of productivity, while no real improvement in production may have been accomplished. Thus, we prefer to assess industrial performance through our two quantitative indicators of industrial performance in conjunction with a qualitative assessment of the social waste (and thus inefficiency) generated by each regime in the form, primarily, of employment instability.[21]

Chapter 2 develops more fully the framework of production politics outlined here, the theoretical and empirical literature that informs it, and the appropriateness of the measures of labor's power and regime performance adopted.

Chapter 3 analyzes the formation of the American auto production regime of segregated inclusion that was consolidated in the 1950s with the Treaty of Detroit. Chapter 4 analyzes the crisis of the US segregated inclusion in the 1970s, and its transformation into the hybrid regime of Jointness in the mid-1980s. Chapter 5 analyzes one variant of a regime of representative integration, the German auto production regime of labor representation, contrasting it to the American regime. Chapter 6 compares the other variant of integrated inclusion, the Japanese auto production regime of incorporative integration, against its American counterpart. The chapters on Germany and Japan, it must be noted, do not offer detailed historical accounts of the origins and historical forces behind these regimes; the emphasis, rather, is on delineating the distinct patterns of labor-capital relations and their consequences on labor's fortunes and industrial performance.

Chapter 7 brings the findings of chapters 4, 5, and 6 together in a three-way comparison of labor's power and efficiency in the auto production regimes of the U.S., Germany, and Japan. We summarize our findings and their fit with our hypotheses; we compare the strengths of our thesis against competing explanations of the observed relationships between labor's power and industrial performance; and we extract the implications of our findings for labor's position in contemporary political economy.

NOTES

1. Data-collection difficulties arising from our temporal proximity as well from the turmoil of the German reunification prevent us from extending the time frame of the analysis beyond the first years of the 1990s.

2. For a succinct discussion of the state-union relationship see Stephen Bornstein, "States and unions: from postwar settlement to contemporary stalemate", in S. Bornstein, D. Held and J. Krieger (eds), *The State in Capitalist Europe* (London: George Allen & Unwin, 1984). See also Michael Goldfield, *The Decline of Organized Labor in the United States* (Chicago: The University of Chicago Press, 1987).

3. George N. Hatsopoulos and Stephen H. Brooks, "The Gap in the Cost of Capital: Causes, Effects, and Remedies," in Ralph Landau and Dale W. Jorgenson (eds.) *Technology and Economic Policy* (Cambridge, Mass., 1986). For the significance of the relationship of financial capital to industrial capital for industrial relations see, Peter A. Hall, *Governing the Economy: The Politics of State Intervention in Britain and France* (New York: Oxford University Press, 1986).

4. The "cost of job loss," for example, is a composite measure of the effects of income support policies and economic activity on industrial relations; variations in the cost of job loss alter the power relations between labor and management by affecting a major determinant of management's authority in the workplace, the effectiveness of its ultimate sanction against labor, the termination of the labor contract. Juliet B. Schor and Samuel Bowles, "Employment Rents and the Incidence of Strikes," *Review of Economics & Statistics*, v. 69 no. 4 (November 1987). For an influential account of the impact of state policy on labor's and nations' fortunes see David R. Cameron, "Social Democracy, Corporatism, Labour Quiescence and the Representation of Economic Interest in Advanced Capitalist Society," in John H. Goldthorpe (ed) *Order and Conflict in Contemporary Capitalism* (New York: Oxford University Press, 1985).

5. Harry Braverman, *Labor and Monopoly Capital: The Degradation of Work in the Twentieth Century* (New York: Monthly Review Press, 1974); Richard Edwards, *Contested Terrain: The Transformation of the Workplace in the Twentieth Century* (New York: Basic Books, 1979); Samuel Bowles, David M. Gordon and Thomas Weiskopf, "Power and Profits: The Social Structure of Accumulation and the Profitability of the Postwar U.S. Economy," *Review of Radical Political Economics* (Spring-Summer 1986). Robert Boyer, *The Search for Labour Market Flexibility: The European Economies in Transition* (Oxford: Clarendon Press, 1988); Alain Lipietz, "Behind the Crisis: The Exhaustion of a Regime of Accumulation. A 'Regulation School' Perspective," *Review of Radical Political Economics*, (Spring and Summer 1986); Harley Shaiken, *Work Transformed: Automation and Labor in the Computer Age* (New York: Holt, Rinehart and Winston, 1984); Michael Burawoy, *The Politics of Production: Factory Regimes under Capitalism and Socialism* (London: Verso, 1985); Chris Howell, *Regulating Labor: The State and Industrial Relations Reform in Postwar France* (Princeton: Princeton University Press, 1992).

6. For a forceful exposition in this vein of the historical origins of the hierarchical factory system in early capitalism see Stephen A. Marglin, "What Do Bosses Do? The Origins and Functions of Hierarchy in Capitalist Production," *Review of Radical Political Economy* (Summer 1974).

7. Capital's collective needs are not obvious and even less obviously served by the policies of state. Thus state policy towards collective bargaining rights may reflect the state's autonomous macro-economic and political needs, which may or may not coincide with capital's. For this type of criticism of the "instrumentalist" view of the state's role in political economy see Peter B. Evans, Dietrich Rueschemeyer, Theda Skocpol (eds.) *Bringing the State Back In* (New York : Cambridge University Press, 1985).

8. Alfred D. Chandler, Jr., *Strategy and Structure: Chapters in the History of American Industrial Enterprise* (Cambridge, MA: MIT Press, 1962); Oliver E. Williamson, *The Economic Institutions of Capitalism* (Detroit: Free Press, 1985); Carliss Y. Baldwin and Kim B. Clark, "Capital-Budgeting Systems and Capabilities Investments in U.S. Companies After the Second World War," *Business History Review* (March 22, 1994).

9. Important works in this perspective include Michael J. Piore and Charles F. Sabel, *The Second Industrial Divide: Possibilities for Prosperity* (New York: Basic Books, 1984); John F. Krafcik, "Triumph of the Lean Production System," *Sloan Management Review* (Fall 1988). James P. Womack, Daniel T. Jones, and Daniel Roos, *The Machine that Changed the World: The Story of Lean Production* (New York: Harper Perennial, 1990).

10. Martin Kenney and Richard Florida, *Beyond Mass Production: the Japanese system and its Transfer to the U.S.* (New York: Oxford University Press, 1993), p. 26.

11. Wolfgang Streeck, "Neo-Corporatist Industrial Relations and the Economic Crisis in West Germany," in John H. Goldthorpe (ed.) *Order and Conflict in Contemporary Capitalism: Studies in the Political Economy of Western European Nations* (New York: Oxford University Press, 1984); ibid, "Successful Adjustment to Turbulent Markets: the Automobile Industry" in Peter J. Katzenstein (ed), *Industry and Politics in West Germany: Toward the Third Republic* (Ithaca, NY: Cornell University Press, 1989); Lowell Turner, *Democracy at Work: Changing World Markets and the Future of Labor Unions* (Ithaca, N.Y.: Cornell University Press, 1991); Kathleen Thelen, *Union of Parts: Labor Politics in Postwar Germany* (Ithaca, NY: Cornell University Press, 1991).

12. Major works in this perspective include Peter Lange, George Ross, and Maurizio Vannicelli, "Unions as Objects of History and Unions as Actors," in Lange, Ross, and Vannicelli (eds.), *Unions, Change and Crisis: French and Italian Union Strategy and the Political Economy, 1945-1980* (New York: Allen & Unwin, 1982); Wolfgang Streeck, "Neo-Corporatist Industrial Relations and the Economic Crisis in West Germany," in John H. Goldthorpe (ed.) *Order and Conflict in Contemporary Capitalism: Studies in the Political Economy of Western European Nations* (New York: Oxford University Press, 1984); idem, "Industrial Relations and Industrial Change: the Restructuring of the World Automobile Industry in the 1970s and 1980s," *Economic and Industrial Democracy*, vol. 8, 1987; Mike Parker and Jane Slaughter, *Choosing Sides: Unions and the Team Concept* (Boston: South End Press, 1988); Lowell Turner, *Democracy at Work: Changing World Markets and the Future of Labor Unions* (Ithaca, N.Y.: Cornell University Press, 1991); Kathleen Thelen, *Union*

of Parts: Labor Politics in Postwar Germany (Ithaca, NY: Cornell University Press, 1991).

13. See, for example, William Lazonick, "Value Creation on the Shop Floor: Skill, Effort, and Technology in U.S. and Japanese Manufacturing," Department of Economics, Barnard College, Columbia University, October 1988; Kenney and Florida (1993); Masahiko Aoki, *Information, Incentives, and Bargaining in the Japanese Economy* (New York: Cambridge University Press, 1988).

14. The distinction between relations of and relations in production belongs to Burawoy, for whom, however, the terms have a different meaning than here. For example, in Burawoy's usage, relations of production is a broader category, including contractual agreements between labor and capital but also the state's support or lack thereof for labor's reproduction. Michael Burawoy, *The Politics of Production: Factory Regimes under Capitalism and Socialism* (London: Verso, 1985).

15. Since we focus on labor's understated role in shaping a production regime, we pay only limited attention to the elements of capital's interests; they include profits (redistributive) and administrative discretion (productivist).

16. From David Montgomery, *Workers' Control in America* (New York: Cambridge University Press, 1979), p. 15, cited in Lazonick (1988).

17. Guenther Roth and Claus Wittich, *Max Weber: Economy and Society* (Berkeley: University of California Press, 1978), p. 53. For the various definitions of power see the collection of writings and Steven Lukes's introduction in idem (ed.), *Power* (New York: New York University Press, 1986).

18. Labor's exit, voice, and fusion-based power is only tangentially related to Albert O. Hirschman's *Exit, Voice, and Loyalty* (Cambridge, Mass.: Harvard University Press, 1970). In Hirschman's sense, exit in industrial relations would connote labor turnover (quits), while we refer to labor's simultaneous and temporary withdrawal from work to redress a grievance. Voice, in Hirschman's usage, refers to the communication of complaints whether the complaints are addressed or not, while we refer to the power to be heard.

19. It may be objected that labor's fundamental interests (and power) are not epitomized by total compensation and employment stability. Meaningful (non-alienating, skilled) work, for example, may be considered as a fundamental labor interests that is not captured by the other two. The problem with alienation and skills is that they are not amenable to operationalization, especially in a cross-national, cross-cultural context. We expect, however, that the relative level of employment stability (along with that of wages) in each case should be quite telling ot the respective levels of alienation and skill

formation. Even if total compensation and employment stability are not exhaustive as indicators of labor's fundamental interests, they are important enough; the claims of the analysis based on them would be more limited but still relevant.

20. Another often cited indicator of performance, market share, is also problematic: it is highly price-sensitive (which is also the case with the balance of trade), and measures the share in the **number** of units (autos) sold by a certain producer rather than the more meaningful share in the **value** of units sold.

21. A quantitative computation of regime efficiency on the basis of employment stability is likely to be marred by the arbitrariness involved in assigning a numerical value to the social waste involved in employment instability.

CHAPTER 2

Production Politics: Labor, Power and Efficiency

As was to be expected, the intensification of cross-national economic competition brought renewed interest to the study of comparative industrial relations.[1] Yet, these studies brought as much illumination to the field as they exposed the inadequacy of its conceptual arsenal to grasp the dynamic changes underway. Comparisons of labor's predicament in the U.S. with that of the U.S.'s main competitors, Japan and Germany, seemed to confirm two contradictory hypotheses about the relationship between labor's power and competitive performance. While comparison of the American case with a presumably "weaker-labor, more-competitive" Japan seemed to confirm the notion that labor's strength and competitive performance were inversely related, comparison with a "stronger-labor, more competitive" Germany suggested a positive relationship between labor's power and competitive performance.

Thus, unless we conclude that labor's power in industrial relations is in fact irrelevant to industrial performance—a rather implausible hypothesis, which is addressed later—these contradictory results call for a re-examination of two underlying concepts. First, the meaning and measurements of industrial performance and related concepts of efficiency, productivity, and competitiveness need to be further specified. Indeed, depending on which aspect of industrial performance is adopted and which particular measurement thereof is utilized, a different ordinal relationship between the U.S., German, and Japanese industrial performance is obtained.[2] Second, the concept of labor's power needs to be redefined. Under the conventional usage of the term,

German labor is considered as stronger than American labor, and Japanese labor is considered as weaker than American labor. However, such characterizations fit uncomfortably with an increasingly relevant dimension of labor's power, the ability to avoid adverse effects that may accompany technological change, deskilling and layoffs. Indeed, the finding that in Japan, where labor is purportedly weaker than in the U.S., workers have been apparently shielded from the adverse effects of technological change much better than the "stronger" workers in the U.S., puts into question the validity of conventional conceptualizations of labor's power that focus on an adversarial relationship to employers and a readiness to strike over wages.

The globalization of production underscores the need to broaden our comparative understanding of industrial relations, and to develop concepts of labor's power and industrial performance that are applicable across national and cultural borders. The analytic framework of production politics, presented below, is an effort to illuminate the relationship between labor's power and industrial performance by comparing modes of labor's inclusion in corporate decision making and industrial performance in the production regimes of the American, German, and Japanese auto industries.

THE CONTROL, ORGANIZATION, AND FLEXIBILITY PERSPECTIVES

A broad range of analyses of contemporary capitalism is in agreement that the private ownership of the means of production and "free" labor have become too detached and insufficient to explain the complex relationship between modern capital and labor[3]. Ownership of the means of production, in particular, is not the only predictor of control over the means of production, while "free labor" has acquired additional rights (collective bargaining) and means of livelihood (social wage) in addition to that of selling its labor power. Authors from various perspectives have identified distinct types of economic organization which the "private ownership" and "free" labor criterion are too broad to discern. Most such typologies of capitalist production systems, however, assign a defining role to the state and/or to capitalist needs and initiatives.

Capitalism's defenders have identified distinct types of capitalism on the basis of the degree of organizational development and. Administrative hierarchies and functional specialization, in particular, are analyzed as methods of minimizing "transaction costs" and inefficiency[4]. Many of capitalism's critics, on the other hand, dismiss efficiency maximization as the central motive force behind transformations in capitalist organization of work. Rather, they periodize forms of capitalist organization on the basis of how control over labor is secured within the workplace and within the political economy at large. Thus "taylorism" is a prominent form of capitalist organization of the labor process that subjugates labor to the dicates of "scientific management" , and stifling its skills and autonomy. "Fordism" refers to a related method of capitalist organization which harmonizes capital's needs to control the labor process with its needs for stimulating effective demand in a context of mass production.[5]

More recently, however, a growing body of literature has attributed significant changes in capitalist organization to a "flexibility imperative" that cannot be understood within the confines of conventional transaction-cost minimizing, nor as yet another method of controlling labor by further subjugating it to the rhythms of the machine or of the business cycle. This body of literature stresses the increasing importance of organizational responsiveness and adaptability in a context of simultaneously global and shifting markets. There is considerable divergence, however, on the further specification of "flexibility" and the respective means through which it is attained.

The framework of production politics builds critically on the insights of the "control," "transaction-cost," and "flexibility" perspectives, but views the form of labor's inclusion in corporate decision making—as opposed to labor control, transaction costs, or flexibility—as the defining principle that differentiates modern capitalist production regimes. Let us first examine the three perspectives above more closely.

(A) THE CONTROL/REGULATION PERSPECTIVE

Harry Braverman's *Monopoly Labor: The Degradation of Work in the Twentieth Century* has had a towering influence over the study of the organization of work in modern capitalism. Focussing on the evolution of the labor process, Braverman makes a compelling case for the long-term trend toward the rationalization and simplification of work, and the structural need for capitalist employers to achieve control over work by separating conception from execution and simplifying jobs.[6] Many subsequent studies have documented this tendency for capitalism to degrade work by encouraging the development and application of technologies that require less and less skill to operate while allowing more and more centralized control by remote decision centers.[7]

A defining characteristic of the organization of work in advanced, or "monopoly" capitalism, is the particular manner through which capital controls labor during the labor process: by wresting any remnants of workers' control over, or knowledge of, the labor process (deskilling, separation of conception and execution), and submitting workers to the presumably impersonal but centrally controlled work rhythm of the assembly line. In this sense, monopoly capitalism is characterized by the prevalence of "technical control" of labor, in contrast to an earlier competitive capitalism's reliance on "direct control."[8]

Braverman's periodization of capitalist control is refined by Richard Edwards, who discerns the more recent evolution of "bureaucratic" control. More importantly, Edwards stresses workers' resistance to capital's preferred modes of control, and the contribution of such resistance to the forms of control adopted in a given period.[9] The work of Michael Burawoy also calls into attention the problematic nature of capitalist control over labor. Labor's resistance to capitalist control during the labor process, accordingly, can be significantly influenced by the mediating role of the state, which can potentially buffer the worker from the ravages of the market.

Like Gartman's, Burawoy's work provides a link between the control school and the regulation school, in that he places capital's control imperative within a broader institutional setting that includes the state. Specifically, Burawoy proposes a typology of factory regimes based on the relationship of institutions of production to the state, which he finds critical for the degree to which labor is buffered from the dictates of the market and thus the degree to which exploitation is based on direct coercion or capitalist hegemony.[10]

The "control" perspective—in Braverman's formulations in particular—has been widely criticized for its functionalism[11] and for its view of "a virtually inert working class, unable to pose any substantial problems for capital either within production or beyond."[12] Braverman's analysis seems ill-equipped to anticipate or account for reversals in the detailed division of labor and in the separation of conception from execution observed in recent years—and particularly in the case of Japan. It remains valuable as a broad guide to the experience of American labor with capitalism until the mid-1970, as long as the control imperative is not considered as endemic to capitalism as such, but to a particular configuration of class forces in the U.S.[13]

David Gartman offers a more nuanced analysis of deskilling. While clearly influenced by the control perspective, Gartman allows for the possibility for less antagonistic labor-management relations, reskilling, and a higher level of productive performance to occur under the broad parameters of a capitalist economy. That more ominous outcomes obtain for American labor,[14] can then be attributed not to advanced capitalism in general, but to the particular configuration of class forces in the U.S.[15] Thus Gartman's work, like Burawoy's can be seen as bridging the control school and the regulation school of capitalist organization.

The relationship between form of work organization and distinct constellations of capital-labor relations are systematically addressed in the quite similar Regulation (or Regime-of-Accumulation)[16] and the Social Structure of Accumulation theories (SSA)[17]. Developed independently in France and the United States at the end of the 1970s, both bodies of work analyze distinct modes of capitalist accumulation and a corresponding set of institutions that regulate or organize social forces in production.[18] The insights of the Regulation and SSA theories have been updated for the 1980s and 1990s in the works of Robert Boyer, Urlich Jurgens et al. and Chris Howell.[19] Boyer identifies significant national differences in the institutional forms of regulation consistent with the same regime of accumulation. However, the identification of such different mechanisms of wage regulation, while they provide more nuance to this perspective, stops short of offering an explanation for their rise and maintenance.

Jurgens et al. develop the concept of "toyotism" as an extension of "fordism," in order to account for the distinctive organization and dynamics of Japanese capitalism. Under toyotism, capitalist paternalism replaces collective bargaining as the form of regulation of labor; it is a form of regulation based on the intensification of the work effort and of capitalist authority in allocating work tasks, in a tacit exchange for stabilizing the labor market.[20] Howell's conceptualization of micro-corporatism, on the other hand, is an effort to capture the apparent balkanization, or enterprise-specific regulation of labor, which is replacing the rigid, nation- or industry-wide regulation characteristic of fordism. The latter, accordingly, is rendered increasingly untenable due to the fragmented and rapidly shifting market conditions that prevail in a globalized economy. However, such micro-corporatism does not represent an advance but a fragmentation of labor's strength.[21]

The Regulation and SSA theories represent important advances in political-economic thought and have influenced the approach taken in this book. However, their level of abstraction remains too high and, yet, their analytic reasoning too complex (particularly in the case of the SSA theory) to adequately illuminate the relationship between industrial relations and industrial performance. Moreover, the Regulation and to a lesser extent the SSA theories leave themselves open to criticisms similar to those levied against the control school: functionalism—elevating conditions compatible with capital accumulation to necessary ones; and definitional vagueness—how narrowly or broadly the "institutional setting" of industrial relations is defined predisposes what kind of consequences are identified. Thus, despite their avowed attention to class struggle, these approaches have analyzed the development of labor unions and associated sanctions against capital's prerogatives, not as mechanisms (however crude or limited) of labor's control over the means of production, but primarily as mechanisms for harmonizing aggregate demand with the aggregate supply of goods in advanced capitalism.

In fact, the SSA and regulation perspectives share with other neo-Marxist perspectives a fundamental ambivalence about the significance of labor's inclusion in corporate decision making processes for the political economy. Some authors stress that labor's inclusion in corporate decision-making is "functional" to the capitalist system: unions serve as mechanisms for industrial peace and demand stimulation. Others, more sensitive to "dialectical" analysis, view such "functional" transformations in relations of production as also exacerbating capitalism's contradictions, contributing to the system's "disfunctioning"[22]. In the neo-classical perspective, on the other hand, labor's inclusion is interpreted as burdening the smooth functioning of the system with a rising level of demands—just as the articulation of a plethora of popular demands on the welfare state precipitates a crisis of "governability" in the political system.[23] The SSA and regulation perspectives do not resolve this ambivalence.

Additionally, these approaches share with neo-classical conceptualizations of the evolution of capitalism the inability to successfully incorporate the evolution of Japanese capitalism into their theoretical foundations. National variations in the organization of capitalism are explained by both schools as reflective of the compatibility of different social arrangements with the same mode and rate of accumulation, both stressing that the latter does not strictly determine but provide limits to such arrangements.

However, for both schools, Japan's more or less uninterrupted productivity growth, and its relative bridging of the conception-execution divide in the labor process, despite its membership in the advanced capitalist group of countries, remains theoretically problematic. Both schools view international variations in the regimes or social structures of accumulation as small enough for their theories to claim general relevance to the dynamics of capitalism in general (as opposed to, say, a national mode of production); at the same time, they view the historical and cultural distinctiveness of Japan from the West as too large to integrate into the institutional setting of western capitalism.[24]

The approach taken in this book limiting its domain to production politics, will attempt to correct such theoretical oversight, by refusing to elevate the historical experiences of only a certain group of countries into a **systemic** logic of a certain phase of **capitalism**. While Japan will not be the central focus of our analysis, its experience with labor-capital relations and productivity growth will be integrated into our theorization of the social dynamics of production in more familiar cases of advanced capitalism.

(B) THE ORGANIZATIONAL EFFICIENCY PERSPECTIVE

A very different view of capitalist transformation analyzes what we call "capital-organizational" structures as independent variables in the determination of industrial efficiency. In this perspective, the historical emergence of factory production and the subsequent hierarchical and detailed division of labor in capitalist organization do not result because of an overriding capitalist imperative for controlling labor—as the control/regulation perspective argues, but because such hierarchies advance the efficiency of the work organization. Alfred A. Chandler Jr. makes the case that "exogenous" (technological and market) changes lead to new business strategies, which, in turn, result in new organizational structures.[25] For example, new business strategies such as large-scale production of standardized products, national and international distribution, vertical integration and diversification, result in new organizational structures that economize and improve upon administrative coordination: the modern "divisionalized" corporation.

In other words, Chandler attributes the growth and development of the modern corporation to the competitive cost advantages gained from the search for ever greater administrative efficiencies in the face of changing markets and technologies.[26]

Oliver E. Williamson builds on these ideas to argue that, the modern multinational corporation, as well as the older corporation, were built upon a new principle or imperative of production: transaction-cost economizing.[27] Ever-larger hierarchies and ever-increasing specialization, accordingly, were adopted for their intrinsic efficiency. Against the "control" perspective, Williamson argues that the transitions from the putting-out system to the factory, and from inside-contracting within the factory to capitalist authority relations, were principally motivated by efficiency considerations. Although the rewards for such innovations were initially captured by their initiators, the new methods were then widely imitated and the benefits were diffused throughout society; the economic pie thus grew larger and all shared in it. The hierarchical organization of the labor process in capitalism is not driven by considerations of power but of efficiency. In Williamson's words,

> there may be more or less preferred types of hierarchy; but hierarchy itself is unavoidable unless efficiency sacrifices are made.[28]

However, some key assumptions that underlie Williamson's approach are becoming increasingly untenable. In fact, the 1980s witnessed developments in capitalist organization that turn some of the prescriptions of the organizational efficiency school on their heads. Williamson presupposes market and technological environments in which scale economies are favored, presuppositions that are increasingly questionable in contemporary conditions of market fragmentation and instability.[29]

Moreover, if a large body of authors agree that capitalist organization evolves as a result of socially-neutral efforts to improve efficiency through changes in "capital-organizational" variables, there is significant disagreement as to what a more efficient organization of capital actually entails. Thus Japanese companies' apparent competitive success over American firms since the mid-1970s is attributed to a variety of "capital-organizational" variables. Some argue that the higher capital costs in the U.S. are the cause of its competitive decline[30], while others point to the "active markets for corporate control" in the U.S.

encourage short-run investment policies among managers which are deleterious to long-term competitiveness.[31]

There is another variant of the organizational efficiency perspective rejects the explanatory power of capital markets for competitiveness differentials.[32] Instead, more complex explanations of competitive performance are developed, such as the internal investment processes and capital-budgeting systems of certain firms. Accordingly, the capital-budgeting and financial-planning systems of firms that arose after the Second World War have systematically obscured the value of investment in organizational capabilities, because such investments were hard to quantify within the widely used financial models. As a result, it has been argued, companies often invested vigorously, but in the wrong things.[33]

"Product development organizations" within firms is yet another critical determinant of competitiveness suggested by another variant of the capital-organization perspective. Kim Clark and Takahiro Fujimoto found striking differences between American and Japanese auto companies in their ability to integrate customers' needs with the process of product design.[34] To discern customer values and preferences, American companies relied on formal market research filtered through reports and meetings. By contrast, the best Japanese firms supplemented market research with direct interaction among designers, engineers, and customers—what the authors call "external integration." This process was complemented by "internal integration" among designers, engineers, and assembly workers. Thus, while between 1982 and 1987 American and Japanese auto companies as groups spent equivalent amounts of money on R&D, the Japanese were able to introduce seventy-two new models, while the Americans launched only twenty-one. While, however, the authors are very convincing concerning the impact of product development organizations on competitiveness, they are less illuminating in explaining why American firms were not as successful at developing such organizations. The authors hint at the significance of integrating labor into the product development process, but do not develop the suggestion.

Works in the capital-organizational perspective display a strong tendency to treat industrial efficiency as a socially neutral relationship between technology, engineers, and operators, between impersonal inputs and outputs, missing the social dimension of efficiency, involving a concrete relationship between direct producers, managers and owners of the means of production. Efficiency maximization may be an important motive force behind transformations in capitalist production, but its realization hinges upon an appropriate organization of the interests as well as functions of the social actors involved in production. Transaction-cost and capital-organization variables, however important they may be as factors of competitive performance, do not operate in a social vacuum, independently of pressures and opportunities provided by labor's position in the organization of production.

Jeffrey Hart's *Rival Capitalists* is an attempt to search for the social preconditions of production efficiency through an internationally comparative analysis.[35] Unfortunately, however, Hart limits his focus to the social preconditions for "the creation and diffusion of technology," which he finds in particular "state-societal arrangements." The first problem here is Hart's presupposition that technological diffusion is synonymous with efficiency. This is highly questionable in light of available evidence that less technologically sophisticated auto plants can be more efficient than highly automated ones,[36] and that similar levels of investment in R&D in autos across the U.S., Germany, and Japan coincide with productivity differences among them.[37] The other problem is that his understanding of particular state-societal arrangements is derived in a rather impressionistic manner, which leads him to very questionable conclusions. Thus he attributes relative British inefficiency (or low level of diffusion of technologies) to Britain's supposedly strong labor movement, weak government and weak business, while Japanese efficiency is attributed to supposedly strong government, strong business and weak labor. Hart's understanding of "the relative weakness of both government and business in the face of a relatively unified and militant labor movement" in Britain[38] might have been more plausible if he was not writing ten years into Conservative governments, ebbing unionization rates, declining real wages and employment security, and dwindling labor militancy.

(C) THE FLEXIBILITY PERSPECTIVE

We can identify three different formulations of the "flexibility" perspective, all of which depart from the control/regulation and capital-efficiency perspectives, in stressing the availability of a range of choices in organizing work and the respective relationship between capital and labor. While all three emphasize the value of corporate responsiveness and adaptability to shifting market conditions, each formulation differs significantly on the specific meaning of flexibility and its social, economic, and technological preconditions.

(C-1) FLEXIBLE SPECIALIZATION

Piore and Sabel's influential work injected a different problematique in the debate on the relationship between industrial relations and productivity. It identified the crisis of U.S. industrial relations as symptomatic of a broader bifurcation of the possible ways of organizing production[39]. A "second industrial divide" between the dominant mass production, fordist paradigm and an alternative, "flexible specialization" paradigm has been confronting industrial societies. In contrast to mass production's reliance on homogeneous markets and low-skill, standardized labor inputs, they argued, flexible specialization is predicated on diversified markets and craft-based, variable production inputs.[40] Rejecting technological determinism, the authors argue that the domination of mass production and fordism, and labor's consequent deskilling and mind-numbing working conditions was not the result of a technological or economic "necessity," but the result of a confluence of factors, including nation-specific policies and historical accident[41].

> ... the triumph of a technological breakthrough over competing adaptations depends on its timing and the resources available to its champions—rather than on its intrinsic superiority. In this view, competition guarantees only that the weak must follow the lead of the strong, not that the strong have found the uniquely correct solution to common problems.

The industrial divide of the 1980s, they argue, could possibly, though not necessarily, result in the triumph of the flexible production paradigm, given the affinity of the latter in dealing with a global economy's rapidly diversifying markets.[42]

Related conceptualizations of "flexible mass production" addressed the observed persistence of many features of mass production (including large production runs, and specialized or dedicated work layouts and labor inputs) alongside new, "flexible" features such as variable product specifications, more malleable production layout, production schedules, and broadly skilled labor inputs—a coexistence facilitated by the diffusion of numerically controlled machine tools, flexible manufacturing systems, and robotics.[43] However, while it became evident that taylorist detailed division of labor and strict separation of conception from execution were being replaced with broader job specifications, job rotation, team work, and the integration of production and quality control functions, questions remained as to the extensiveness of such changes and their significance for labor, capital and society at large[44].

The affinity of flexible production to "cooperative" labor-management relations is a consequence of the broad skills of the workforce and quick adaptation to market signals on which it is predicated—in contrast to the traditional "adversarialism" associated with the mass production paradigm that result from the narrow skills of the workforce and large-standardized production layout. While dissenters criticized labor-management cooperation as a mirage obscuring intensified exploitation of labor,[45] it would prove more difficult to "argue with success." The affinity of flexible production to productivity/competitiveness, mostly associated with its aptitude for responding to rapidly shifting global market conditions, was impressively illustrated by the successes of certain Italian industrial districts, and even Japan's industrial success was attributed to its adoption of flexible specialization.

While Piore and Sabel took pains to explain that the domination of one production paradigm over another is not necessarily the result of its intrinsic superiority but of a historical confluence of economic and political factors, the crisis of American mass producers of the early-1980s indicated that traditional mass producers had in fact little choice but to switch to flexibility if they were to survive in the new globally competitive environment. Had the paradigm of "flexible specialization" become a victim of its success? Was it a "catch-all concept—open, indeterminate, and unspecified, [often changing its] meaning to fit new situations?"[46]

The diversification of the world auto market as well as the development of re-programmable automation technologies seemed to be developments particularly rewarding for Japanese industrial relations,[47] whose cooperative and flexible nature gave them an edge in adaptability and thus enhanced their competitiveness.[48] Cross-national surveys of auto plants by researchers at M.I.T. and accompanying research showed that Japanese auto plants, in Japan as well as in the U.S. ("transplants"), were producing autos with fewer defects and faster[49]. What was urgently needed, accordingly, was a philosophical renaissance of American management which would lead to the adoption of more flexible and cooperative methods of organizing production.[50]

What still remained largely under-analyzed, however, were the social preconditions for flexible production. Thus, rather puzzlingly, while Piore and Sabel argue that social and political struggles are critical for the consolidation of a particular production paradigm, and while they acknowledge that unique national constellations should thus affect which production paradigm is adopted[51], they actually devote only a couple of pages to the distinct evolution and shape of national production systems. Thus their analysis leads to the disappointing conclusion that there is a functional equivalence between different social preconditions of flexible production: flexible production could triumph just as well in a social setting where labor has little influence as in one in which its influence is substantial. Thus, beyond suggesting the possibilities for the reincarnation of the "craft model" of organizing production in a modern context, they provide us with little conceptual guidance and empirical evidence for the social preconditions of flexible production.

(C-2) FLEXIBLE DEMOCRATIC CENTRALISM

Among attempts at clarifying the social preconditions for flexible production, the work of Altshuler et al. stands out for its breadth as much for its excessive eclecticism.[52] Thus Japanese competitive advantage is attributed to all of the following:

- the organization of corporate groups (core-supplier networks), that reverses Western models of competitiveness that put a premium on vertical integration;[53]

- the organization of multi-sector conglomerates (Keiretsu);[54],

- management's philosophical preference for improving quality over reducing costs;[55]

- the high level of company training provided to labor;[56]

- the high levels of trust between labor and management;[57]

- labor's acceptance of limited wage increases[58].

In contrast to the excessively eclectic approach of Altshuler et al., Kelley and Harrison's study of machine shops across the U.S. seeks to isolate the contribution of labor organization, or lack thereof, to productivity. The authors are, in a way, revisiting a previous study which claimed that "Japanese-style" institutions of worker involvement, such as quality-of-working-life, employee-involvement, and quality circles programs had only a negligible effect on productivity.[59] Kelley and Harrison's study concludes that the degree of unionization and the union's support of management plans is decisive for realizing the productivity potential of cooperative labor-management institutions.[60] Similarly, some union activists conclude that productivity improvements are not likely to accompany innovative labor-management arrangements unless management and the union implement them "vigorously, thoroughly, openly, with full commitment and mutual trust."[61]

Why did American companies not seek accommodation with their unions before embarking on efficiency-advancing changes? A sizeable portion of the literature places the blame on the anti-union animus of the employers and the political leadership. Indeed, researchers provided ample documentation of an anti-union offensive waged by employers and government alike in the 1980s.[62] These analyses fail, however, to provide convincing explanations for labor's failure to defend itself against such offensives. After all, bureaucratized unions, technological change, and foreign competition—the key explanations advanced for the effectiveness of employer and government opposition—were also present in earlier decades as well but with very different effectiveness. Kochan et al., however, do suggest that the postwar transformation of American industrial relations does not have to end with labor's defeat as it also brings with it new opportunities for unions; labor could reverse its downward trend if its participation in quality circles and related shop floor forums of labor-management cooperation is extended "upward," so that labor participates in the "strategic business decisions."[63]

The "strategic choice" perspective advanced by Kochan, Katz, and McKersie offers an important modification to John Dunlop's systems approach to industrial relations,[64] in order to account for the role played by key actors' strategic choices in the actual configuration of the system.[65] Thus the traditional adversarialism of American industrial relations system, for this perspective, is the result of the choices which the government, management, and unions have made with respect to their mutual relations.

However, the highly suggestive agenda of these authors' research ends up focussing on only one of the elements determining the nature of industrial relations, management ideology. While they are correct in pointing out the impediments which management's anti-union ideology poses for cooperative industrial relations, they are less convincing about labor's role in the making (and thus the undoing) of the postwar industrial relations system. The inadequacy of their framework becomes clearer when one considers the very different configuration of Japanese industrial relations, where anti-union animus in the formative postwar years was unparalleled yet cooperative relations thrived.

Wolfgang Streeck takes the analysis a step further, arguing that what is critical for industrial performance is not labor organization as such, but a particular **form** of unionization, one which ensures labor influence in and responsibility for corporate performance.[66] Thus Streeck argues that the success of German auto industry in overcoming the severe crisis of the mid-1970s, is related to a labor-management cooperation predicated on centralized, co-determining, and responsible union organization. If industrial success is predicated on flexibility, the latter is predicated on labor-management cooperation, which, in turn, is predicated on robust German unionization.[67] Unfortunately, however, Streeck goes on to cast doubt on the necessity of such social preconditions for flexible production, when he extends his analysis to Japan. He suggests that flexibility there is predicated on an almost the opposite set of social preconditions, positing a "functional equivalence" between strong-labor (Germany) and weak-labor (Japan) contexts of flexibility.[68]

In a similar vein, Lowell Turner's otherwise stimulating study of the impact of labor organization and participation in corporate decisions on industrial restructuring and performance remains captive of social-democratic or neo-corporatist conceptions of unionization that also inform Streeck's work.[69] While Germany is said to outperform the U.S. in both labor-friendliness and in industrial performance in general, this is attributed to American unions' relative lack of centralization and lack of articulation to the state through a social-democratic political party— all the while Japanese industrial success takes place in a context of even less union centralization and articulation to the state than in the U.S..[70]

(C-3) FLEXIBLE INTEGRATION

Kenney and Florida's work is refreshing for its attempt to steer away from the prevalent "super-exploitation" explanations of Japanese productivity which permeate the above perspectives.[71] What is critical for Japanese industrial performance is Japan's success in adopting the model of "innovation-mediated production," which refers to the "integration of innovation and production, of intellectual and physical labor."[72] However, while the authors trace the origins of Japan's production regime to the widespread worker militancy in the postwar period, they understate the significance of workers' power in the consequent operation of the regime, preferring to focus instead on the importance of a particular organization of capital for optimal industrial performance. The works of Lazonick and Aoki are also competent attempts at a synthesis of the insights of the control and the capital-organization perspectives. They are among a group of authors that examine how different constellations of the balance of power between capital and labor—differences that are detectable across national economies—are intimately related to the forms of capitalist organization, as well as the degree to which efficiency is maximized.

The work of Lazonick suggests that international differences in the position of labor in the labor process should neither be understood simply as variations in the form of capital control over labor, nor as the result of a benevolent pursuit of efficiency through fragmentation of work and progressive specialization of functions [73]. Tracing the evolution of American, British and Japanese industrial relations (with comparative illustrations from Germany) from the interwar period to the early 1980s, Lazonick examines their differences with respect to the "mode of incorporation of labor into the company hierarchy." The company hierarchy, viewed from the perspective of the division of labor, consists of generalists at the top, operatives at the bottom, and specialists in the middle.

Lazonick traces the differential ability of these industrial relations systems in "creating value at the shop floor" to the ability of capital to **elicit** workers' effort and cooperation, and the latter to the organizational integration/segmentation of production. Thus he offers a more nuanced framework for the evolution of the labor process under capitalism than either neo-classical or neo-Marxist accounts.

These cross-national differences in organizational integration manifest the British failure to restructure its economic institutions in response to American managerial capitalism, and the American failure to restructure its economic institutions in response to Japanese collective capitalism.[74]

It is important to note that for Lazonick the cooperative character of Japanese industrial relations, notable also for their aptitude for smooth incorporation of new technologies, wase not the consequence but rather the cause of the rapid incorporation of such technologies. Japanese industrial relations were shaped **before** the introduction of new technologies; they were shaped by the structure of market forces surrounding Japanese firms and the massive labor unrest following the Second World War.

Aoki, using a game-theoretic analysis of capitalist organization in the U.S. and Japan, also argues that in Japan, philosophical traditions, market conditions but also institutional arrangements following labor struggles in the 1950s resulted in the emergence of a form of capitalist organization wherein the capital-labor relationship is less antagonistic and more efficient than in the U.S.. He contrasts the "centralized-hierarchical" prototype of coordination found in American firms, which is based on the principle of specialization, to the "decentralized-horizontal" prototype of coordination found in Japanese firms, which is based on knowledge sharing ("learning by doing").[75]

Aoki is most compelling when he points to the relative inefficiency of the American prototype in responding to rapid "shocks" facing the firm, either due to unforeseen malfunctions in the labor process or due to changing market signals. The specialization in functions (management v. labor) as well as within functions (operator v. maintenance), while it may involve gains in efficiency during "normal" times, it can prove very costly when the firm needs to adapt to unforeseen changes. The "adaptive cost of specialization" is likely to be increasing as the size of the market (or of the certainty for conditions of the circumstances of production) decreases. Thus Aoki gives a novel meaning to Adam Smith's dictum:

the degree of specialization is limited by the extent of the market.][76]

PRODUCTION POLITICS AND EFFICIENCY

In modern capitalism, the social relations developed around the process of production are institutionalized in a production regime, which may be considered a political structure regulating the distribution of power among the relevant social actors, labor and capital/management. I am using "power" in Weber's sense, as

> the probability that one actor within a social relationship will be in a position to carry out his own will despite resistance.[77]

This usage is not as different as one might think from Poulantzas's who defines class power as

> the capacity of one or several classes to realize their specific interests . . . The capacity of one class to realize its interests is in opposition to the capacity (and interests) of other classes: **the field of power is therefore strictly relational.**[78]

Thus for both Weber and Poulantzas power is not something that an individual or group/class of individuals either have or do not have, but something that can be possessed in increments. Thus we can talk of "labor's power in corporate decision making" without ignoring capital's (superior) power therein. "Labor's power" in production calls attention to the contestation through which labor shares in the benefits of production. Thus, for example, high wages can be seen as the result of labor's power, the presumed "functionality" of such wages for fordist regulation notwithstanding.[79] And lifetime employment guarantees in Japan, as we will argue later, were actually forced on Japanese employers by workers through the intense industrial confrontations of the immediate postwar period, even if they also proved useful for the stability of that production system.

In contrast to the classical model of capitalism, where labor's position in production is little different from that of a commodity[80], in modern capitalism labor is included into the production regime as a pertinent social actor. The legitimation of labor's collective organization, which is completed in the major industrial countries under consideration by the 1950s, accords it a definite influence over the deployment of the means of production and particularly its labor power. This influence, however limited it may be for radically transforming the capitalist mode of production, introduces new dynamic elements into the particular capitalist production regimes that it defines.

Depending on the mode of labor inclusion into the production regime, corporate decisions on a range of issues are no longer the exclusive domain of capital, but are subject to legitimized contestation by (organized) labor. In other words, depending on the basis and scope of labor's inclusion into the production regime, not only is the labor market politicized, but so are a range of corporate decisions: wage levels, training levels, technological choices, employment stability, work allocation, discipline, and others. While private ownership in the means of production and the market continue their systemic prominence, unions have various degrees of success in "taking wages out of competition" (in some sectors of the economy) or even, under certain production regimes, in "taking employment out of competition."

A major source of confusion surrounding the application of the concept of power to the relations of production is a traditional over-reliance on only one dimension of power, redistributive power. Indeed, labor's power has been analyzed, predominantly, in terms of organized labor's capacity to redistribute the wealth produced by improving its reward/effort ratio and reducing related disciplinary and administrative arbitrariness during production: wages, work intensity and grievance arbitration.

A central methodological proposition informing the framework of production politics is that the redistributive denotations that dominate conceptualizations of labor's power (wages, work intensity, grievance arbitration) need to be supplemented by productivist ones (fulfilling work, reskilling, employment stability). This is because **what** as well as **how** something is produced is highly consequential for the skills and the employment levels that will be needed to produce it, just as **why** something is produced is consequential for labor's share in the proceeds of production (is it produced primarily for the near-term/long-term benefit of investors/the community/workers?). Labor has a fundamental interest in being paid well today but also in having a job tomorrow. Thus we can distinguish between two types or dimensions of labor's power. Redistributive power pertains to the capacity to secure redistributive policies that entail high wages and rational working conditions. Labor's productivist power pertains to its capacity to secure production methods that entail meaningful, skilled inputs and stable employment. Consideration of these two dimensions of labor's power is paramount for understanding the distinct patterns of influence exercised by American, German, and Japanese workers in their respective production regimes, as well as the different levels of industrial performance attained by each of these regimes.

POWER AND INDUSTRIAL PERFORMANCE

There are four central reasons why labor's power in a production regime may be paramount for the level of industrial performance attainable by the regime. One reason is associated with labor's redistributive power, and the other three to labor's productivist power. The effect of labor's redistributive power on capitalist productivity and dynamism is suggested in an early article by Robert Brenner: if you can't make them work harder, better make them work smarter. Brenner makes his point through a historical comparison of the transition from feudalism to capitalism of Western Europe and Eastern Europe.[81] In Western Europe, the failure of feudal lords to crush rebellions challenging their attempt to intensify **absolute** surplus extraction led to the transformation of these feudal lords into capitalists: they became directly involved in the organization of production and invested in technologies and methods that increased the amount of surplus produced. Thus landlord-entrepreneurs attained ever higher living standards without further squeezing those of the agricultural laborers; they enriched themselves through **relative** surplus extraction. By contrast, in Eastern Europe, the serfs' rebellions against absolute surplus extraction were crushed in blood, which in turn condemned Eastern Europe to a prolonged transition to capitalism, marked by land erosion, depopulation, and underdevelopment. The effectiveness of labor's redistributive pressures in the West was thus a key parameter in that region's strides in productivity and development.

Industrial performance may also improve as a result of labor's productivist power. In a production regime where labor can influence which production methods are adopted, it can use its influence to preclude the adoption of certain nominally efficient but actually wasteful production methods. For example, labor can preclude the adoption of the wasteful hire-and-fire method of adjusting employment (and production) levels to changes in demand. This method is seen as efficient from the point of view of the individual capitalist, but in fact it is quite wasteful of human capital and thus it is not as efficient from the point of view of the regime as a whole. The hire-and-fire method includes costs that are not borne by the capitalist but "externalized" to labor and the community in the form of boredom, demoralization, alienation, alcoholism, and associated ills of unemployment.[82] The preclusion of such kind of innovation in effect forces capital to seek profits through the adoption of more genuine improvements in productive efficiency—ones that harness, not repress, the creativity and variability of human labor, and involve investing in, wasting, human capital.

A third reason why labor's power may be positively associated with strong industrial performance is the affinity of labor's power to functional integration and flexibility. Recent interest in flexibility in the organization of production and the deployment of labor has led to the demonstration of the close relationship between functional integration (of managerial and operative tasks) and flexibility. What was left unexplored, however, was that functional integration is predicated on interest integration (of capital/management and labor interests).

Flexibility, or a high level of responsiveness and adaptability of the production layout to shifting market stimuli, necessitates that the functions of management and of labor be not rigidly separated; workers must have broad enough skills (including coordinating ones), and managers must posses sufficient knowledge of operative tasks for the two sides to be able to cooperate in a process of continuous adaptation and improvement.

Most important, however, is that functional integration and flexibility are not likely to flourish in a production regime as long as there is little interest integration, namely, when certain of labor's fundamental interests (usually productivist ones) are excluded from corporate decision making. This is so for three reasons. One, bereft of productivist power, labor is not likely to have the training needed to undertake coordinating functions, nor the requisite trust in the company to willingly cooperate in productivity-enhancing changes in production (fearing that the latter may cost jobs). Two, in a context where labor's productivist interests are excluded from corporate decision making, where manning levels, production schedules and skill formation are the exclusive prerogatives of management, the latter are likely to lack the requisite confidence in (or social predisposition to accept) workers' ability to actively contribute to the continuous adaptation of the organization of production to changing market conditions. Three, lacking interest integration, or when labor's position in the corporation is tenuous, labor is not likely to willingly cooperate with management in its demands for flexible deployment or actively contribute to productivity improvements, since the latter may well result in the loss of jobs.

FROM THE POLTICS OF PRODUCTION TO PRODUCTION POLITICS

The significance of labor's inclusion in corporate decision-making, as such, needs not be exaggerated as "industrial democracy" nor de-emphasized as a "smokescreen for exploitation." Both such interpretations miss the pertinence of labor in modern capitalism. International differences in labor-capital relations, as will be shown, reveal distinct ways in which (organized) labor's resistance to capitalist prerogatives have transformed the capital-labor relationship, not only in form but also in substance.

While labor's position is clearly subordinate to capital's, labor has managed to successfully challenge the monopoly of the owners of the means of production over the conditions under which these are utilized. We can distinguish among different kinds of capitalism—not on the basis of the state's intervention in production, which has been amply examined, but on the basis of labor's intervention in corporate decision making. The type of labor's inclusion in corporate decision making, or the articulation of capital's and labor's interests around production, is critical for the type of relationship that exists between capital (management) and labor during production, or the organization of functions, with important implications for the production efficiency of the regime.

This book, reversing the tendency among many neo-Marxist analyses to distinguish between production systems on the basis of types of capital's control over the means of production and labor, is based on a framework of analysis centered on labor' (however limited) control over capital's use of the means of production. The underlying premise of our approach is that the historical outcomes of postwar labor-capital confrontations over the utilization of the means of production were not settled as capital's triumphs (as could be inferred by the fact that capital maintained its dominance in the system of production), but were rather **Pyrrhic victories** for capital: capital's domination was maintained at the price of recognizing labor's right to contest a range of issues that were until then a capitalist prerogative. It will be argued that a typology of production regimes based on labor's control over corporate decision-making can explain the different dynamics underway in capital-labor relations in different advanced capitalist countries; and it can also illuminate the disadvantages inherent in the production regime of the United States with respect to industrial efficiency, compared to other possible configurations of capital-labor relations, namely, the production regimes of Germany and Japan.

The framework of production politics adopted here echoes Gosta Esping-Andersen's analysis of how the social composition of ruling coalitions influences policy, although our analysis is not of state-oriented politics but of workplace governance.[83] The two levels, state and production, are certainly interrelated. Our treatment of the level of production as though it were autonomous of the state is certainly a simplification. It is meant to highlight a relatively neglected area of politics rather than to elevate it to a veritably autonomous field of social action. Production politics is an effort to identify the micro-foundations of political economy.

The "politics of production" have been analyzed by Michael Burawoy as the "micro-foundations" of political economy, in his cross-national analytic framework of factory regimes.[84] However, Burawoy's conceptualization of "politics of production" is tainted by the determining role he ascribes to the mode of state intervention into the relations of production—the key parameter in Burawoy's typology of factory regimes[85]. Abstracting thus from sources of labor strength that are not directly related to the degree of state intervention in the factory regime, Burawoy's typology identifies the Japanese working class as the weakest in the advanced capitalist world, incapable of ever obtaining more than "few concessions"[86]. Thus the distinction between "macro- and micro- foundations" in political-economic analysis remains ambiguous.[87] Our framework of production politics attempts to fill that conceptual gap, by exploring the relatively autonomous (from the state) dynamics of labor-capital relations in the sphere of production.[88]

A major difficulty in conceptualizing an economically and politically relevant production politics within capitalism is that the concept itself seems to defy some central assumptions of classical capitalism. After all, isn't the de-politicization of production relations under the rule of the market a defining characteristic of capitalism that distinguishes it from feudalism? It is true that Marx's work has demonstrated the political underpinnings of such apparent de-politicization (the capitalist class's "wresting of the means of production" from the workers), but did not include the veritable power relations between capital and labor in his model of capitalism. In his political writings, Marx emphasized the centrality of class struggle or labor-capital politics, but focussed on the arena of the state. Working class politics would be crucial in implementing the transfer of the ownership of the means of production from capitalists to the workers through violent or electoral conquest of the state. Social scientists coming from a Marxist tradition have similarly focussed their analyses of working class politics on state politics. Relations of production were seen mostly as reflections of political relations at the state level, as the background to state politics, or reflective of the "phase" of capitalist development ("monopoly" or "late" capitalism).

Thus, in the classical model of capitalism the only political act in production is the (often violent) wresting of the means of production from the worker[89]. After that, politics in the sphere of production effectively "ceases," as the individual worker has no source of power to contest that of his employer[90], except that accorded by the market, the option to sell his labor power to a more "generous" (because more productive?) employer. Conversely, the employer's power over the worker seems to be limited only by the generosity of the next employer, since the worker can do nothing to affect the policies pursued by his employer. Ultimately, it is the labor market, or the size of what Marx called the "industrial reserve army" of the unemployed that determines variations in production decisions such as the level of employment, compensation levels, etc.. Thus production politics once again becomes vacuous (or a misnomer for state policies or demographic forces that affect the size of the "industrial reserve army").

However, as soon as the individual worker is no longer atomized, but becomes a member of a union, the possibility arises that a simultaneous withdrawal of all the workers in a given firm or a whole industry from work (strike) will force the employer(s) to deal with a real counter-power to the way and purpose he uses the means of production. The ability of labor to deactivate the means of production by withdrawing its labor power introduces a veritable process of contestation (as opposed to mere resentment) over the uses of the means of production between capital and labor. In neo-classical analyses this is referred to as the (political?) "distortion" of the functioning of the labor market, through unions' monopolistic hold over it.

A political understanding of the organization of production in modern capitalism, one that goes beyond the tautological premise of capital domination of the organization of production, assumes that there is a **range** of possible configurations of labor-capital relations consistent with capitalism's fundamental definition[91]. Distinct types of such configurations represent distinct dimensions of labor (or capital) power over the use of the means of production, which are determined by (a) the distinct **strategic choices** that identify the terrain of contestation between capital and labor during the formative years of a regime, and (b) the distinct **institutions of production** that crystallize the outcomes of those class battles and which inform the consequent strategies of the parties.

PRODUCTION REGIMES OF LABOR INCLUSION

The production regimes of the United States, Germany and Japan that we will analyze, are all regimes of labor inclusion, to be distinguished from most pre-war/pre-unionization regimes of labor exclusion. Unlike regimes of labor exclusion, characteristic of "classical" capitalism, contemporary regimes of labor inclusion express labor's qualitative leap in its relationship to the means of production. The recognition of organized labor by capital was generalized in the large manufacturing industries of advanced capitalist countries by the 1950s, and it marked the transformation of labor into an actor in the political structure of the corporation, capable of injecting its own interests into (certain) important corporate decisions through a specified structure of influence. While the particular manner in and degree to which labor has been included into production politics is highly consequential for the level of labor's influence and will be addressed below, it is important to stress at this point that the very fact of labor's inclusion amounts to a nascent de-commodification of labor: labor can no longer be considered as a mere commodity, inasmuch as it exercises an autonomous, legitimate influence over the price at which it is "sold" and the conditions under which it is used.

Thus, labor's position in the corporation and its power over decision-making determine a certain type of relationship between key labor interests and capital interests in the formulation of corporate decisions. This relationship between labor and capital is institutionalized as a specific production regime. The following two categories/criteria are used to distinguish between modes of labor

influence in corporate decision making, which in turn define a typology
of production regimes.

Criterion I: *Scope of Inclusion*
—segregation: labor's scope of influence separated from capital's;
                 labor is included only in redistributive decisions

—integration: areas subject to labor influence are   integrated with
                 those subject to capital's influence; labor is included in
                 redistributive and productivist decisions

Criterion II: *Basis of Inclusion*
—exit: labor's ability to strike against certain unfavorable
                 decisions (collective bargaining)
—voice: labor's voting strength in decision making
                 (representation)
—fusion: labor's amalgamation with capital   (incorporation)

With respect to the organization of labor's and capital's functions in
production, we can distinguish between regimes that rely on a rigid
hierarchy of tasks, and those that, while maintaining functional
hierarchies, allow for porous lines of demarcation in functional
hierarchies. In other words, we can distinguish between regimes where
the execution of tasks is strictly separated from the
conception/coordination of tasks and regimes where there is significant
overlap in the kinds of tasks performed by labor and by management.
This distinction corresponds to the one between narrow specialization
predicated on economies of scale and flexible, broad job specifications
predicated on flexibility and adaptation through learning-by-doing.

On the basis of these criteria we construct the following typology
of production regimes of labor inclusion (Table 1). It will be noted that
there is a correspondence between forms of interest organization
(relations of production) and forms of functional organization (relations
in production). The hypothesized mechanism through which the mode
of labor's inclusion in an integration regime results in industrial success
can be schematically presented as follows:

inclusion of labor's redistributive and productivist interests ==>
interest integration ==> functional integration ==> flexibility ==>
superior manufacturing

Table 1: Production Regimes of Labor Inclusion

Organization of interests of labor and capital	Segregation	Integration	
		Representative	Incorporative
—basis of labor's inclusion	exit	exit voice	exit fusion
—scope of labor's inclusion (issues)	redistributive	redistributive productivist	redistributive productivist
Organization of functions of labor and capital			
—labor's functions in production	execution	execution conception	execution conception
—contribution of labor to performance	indirect	direct	direct
Cases	pre-1984 USA	Germany	Japan

Segregation and Integration

The concept of labor inclusion, important as it is to delineate post-war production politics from their predecessors, is also too broad to capture the historical differences among patterns of labor inclusion that prevailed in different countries. By narrowing the concept of labor inclusion we may look for how extensive labor's inclusion in corporate decision-making is, by asking what portion of the workforce is included (extent of inclusion). Or, we may look for what areas of decision-making are open to labor's inclusion (scope of inclusion). Thus, we differentiate regimes of labor inclusion further into regimes of segregated inclusion (or "segregation" regimes, for short) and of integrated inclusion (or "integration" regimes, for short), according to the scope of corporate decisions in which labor exercises a significant, institutionalized influence.

The term "segregation" is chosen here because of its resonance with the type of inclusion of African-Americans into the civic body of the U.S., particularly after the Reconstruction. Segregation of the races was justified by the "separate but equal" doctrine, which the U.S. Supreme Court's 1896 *Plessy v. Ferguson* decision upheld as consistent with the 14th Amendment's "equal protection of the laws" clause. African-Americans' segregated inclusion in the political regime was certain a tremendous advancement over their pre-Civil War exclusion, yet as the Supreme Court concluded in the 1950s, "separate" inevitably precluded "equal."

In segregation (or segregated inclusion) regimes, labor is included in a narrow range of corporate decisions—predominantly "redistributive" decisions of wage and hour bargaining). In integration (or integrated inclusion) regimes labor is included in a broader range of corporate decisions—"productivist" decisions that include investment decisions related to technology, employment, training, work organization). The terms "segregation" and "integration" encapsulate not only the type of relationship between capital's and labor's interests that pertain to production, but also the relationship between capital's and labor's functions in production. In segregation regimes, there is a strict separation between the functions of execution and of conception, with labor restricted to execution of functions conceived exclusively by capital (or its representatives). In integration regimes, labor is involved in both the execution and conception functions, even though management specializes in the latter.

Even when we assume that the weapon of the strike introduces elements of labor control over the means of production, it is not immediately apparent that a veritable political process is underway. The "mini-democracy" view of industrial relations by "industrial pluralists" (Dunlop et al.) ignores the structural inequality of the capital-labor relationship: capital can ultimately outlive labor in a strike, because of its larger reserves of wealth; and it is harder for labor than it is for capital to define and orient its strategies[92]. In other words, if the basis of labor's power to influence the production and appropriation of wealth is the legitimation of its **right to exit** from the social arrangements with capital, it is certainly a power inadequate to match the power which capital derives from its **ownership rights**.

Labor can inflict costs on capital for certain unfavorable decisions (such as higher pay for overtime, severance pay for dismissals) but cannot change the general direction of the policy that lead to those decisions. That is particularly so under certain regimes of inclusion (such as the postwar United States and French production regimes), where labor is included only in a narrow scope of corporate decisions (mainly, wage bargaining). Thus labor in such regimes has found itself in the unenviable position of having to influence a part of corporate decisions without any perspective of the corporation's general strategy. Labor, in such regimes, has had to perform a redistributive function in isolation from a productivist strategy reserved for capital. As long as labor is thus not **integrated** into the general process of policy formulation, it cannot propose alternative decisions but only amendments to already formulated policies of a narrow scope. However, in regimes of labor integration (or integration regimes, for short), such as the German and Japanese variants discussed below, labor is not limited to exercising its influence "from outside" the corporation, or in isolation from the corporation's productivist concerns, but its influence is endogenous to the corporate decision-making process; labor's demands and capital's demands are articulated in a common arena of decision-making, neither sequentially nor hierarchically.

The distinction which we make between segregation and integration regimes is also expressed in the different types of instruments available to labor in the process of its inclusion in corporate decision-making:

(a) exit. We are thus referring to the weapon of strike. This is the main instrument available to labor in segregation regimes. Exit is also available in integration regimes, but its significance is diminished by other kinds of instruments that are also available to labor in such regimes. In what became integration regimes labor was successful in using exit as a means of acquiring qualitatively new instruments (see below), while in segregation regimes exit was not (successfully) used for regime-transforming ends.

(b) voice. We are referring to labor's right of representation on the board of directors, and, thereby, its right to voice its concerns with a reasonable chance to persuade without having to resort to exit. It is found in representation regimes, and only in elementary form (on a consultation basis) in incorporation regimes. In segregation regimes labor lacks voice; collective bargaining rights, should not be confused with voice, since the outcome of such bargaining is predicated only on the feasibility of exit. Thus we are conceptualizing "voice" in a narrower manner than Hirschman or Medoff and Freeman, who would call any form of labor-capital dialogue "voice."[93] In segregation regimes, in meetings of the board of directors, labor does **not** have a voice; its influence there, when it is felt at all, is more akin to "noise" than to "voice." We thus reserve the term "voice" for the type of influence that is based on labor's power to inject its interests in corporate decisions by participating in a regularized discourse with capital's representatives over corporate policy (see Chapter 3).

(c) fusion. We are referring to labor's right to remain an inseparable, indispensable component of the corporation. This instrument prevails in incorporation regimes and, in the case of Japan, it is based on lifetime employment guarantees. It ensures that capital, unable to "rid" itself of labor, is obligated to maintain labor's motivation and skills. We differentiate between voice and fusion because the latter instrument does not accord labor an autonomous forum for expressing its interests/demands. In incorporation regimes, labor maintains an autonomous presence only in wage bargaining, yet the protection of its skill-formation and employment interests are "built in", and derive "automatically" from its inseparability from the corporation.

In regimes where the main source of labor's power is the option of exiting from any form of cooperation with capital in production, labor's social position vis a vis the corporation is that of **contracted help**— with the pejorative connotations of "help" acknowledged. In regimes where labor's source of power is not only exit but also voice, labor's social position is that of **junior partner**. In regimes where labor's source of power is exit and fusion, labor's social position is that of **tenured member**.

Labor's basis and scope of influence in decision making, or the organization of interests correspond to distinct types of division of labor between capital (management) and labor; such degree of functional specialization, in turn, determines the type of labor's contribution to industrial performance. Thus in segregation regimes (basis of inclusion: exit; scope of inclusion: redistributive issues; labor's execution functions strictly separated from conceptual functions), labor's contribution to productivity is indirect and incidental. Labor in regimes where it is contracted help and its source of power is the option of exit is not active in improving the corporation's productive performance, nor is it expected from capital to do so. The responsibility for industrial performance lies exclusively with capital (management). However, through its concerted ability to push for increasing wages under the threat of a strike, labor in such regimes has the indirect but important effect of forcing management to undertake strategies of productivity improvement that can satisfy labor's demand for rising wages.

In other words, in segregation regimes, unlike in previous regimes of exclusion, labor contributes to real productivity increases for the regime by precluding (inasmuch as its power to exit and social position as contracted help allow) managerial options for only **apparent** productivity increases: namely, productivity increases for the corporation but not for the regime as a whole; gains can be achieved simply by lowering real or even nominal wages (super-exploitation). One cannot overemphasize the significance of this point. The ability of the lower class to put limits to its exploitation is an integral part of the dynamism of the economic system, a dynamism otherwise attributable exclusively to the innovative genius of the upper class and/or to the creative role of markets[94].

In representation regimes (basis of inclusion: exit and voice; scope of inclusion: redistributive and productivist issues; labor's execution functions integrated with certain conception function), labor's contribution to productivity is quite positive, which is to be expected from the fact of its participation in corporate strategy formulation. It should be added, however, that labor's contribution to improving productive performance in representation regimes is direct but conditional; its contribution can be extended or withdrawn, depending on management's cooperation with key labor demands during the process of corporate strategy formulation (particularly on the issue of preventing layoffs and deskilling).

Lastly, in incorporation regimes (basis of inclusion: exit and voice; scope of inclusion: redistributive and productivist issues; labor's execution functions integrated with certain conception function), labor's contribution to productivity is direct and unconditional, reflecting the permanent, or constitutionally embedded nature of lifetime employment guarantees. Labor, in such regimes, has a definite interest in enhancing productivity, since, as a matter of company-constitutional principle, it is assured that productivity improvements can only enhance labor's interests, since layoffs are unthinkable even in bad market conditions and wages are explicitly tied to productive performance. Unable to shed "excess" labor and thus motivated to maximize the productivity of a permanent labor force, management, in such regimes, also has a strong incentive to ensure that labor remains capable of adapting to changing work needs, and motivated to readily contribute its hands-on knowledge into the process of productivity improvements.

The segregation, representation, and integration regimes defined in our framework are "ideal types." Their historical/empirical denotations will be presented in the following examination of the production regimes of the United States, Germany, and Japan. Through these presentations it will become clear that, while the production regimes of Germany and Japan have changed little since the 1950s, that has not been the case in the United States. During the 1980s, the segregation regime of the United States, it will be argued, unable to compete with the more efficient integration regimes of Germany and Japan, has made hesitant yet significant moves away from segregation.

MEASURING LABOR'S POWER AND INDUSTRIAL PERFORMANCE

In Chapter 1 we defended the choices which shaped our research design. We also justified our methods for assessing labor's power and industrial performance through qualitative and quantitative analyses, by comparing the institutional structures and substantive outcomes of automobile production regimes. The highly contested nature of the concepts of labor's power and industrial performance, however, make it necessary to it necessary to elaborate on our justifications for the operationalizations and measurements adopted.

Measuring Labor's Power

The notion that labor's power could have a positive effect on efficiency received a strong impetus by Freeman and Medoff's influential econometric analysis of unionization and productivity.[95] They argued that the neo-classical view of unions's "monopoly" function in the labor market captures only one of two functions which unions have, the other being their "voice" function. The latter, accordingly, enhances productivity by institutionalizing better communication between labor and management, thus reducing worker turnover and retraining costs for replacement workers. However, their cross-industry and cross-sectoral econometric analysis showed that unionization had a weak but positive impact on productivity, but this and subsequent analyses were not entirely convincing.[96]

For one thing, some challenged the conclusion that unionization contributed to productivity, despite the documented correlation. The data, it was argued, was compatible with a different interpretation, namely that unions are likely to flourish in the most productive industries; that unions were a symptom, not a cause, of productivity.[97] Moreover, "unionization" was too broad as an indicator of labor's power in the firm. Was it appropriate to consider the impact on productivity of "unionized" firms despite the disparate types and degrees of unionization that existed? Was the apparent decline in American competitiveness attributable to the American type of unionization than to the degree of unionization?[98]

Here we shall assess labor's power in two complementary ways. First, we review "qualitative" indicators of labor's power in corporate decision making: institutions through which labor's fundamental interests are included in corporate decision making, such as collective bargaining, codetermination, lifetime employment. Here we differentiate between labor's fundamental redistributive (wages, benefits) and productivist interests (employment security, skills), and examine the extent of inclusion of each type of interest granted by each regime.

Second, we analyze "quantitative" indicators of labor's power through a proxy for labor's power, substantive outcomes for labor's key interests. In other words, we analyze labor's power through its intended consequences, the satisfaction of its redistributive and productivist interests. After all, in line with Weber's definition of power (see above), the ability to satisfy one's interests (against resistance by others) is tantamount to having power. Thus, lest our demonstration of labor's "procedural ability" to secure its interests is not convincing enough, we provide evidence of labor's "substantive ability" to do the same.

We are arguing that the procedural inclusion and the substantive satisfaction of labor's fundamental interests in corporate decision making are evidence of labor's power therein. But is it not possible that, rather than reflecting labor's power in corporate decision making, the said procedures and outcomes reflect the operation of other forces, such as economic conditions, or the state's incomes policy? Possibly, but not likely.

While favorable economic conditions undeniably contribute to favorable economic outcomes for labor, they do so largely by augmenting labor's power in corporate decision making: whatever its origins, labor's power remains the immediate and critical determinant for the satisfaction of its interests. Low unemployment, for example, does not automatically raise wages. Rather, low unemployment augments labor's bargaining power vis a vis its employers by making labor more scarce and increasing the cost of job loss[99], which in turn brings about more labor-friendly decisions on wages.

A further specification in measuring labor's power is necessary. It may be objected that labor's fundamental interests (and corresponding power to satisfy them) are not confined to total compensation and employment stability. Meaningful (non-alienating, skilled) work, for example, may be considered as a fundamental labor interest that is not captured by employment security. The problem with alienation and labor skills is that they are very difficult to quantify, let alone compare systematically across cultural borders. For example, "years of job training" may be considered a measurement of skill, but a very unreliable one, given the possibly wide cross-national gaps in the quality of training provided. Moreover, far from ignoring the significance of labor's skills, we shall argue that (relatively) skilled work is likely to coexist with (relatively) high wages and employment stability.

Even if total compensation and employment stability are not exhaustive indicators of labor's fundamental interests, they are important enough; the claims of an analysis based on them might be more limited but still highly pertinent.

Measuring Industrial Performance

The operationalization but also the very conceptualization of productivity and efficiency remain highly problematic tasks. Was Japan more efficient than the U.S. in the 1980s, or had it only narrowed the American lead in efficiency? Was Germany more efficient or less efficient than the U.S.? Even when the efficiency of the same industry is analyzed, vastly different assessments emerge. For example, while the M.I.T. studies cited above documented a large productivity gap between Japanese and American auto production, another 1992 study of the international auto industry reported only a small Japanese lead. The same study placed German auto productivity at a mere 57% of Japanese levels.[100] Another sophisticated study pointed out that the output per employee of Japan's auto industry was 36% lower than that of the U.S., and even 14% lower than Canada's.[101]

Part of the problem could be addressed if the basic measure of productivity, benefit as a function of cost, is made sensitive to cross-national variations in capacity utilization, degree of vertical integration, factor prices, etc—although the "weights" assigned to such variables could themselves be a source of distortion in cross-national productivity assessment.

But there is still a fundamental problem; that **the point of reference** of productivity is, intentionally or not, the stockholders and their managers rather than the production regime as a whole. Thus, most measures of productivity or efficiency are calculations of the costs and benefits of production for the capitalist, completely ignoring, for example, those costs of production which the capitalist may "externalize" to the rest of the production regime, particularly to the worker, in the form of unemployment, deskilling, alienation, adverse health effects, pollution. To wit, slavery was a very wasteful (of human and natural resources) production regime, although near-zero production costs to the slave owner pushed the output/input ratio of "productivity" through the roof.[102]

The research strategy adopted here is to measure industrial efficiency indirectly, through two complementary types of indicators. In order to avoid the shortcomings of the alternatives mentioned above and the intricacies of operationalizing the costs of production externalized to labor, we compare levels of industrial efficiency through a comparison of pertinent **effects of** industrial efficiency: consumers' evaluations of the products of a certain regime over another's. We base this strategy on the plausible stipulation that, *ceteris paribus*, superior production efficiency will be reflected in superior products.

We propose to measure relative consumer preferences for the autos of each regime through the complementary use of a price-sensitive and a non-price-sensitive indicator, product reliability surveys and auto balance of trade, respectively.

Why is consumer preference a better indicator of a regime's performance than the more widely used indicators, such as productivity? Isn't consumer preference as misleading as productivity—directly expressive of or coterminous with the rate of exploitation? The automobile balance of trade and auto reliability surveys, to be sure, might also be expressive of the rate of exploitation. That is why we compare the regimes' industrial performance in juxtaposition with labor's power/fortunes therein. Moreover, our indicators of industrial performance, are further separated from and not coterminous with the rate of exploitation. Unlike "output per hour," "unit labor cost," or "return to investment," the indicators we adopt do not vary in (inverse) proportion to wage or employment levels.

Thus, for example, while an increase in the rate of exploitation in a production regime (reduction in wages or in employment) will be reflected in commensurate increases in its measure of "productivity" (output per hour, or unit labor cost), it is less likely that its balance of trade or its product reliability ratings will be affected in the same degree, if at all. That is because the effect of a change in labor costs on the balance of trade is mediated by the price elasticity of demand for the product (which in turn depends on consumer perceptions of the product's quality. The effect of a change in labor costs is even less likely to affect product reliability ratings, as product quality is clearly not a direct function of labor costs.

The most dependable source of auto reliability surveys is the *Consumer Reports* and their annual frequency-of-repair records, which date back to the early 1970s. The non-profit nature of the Reports as well as their long experience single them out as the best available source of consumer surveys of auto reliability.[103]

Additionally, we provide data from J.D. Power & Associates' Vehicle Dependability Study, which dates back to 1985.[104]

It is noteworthy that the most frequently cited J.D. Power index of auto quality, the Customer Satisfaction Index (CSI), is not, as one might think, an index of auto reliability. The CSI results from the combination of **two** major factors affecting customer satisfaction, only one of which reflects industrial performance. Indeed, the CSI results from a combination of an index of Customer Handling, which addresses primarily dealership service, and which has little to do with production efficiency, and the index of Vehicle Repair and Reliability. Thus, more suitable for our purposes is a lesser-known but more pertinent measurement of quality of manufacturing, J.D. Power's Vehicle Dependability Study, which measures problems per 100 vehicles and their impact on satisfaction after five years of ownership.[105]

Telling as the above reliability surveys may be of the relative quality of American, German, and Japanese autos, it suffers from its complete abstraction from the respective prices at which these autos are available—the inverse weakness of indicators that measure costs with no regard to quality. An economically relevant assessment of industrial performance cannot be limited to the quality of the product but must also include an evaluation of the competitiveness of the product, or consumers' evaluation of the product's "value" (quality/price). The balance of international trade in autos satisfies this requirement, as it registers, *ceteris paribus*, the preferences of consumers for the autos of the respective regimes.

One may plausibly object at this point that a favorable balance of trade, even if it does not directly reflect national differences in cost structure, might still be less a reflection of the production regime's efficiency in transforming inputs into outputs than of the state's trade and industrial policy and/or of currency fluctuations. It will be shown, however, through the long time frame of our comparative analysis, that the observed cross-regime variations in the auto balance of trade are only marginally affected by changes in state involvement in auto production or by changes in trade policies or in exchange rates.

Moreover, our stipulation that the auto balance of trade is an appropriate gauge of industrial performance is independently confirmed by the fact that the evolution of the auto balance of trade of the three regimes over time closely mirrors the evolution of industrial performance as registered by our other indicator, auto reliability ratings. Whether labor's power and industrial performance are causally related or simply covary will be discussed in the concluding chapter's review of alternative explanations of the performance differentials among the three regimes. Here, it should suffice to suggest that the long time frame of our analysis allows us to control for the undeniable contribution of various other factors to industrial relations and performance.

NOTES

1. For an overview of the industrial relations literature see Greg J. Bamber and Russel D. Lansbury (eds), "Studying International and Comparative Industrial Relations," idem (eds.), *International and Comparative Industrial Relations: A Study of Developed Market Economies* (London: Allen & Unwin, 1987).

2. Competitiveness is indicative of relative efficiency and productivity, but it refers more directly to the ability to compete in the market. It can be understood as a consequence of the efficiency and/or productivity of a firm at the level of market performance: the ability to sell or to produce products of

relatively high "value," i.e. quality/price. It can be measured as the balance of trade in a given good, or it terms of market share.

3. Marx uses "free" labor sarcastically as well as literally. Literally, free labor refers to labor's freedom under capitalism to sell its capacity to produce to the employer of its choice (in contrast to serfs under feudalism). Sarcastically, free labor refers to labor's obligation to sell its labor power to an employer, given that it is bereft of any means of production of its own.

4. The most authoritative exposition of the "transaction cost" approach to capitalist organization is Oliver E. Williamson, *The Economic Institutions of Capitalism* (Detroit: Free Press, 1985).

5. "Fordism" is closely related to taylorism, but does not refer so much to the labor process as to the more macro-level, political context of taylorism: stifling of labor opposition to taylorism through higher wages; the latter are not seen as a reward for labor but as a method of stimulating aggregated demand. See the works of Braverman, Edwards, Gordon et al., Marglin, Gartman, Boyer, Howell. "Post-fordism" expressed an acknowledgment that fordism is in eclipse, although an alternative system is yet to be crystallized. See Sabel (1982), Jurgens et al. (1993). See the following discussion of "toyotism" and "micro-corporatism" as updates of the control/regulation approach to capitalist organization.

6. Braverman (1974). See also the briefer treatment by Stephen A. Marglin, "What Do Bosses Do? The Origins and Functions of Hierarchy in Capitalist Production," *Review of Radical Political Economy* (Summer 1974).

7. Andrew Zimbalist (ed.), *Case Studies on the Labor Process* (New York: Monthly Review Press, 1977). The literature on technology is extensive. See David F. Noble, *Forces of Production: a Social History of Industrial Automation* (New York: Knopf, 1984); Shaiken (1988), *Work Transformed Automation and Labor in the Computer Age* (Lexington, MA: Lexington Books, 1994); and Barbara Garson, *The Electronic Sweatshop* (New York: Penguin Books, 1988).

8. For a good review of the labor process school see Peter Meiksins "'Labor and Monopoly Capital' for the 1990s: A Review and Critique of the Labor Process Debate" *Monthly Labor Review*, Special Issue: Commemorating Harry Braverman's 'Labor and Monopoly Capital,' (November 1994).

9. Edwards (1979).

10. Burawoy, *op. cit.*

11. One of the best compilation of critiques of Braverman and of the control perspective is Stephen Wood (ed), *The Degradation of Work? Skill, Deskilling and the Labour Process* (London: Hutchinson & Co., 1982).

12. Tony Elger, "Braverman, Capital Accumulation and Deskilling," in Wood, *op. cit.*, p. 25.

13. For a critique of Braverman's work as US-centric see Craig Littler, *The Development of the Labor Process in Capitalist Societies* (London: Heinemann, 1982).

14. For stark accounts of the condition of U.S. labor in the 1980s see, for example, Donald Wells, *Empty Promises: QWL Programs and the Labor Movement* (New York: Monthly Review Press, 1987); Parker and Slaughter (1988); Elly Leary and Marybeth Menaker, *Jointness at General Motors: Company Unions in the 21st Century* (New Directions, Internet access, 1995). For a longer-range account see also Leo Troy, "The rise and fall of American trade unions: the labor movement from FDR to RR," in S.M. Lipset (ed.), *Unions in Transition: Entering the Second Century* (San Francisco: ICS Press, 1986).

15. Gartman (1982), p. 72.

16. See, for example, Michel Aglietta, *A Theory of Capitalist Regulation: The U.S. Experience* (London: Verso 1979), Lipietz (1986); and Boyer (1988).

17. See David Gordon, "Stages of Accumulation and Long Economic Cycles," in T. Hopkins and I. Wallerstein (eds), *Processes of the World System* (Beverly Hills: Sage Publications, 1980); D. Gordon, R. Edwards and M. Reich, *Segmented Work, Divided Workers* (Cambridge: Cambridge University Press, 1982); Bowles, Gordon, and Weisskopf, *Beyond the Wasteland: A Democratic Alternative to Economic Decline* (Garden City: Anchor/Doubleday, 1983).

18. For a comparative analysis of the two schools see David M. Kotz, "A Comparative Analysis of the Theory of Regulation and the Social Structure of Accumulation Theory," *Science and Society"* (Spring 1990, pp. 5-28).

19. Boyer (1988);. Urlich Jurgens, Thomas Malsch and Knuth Dohse, *Breaking from Taylorism: Changing Forms of Work in the Automobile Industry* (Cambridge: Cambridge University Press, 1993); Howell (1992).

20. This understanding of 'toyotism' resonates in Michael Burawoy's classification of contemporary Japanese production as a "despotic factory regime," akin to that found in the West during 19th-century capitalism. Burawoy (1985), p. 143.

21. Howell (1992).

22. James, O'Connor, *The Fiscal Crisis of the State* (New York: St. Martin's Press, 1973); Claus Offe, *Contradictions of the Welfare State*, (John Keane, ed.) (Cambridge, Mass.: MIT Press, 1984).

23. According to Samuel Huntington, "That which Marxists erroneously ascribe to the capitalist economy is in reality a result of the democratic political

process." Idem, "The United States," in Michel Crozier (ed), *The Crisis of Democracy: Report on the Governability of Democracies to the Trilateral Commission* (New York: NYU Press, 1975), p. 73.

24. Alain Lipietz views Japanese capitalism represents a special way of harvesting workers' manual as well as intellectual skills. Alain Lipietz, *Mirages and Miracles* (London: Verso, 1987).

25. Alfred D. Chandler, Jr., *Strategy and Structure: Chapters in the History of American Industrial Enterprise* (Cambridge, MA: MIT Press, 1962).

26. Alfred D. Chandler, Jr., "The Competitive Performance of U.S. Industrial Enterprises since the Second World War," *Business History Review* 68 (Spring 1994).

27. Oliver E. Williamson (1985). A transaction occurs when a good or service is transferred across a technologically separable interface.

28. Oliver E. Williamson (1985), p. 231.

29. See Masahiko Aoki, *Information, Incentives, and Bargaining in the Japanese Economy* (New York: Cambridge University Press, 1988), p. 29. For a neo-Marxist critique of the transaction-cost approach see Marilyn Kleinberg Neimark, *The Hidden Dimensions of Annual Reports: Sixty Years of Social Conflict at General Motors* (New York: Marcus Wiener Publishing, Inc., 1992).

30. See, for example, Hatsopoulos and Brooks (1986).

31. Among the first to make the argument for US managerial "myopia" were Robert H. Hayes and William A. Abernathy, "Managing Our Way to Economic Decline," *Harvard Business Review* 58 (July-August 1980).

32. The capital markets argument is refuted in cross-firm analyses. A large number of US companies—including General Motors, Ford, Du Pont, ITT, and Goodyear—appear to have overinvested by a substantial margin in physical capital and traditional R&D. In such cases, massive spending on facilities and R&D failed to secure technological or market leadership. See Michael Jensen, "The Modern Industrial Revolution: Exit and the Failure of Internal Control Systems," *Journal of Finance* 48 (July 1993).

33. Carliss Y. Baldwin and Kim B. Clark (1994).

34. Kim B. Clark and Takahiro Fujimoto, *Product Development Performance: Strategy, Organization, and Management in the World Auto Industry* (Boston, Mass.: Harvard Business School Press, 1991).

35. Jeffrey A. Hart, *Rival Capitalists: International Competitiveness in the United States, Japan, and Western Europe* (Ithaca, N.Y.: Cornell University Press, 1992).

36.

37. The McKinsey Global Institute, *Manufacturing Productivity* (Washington, D.C.: McKinsey & Co., 1993); Carliss Y. Baldwin and Kim B.

Clark, "Capital-Budgeting Systems and Capabilities Investments in U.S. Companies After the Second World War," *Business History Review* (March 22, 1994).

38. Ibid, p. 285.

39. Piore and Sabel (1984). The brevity of our presentation of their work is due to the familiarity of their work.

40. This argument is foreshadowed in Charles F. Sabel, *Work and Politics: The Division of Labor in Industry* (Cambridge, Mass.: Cambridge University Press, 1982), chapter 5.

41. Piore and F.Sabel (1984), p. 15 and p. 222.

42. Recently, Sabel has rejected his earlier mode of ascribing central tendencies to different periods. He now stresses a continuous experimentation with diverse modes of work organization. Historical agents, he now argues, have rarely committed themselves to a single model of work organization, preferring to continuously adapt their actions to changing circumstances and to hedge their bets against contingencies. Sabel, Charles F. and Jonathan Zeitlin, "Stories, Strategies, Structures: Rethinking Historical Alternatives to Mass Production," in idem (eds.), *Worlds of Possibility: Flexibility and Mass Production in Western Industrialization* (Cambridge, Mass.: Cambridge University Press, forthcoming).

43. Benjamin Coriat, *Penser a l'envers: travail et organization dans l'enterprise japonaise* (Paris: Christian Bourgeois Editeur, 1991). See also the regulationist account of Japan's transcendence of the mass production paradigm in Alain Lipietz (1987).

44. See the contributions to Wood (1982); Richard Hyman, and Wolfgang Streeck, *New Technology and Industrial Relations* (New York: Blackwell, 1988); Tolliday, Steven and Jonathan Zeitlin (eds) *The Automobile Industry and its Workers: Between Fordism and Flexibility* (Cambridge: Polity Press, 1986); Christian Berggren, *Alternatives to Lean Production: Work Organization in the Swedish Auto Industry* (Ithaca, N.Y.: ILR Press, 1992); Jurgens et al. (1993).

45. Mike Parker and Jane Slaughter have characterized U.S. versions of labor-management cooperation and flexible work organization as "management by stress." Idem (1988).

46. Kenney and Florida (1993), p. 26.

47. On the particular affinity of micro-electronic technologies to labor-management cooperation see Peter Brodner, *Skill Based Automation: Proceedings of the IFAC Workshop, Karlsruhe, FRG, 3-5 September, 1986* (New York: Pergamon Press, 1987); Gustavsen, Bjorn, Peter Grootings, Lajor

Hethy (eds), *New Forms of Work Organization in Europe* (New Brunswick, N.J.: Transaction Books, 1989).

48. David Friedman considers Japan as a hybrid economy, with features of mass production coexisting with features of "flexible specialization." *The Misunderstood Miracle: Industrial Development and Political Change in Japan* (Ithaca, N.Y.: Cornell University Press, 1988).

49. Womack et al. (1990); Krafcik (1988); John F. Krafcik and John Paul MacDuffie, "Explaining High Performance Manufacturing: The International Automotive Assembly Plant Study," (Cambridge, Mass.: MIT Press, 1989).

50. For a critique of the methodology and prescriptions of "lean production" see Karel Williams, Colin Haslam, John Williams, Tony Cutler, Andy Adcroft, Johal Sukhdev, "Against Lean Production," *Economy and Society* (August 1992). See also Christian Berggren (1992).

51. The authors argue, for example, that the mass production system was adopted in a national-specific form, shaped by the producers' relationship to (a) the world market, (b) the state (c) the postwar labor movement. Piore and Sabel (1984), p. 222.

52. Alan Altshuler, Martin Anderson, Daniel Jones, Daniel Roos, and James Womack, *The Future of the Automobile: The Report of MIT's International Automobile Program* (Cambridge: MIT Press, 1986).

53. "The key to the successful implementation of this new Japanese system is the industrial group." Ibid., p. 147.

54. " . . . the Japanese have developed relationships among the automotive industrial groups, their financing sources, and industrial groups in other sectors that seem to carry competitive advantages over typical arrangements in the United States and some of the European Auto Program countries." Ibid, p. 149.

55. "The notion that quality costs more has been reversed [in Japan]. Defect prevention turns out to cost less. Similarly, the traditional assumption that large inventory buffers are needed for high process yield has been turned around . . . A large number of good parts per unit of operating time, seems most likely to be obtained with very low buffers." Ibid, p. 146.

56. " . . . the Japanese producers have learned that moving knowledge, skills, and decision making down the system into the hands of the primary work force makes the old supervision and information-gathering systems redundant." Ibid, p. 146.

57. Ibid, p. 207.

58. Ibid, pp. 209-210.

59. Harry C. Katz, Thomas A. Kochan and Kenneth R. Gobeille, "Industrial Relations Performance, Economic Performance, and QWL Programs: An Interplant Analysis," *Industrial and Labor Relations Review*, (October 1983).

60. Maryellen R. Kelley and Bennett Harrison, "Unions, Technology, and Labor-Management Cooperation," in L. Mishel and P. Voos (eds), *Unions and Economic Competitiveness* (New York: M.E. Sharpe, Inc., 1992). For a similar conclusion see also Paula B. Voos, "The Influence of Cooperative Programs on Union-Management Relations, Flexibility, and Other Labor Relations Outcomes," *Journal of Labor Research* (Winter 1989).

61. Barry Bluestone and Irving Bluestone, *Negotiating the future: a labor perspective on American business* (New York: Basic Books, 1992), p. 14. The Bluestones advocate what they call an "Enterprise Compact" between labor and management in the organized sector, which would include labor representation on the Board of Directors and the abolition of traditional management rights clauses.

62. Goldfield (1987); Thomas Kochan, Harry C. Katz and Robert B. McKersie (eds), *Challenges and Choices Facing American Labor* (Cambridge: MIT Press, 1985); Idem, *The Transformation of American Industrial Relations* (New York: Basic Books, 1986); Parker and Slaughter (1988).

63. Kochan et al. (1986), pp. 203-205. Sabel makes a similar argument in "A Fighting Chance: Stuctural Change and New Labor Strategies," *International Journal of Political Economy* (Fall 1987).

64. John T. Dunlop, *Industrial Relations Systems* (New York: Holt Rinehart, and Winston, 1958).

65. Kochan et al. (1986).

66. Wolfgang Streeck, *Industrial Relations in West Germany: A Case Study of the Car Industry* (New York: St. Martin's Press, 1984).

67. Streeck, Wolfgang, "Industrial Relations and Industrial Change: the Restructuring of the World Automobile Industry in the 1970s and 1980s," *Economic and Industrial Democracy*, vol. 8, 1987.

68. Ibid., p. 458.

69. Turner (1991).

70. Christian Berggren's highly suggestive analysis of the Swedish alternative to flexible production is also too deeply rooted in social-democratic criteria for assessing labor's power. Berggren (1992).

71. Kenney and Florida (1988); and idem (1993).

72. Ibid., p. 14.

73. Lazonick, William, *Business Organization and the Myth of the Market Economy* (New York: Cambridge University Press, 1991); also idem (1988).

74. Ibid., pp. 37-38.

75. Aoki (1988), esp. p. 26.

76. Ibid., p. 31.

77. Weber, 1978, p. 53. For the various definitions of power see the collection of writings and Steven Lukes's introduction in Lukes (1986).

78. Nicos Poulantzas, *State, Power, Socialism* (London: Verso, 1978), p. 147 (emphasis in the original).

79. Poulantzas's "objective class interests" is problematic for his relational definition of class power. If the objective interest of labor is understood in a maximalist sense, as the overthrow of capitalism, any expression of labor's power short of revolution is meaningless, inasmuch as it contributes to the continuation of capitalism if in a modified form.

80. The "commodification" of labor under classical capitalism is a systemic tendency, rather than a **fait accompli**; labor has resisted its commodification through work stoppages, food riots, and industrial sabotage (e.g. the Luddites). According to Marx, it is this tendency of commodification that reveals labor's "negation" by the capitalist system, and foreshadows the "negation" of the system by labor.

81. Robert Brenner, "The Origins of Capitalist Development: A Critique of Neo-Smithean Marxism," *New Left Review* (July-August 1977).

82. "Externalities" are a cause of "market failure." They are defined as "the effects of the output of private goods and services on persons other than those who are directly buying or selling or using the goods in question." Robert L. Heilbroner and James K. Galbraith, *The Economic Problem* (Englewood Cliffs, N.J.: Prentice-Hall, 1987), p. 484. The authors do not refer to the hire-and-fire method, but to general "disutilities" involved in a process of production. Another famous economist suggest that "wherever there are externalities, a strong case can be made for supplanting complete individualism by some kind of group action [. . .] in the interest of all." Paul A. Samuelson, *Economics* (New York: McGraw-Hill, 1973), p. 475.

83. Gosta Esping-Andersen, *Politics against Markets: The Social Democratic Road to Power* (Princeton: Princeton University Press, 1985).

84. Burawoy (1985). The difference between the concept of "production politics" developed here and Burawoy's "politics of production" is not only a matter of linguistic style but substantive—analogous to the difference between "political sociology" and "sociology of politics," discussed in Giovanni Sartori's early article. "From the Sociology of Politics to Political Sociology," in Seymour Martin Lipset (ed.), *Politics and the Social Sciences* (London: Oxford University Press, 1969).

85. Burawoy (1985), p. 12.

86. Ibid., p. 144.

87. This is identified but not resolved in the Przeworski-Burawoy debate about the relationship of the working class to capitalism. See Michael Burawoy,

"Marxism without Micro-Foundations," and Adam Przeworski, "Class, Production and Politics: A Reply to Burawoy," in *Socialist Review* (2, 1989).

88. For recent analyses with a broader focus than our own, exploring the relationship between social organization and economic policy making at the national level, see the review article by Mark Kesselman, "How Should One Study Economic Policy-Making? Four Characters in Search of an Object," *World Politics* (July 1992).

89. One of the most dramatic expression of such acts is the Enclosure movement in England and Spain during the 16th century (Wallerstein, 1974, ch. 5).

90. Even the worker's labor power is no power against an employer since the worker can withhold it only by risking starvation.

91. "Free" (from means of production and feudal obligations) labor and private ownership in the means of production.

92. Claus Offe and Helmuth Wiesenthal, *Two Logics of Collective Action Theoretical Notes on Social Class and Organizational Forms.* In Maurice Zeitlin (ed.), *Political Power and Social Theory* (Greenwich, CT.: JAI Press, 1980).

93. Ibid. See also Richard B. Freeman and James L. Medoff, *What Do Unions Do?* (New York: Basic Books, 1984).

94. The critical role of a subordinate class in facilitating the productivity and dynamism of a production system by resisting repressive forms of exploitation (absolute vs. relative surplus extraction), is impressively argued by Brenner (1978) against the more "technology-" and "market-determinist" approaches to the transition from feudalism to capitalism of Frank (1969), Wallerstein (1974), Sweezy (1976).

95. Richard B. Freeman and James L. Medoff, *What Do Unions Do?* (New York: Basic Books, 1984). That unionization can have a positive effect on productivity was suggested earlier by Sumner Slichter, *Union Policies and Industrial Management* (Washington, D.C.: The Brookings Institution, 1941). Unions may "shock" management into more efficient production by raising the costs of inefficiency. Higher labor costs would lead firms to restructure and become more businesslike, hire better managers, and implement production standards along with monitoring and review processes.

96. For a good review of the vast econometric literature on unionization and productivity, see Dale Belman, "Unions, the Quality of Labor Relations, and Firm Performance," in Larry Mishel and Paula Voos (eds), *Unions and Economic Competitiveness* (Armonk, N.Y.: M.E. Sharpe, Inc., 1991). For an early treatment of the subject see Seymour Melman, *Decision-Making and Productivity* (Oxford: Blackwell, 1958).

97. See, for example, Jeffrey H. Keefe, "Do Unions Influence the Diffusion of Technology?" *Industrial and Labor Relations Review*, vol. 44, no. 2 (January 1991).

98. The effect of various types of unionization on industrial performance and on labor is addressed, albeit only partially, in Richard B. Freeman, (ed.), *Working Under Different Rules* (New York: Russel Sage Foundation, 1994). Conspicuously absent is analysis of Japanese unionization.

99. Samuel Bowles, "Post-Marxian economics: labour, learning and history," *Social Science Information* (September 1985).

100. McKinsey Global Institute, *Manufacturing Productivity* (Washington, D.C.: McKinsey & Co., 1993).

101. Melvin A. Fuss and Leonard Waverman, *Costs and Productivity in Automobile Production: The Challenge of Japanese Efficiency* (Cambridge: Cambridge University Press, 1992), p. 39. The authors find this measurement as too crude and unacceptable.

102. For an econometric account of how slavery in the US was unproductive even from the perspective of the slave-owner see Robert William Fogel, *Time on the Cross: The Economics of American Negro Slavery* (New York: W.W. Norton, 1979 and 1989).

103. For the derivation of reliability data from Consumer Reports, see Appendix.

104. J.D. Power & Associates is an Agoura Hills-based international marketing information firm, specializing in consumer opinion and customer satisfaction studies. Its annual surveys of auto customer satisfaction are among the most highly regarded in the industry.

105. For the derivation of J.D. Power data see Appendix.

CHAPTER 3

Segregation in U.S. Auto Production

This chapter explores the dual significance of unionization in the U.S. from the mid-1930s to the end of the 1970s: the inclusion of labor's redistributive interests in corporate decision making, and the exclusion of its productivist interests from corporate decision making. The resulting regime of segregated inclusion in the auto industry is presented in three steps: the legislation of segregated inclusion, the institutionalization of segregated inclusion, and the performance of segregated inclusion.

1. THE LEGISLATION OF SEGREGATED INCLUSION

At least since the Wagner Act, ownership in the means of production has become increasingly distinct from control over their utilization. The distinction is based not only on the dispersal of ownership characteristic of the modern corporation, or the rise of a professional cadre of managers who manage large corporations on behalf of shareholders.[1] Control over the means of production has stopped to automatically reside with the owners because labor has gained legal rights that challenge capital's monopoly over corporate decision making. Workers fought for these rights, and employers against them.

The Road to Wagner

The earliest comprehensive national statutory regulation of labor's rights and labor-management relations passed Congress in 1926. The Railway Labor Act, for the first time granted the national government's specific recognition of the right of employees to form unions and engage in collective bargaining. However, the Act covered only railroad employees (in 1936 it included airlines as well).

The 1932 Norris-LaGuardia Act, prohibited federal courts from issuing injunctions against strikes regardless the strike's purpose. Until then, strikes, labor's main bargaining leverage against capital, could be preempted by court orders, either as violations of state laws (protecting private property or barring "conspiracies"), or, when the former venue was not available, as violations of federal law. Courts would frequently issue injunctions against a strike, citing the federal Sherman Antitrust Act of 1890: a strike could be found to interfere with the free flow of goods in commerce and thus be considered a combination or conspiracy in restraint of trade. The Norris-LaGuardia Act thus protected the initiation of strikes but was silent on the right to organize or the right to collective representation. Labor's rights were regulated by individual states, where business-dominated legislatures and courts ensured their marginalization.

In 1933 the National Industrial Recovery Act, Section 7A provided the second legislative blow to capital by recognizing workers' right to "organize unions of their own choosing" and the right to collective bargaining. The NIRA did not establish enforcement provisions, and employers repudiated its legality. Nonetheless its symbolic impact on workers was enormous; that year, following NIRA's passage, a million workers went on strike, almost four times the average number of strikers of the previous ten years; in 1934, 1,500,000 workers were on strike.[2] In 1935 the Supreme Court ruled the NIRA unconstitutional.

The Wagner Act

However, it was the 1935 National Labor Relations Act (NLRA), often referred to as the Wagner Act, that went much further than any previous legislation, by establishing a comprehensive legal framework of labor-management relations. In this new framework labor was recognized as a central actor with rights to organize for collective representation and industrial action aimed at influencing certain corporate decisions. To the immense consternation of the whole business sector, the NLRA severely undermined the rights of capital owners, reversing the time-honored legal tradition of giving primacy to property rights when they collided with political rights, such as the First Amendment rights of free expression and association. Henceforth, owners of capital (in the non-agricultural, non-domestic, private sector) would be obligated to bargain with their employees' collective representatives over a range of corporate decisions, should the employees choose to be so represented. And, lest capital tried to circumvent its obligations, a special administrative board was created to facilitate the implementation of labor's federally guaranteed rights at the workplace. Here are the main provisions of the NLRA:

- It granted employees the right to be collectively represented by a union for purposes of bargaining with their employers (Section 7).

- It prohibited employers from infiltrating unions or from setting up employer-dominated, "yellow" unions (as was done during Welfare Capitalism), and provided for federal board-monitored procedures for certifying the employees' collective representatives (union representation elections by secret ballot or the signing of union cards—Section 9), and prohibition of union membership to non-supervisory managers, independent contractors and immediate family members of employers (Section 2(3)).

- It prohibited employers from interfering with employee rights to freely choose representation (Section 8(a)(1)).

- It prohibited an employer from discriminating against an employee because of union membership (Section 8(a)(3)).

- It mandated that an employer bargain in good faith with employees' representatives (8(a)(5)).

- It affirmed the right to strike: "Nothing in this Act, except as specifically provided for herein, shall not be construed so as either to interfere with or impede or diminish in any way the right to strike, or to affect the limitations or qualifications on that right" (Section 13).

- It established the National Labor Relations Board as the authority for enforcing the Act's provisions (Section 3).

The National Labor Relations Board (NLRB), originally consisting of three members appointed by the President, was established by the Act as an independent Federal agency. The NLRB was given power to determine whether a union should be certified to represent particular groups of employees, using such methods as it deemed suitable to reach such a determination, including the holding of a representation election among workers concerned.

Employers were forbidden by the Act from engaging in any of the five categories of unfair labor practices. Violation of this prohibition could result in the filing of a complaint with the NLRB by a union or employees. After investigation, the NLRB could order the cessation of such practices, reinstatement of a person fired for union activities, the provision of back pay, restoration of seniority, benefits, etc. An NLRB order issued in response to an unfair labor practice complaint was made enforceable by the Federal courts. Among those unfair labor practices forbidden by the Act were:

1. Dominating or otherwise interfering with formation of a labor union, including the provision of any financial or other support.

2. Interfering with or restraining employees engaged in the exercise of their rights to organize and bargain collectively.

3. Imposing any special conditions of employment which tended either to encourage or discourage union membership. The law stated, however, that this provision should be construed to prohibit union contracts requiring union membership as a condition of employment in a company—a provision which, in effect, permitted the closed and union shops. (In the former, only pre-existing members of the union could be hired, in the latter new employees were required to join the union.)

4. Discharging or discriminating against an employee because he had given testimony or filed charges under the Act.

5. Refusing to bargain collectively with unions representing a company's employees.

However, much as the NLRA granted American workers rights to an extent they had never been granted before, it did not elevate the position of labor against capital from that of hired help; it bestowed granted a certain dignity in the conditions of labor's employment without, however, recognizing any labor rights to employment. The provisions of the NLRA listed above, at the same time as they conferred labor significant rights, also carefully and importantly circumscribed those rights. As a result, labor's inclusion in corporate decision making is not entirely analogous to the participation of a social group in a political regime, (such as the inclusion of the working class in politics through the extension of the suffrage). What the NLRA sanctions is a segregated inclusion of labor in corporate decision making. The characterization the nature of labor inclusion under the NLRA as "segregated" is approptiate, considering the following legal limitations on labor's participation in corporate decision making:

(a) The law identifies as "mandatory" subjects over which capital must bargain with labor's representatives "wages, hours, and other terms and conditions of employment"[3]. What are the "other terms and conditions of employment?" The law is vague enough to allow court interpretations that distinguish between workers' rights to bargain with capital over wages, hours and promotion procedures, and capital's rights to unilaterally make "managerial" or "capital" or investment decisions. This distinction, in effect, segregates labor's redistributive/disciplinary interests from its productivist interests, and puts labor in the precarious position of having to protect the former without any control over the latter. Indeed, as we will see, labor in the auto industry initially insisted on a broader definition, that would have secured its inclusion in every type of corporate decision, including investment decisions. By the end of the 1940s, however, labor conceded "managerial" decisions to management; later, in the few instances when it sought to challenge managerial prerogatives over "managerial" decisions, labor was rebuffed by the courts. Indeed, this section has been interpreted by the courts to exclude certain basic "managerial" decisions, involving "the scope and direction of the enterprise" from the field of mandatory subjects of bargaining[4].

(b) The law states that an employer must bargain with the union before changing any conditions of employment. However, if such changes result from managerial decisions that are deemed as managerial prerogative, then there is no obligation on the part of the employer for prior bargaining over the **decision** itself, only the obligation to bargain over the decision's **effects** on the employees, after the implementation of the changes and the manifestation of negative effects in working conditions[5]. A 1964 Supreme Court decision ruled that certain subcontracting decisions are mandatory subjects of bargaining, if the subcontracted work is done under the same working conditions as before[6]. Thus an employer can unilaterally, without prior bargaining, institute a new policy, if the policy stems from "a basic capital decision on the scope and ultimate direction of the enterprise"[7].

(c) Labor's right to collective bargaining over a certain range of corporate decisions may result in the *de facto* inclusion of certain labor interests in corporate decisions, reflected, for instance, in steadily rising compensation decisions. But labor's legal rights are not so constituted as to recognize labor as a member of the enterprise's decision making body. Labor is segregated, kept away from managers and corporate boards, having a legitimate right to exercise its influence over corporate boards from outside. In fact the bargaining forum is distinct from the decision making forum of the corporation, the latter being reserved for (the representatives of) the employers. As a direct consequence of this segregation of forums, labor must pursue its interests without the perspective of the general condition and plans of the corporation.

(d) An employer's duty to bargain with the union, over issues relating to labor's narrowly construed, immediate interests, not pertaining to the direction of the enterprise, is further weakened by the requirement to bargain only "to an impasse": the employer cannot be required to agree to a proposal or make a concession (nor can the union); he may lawfully bargain for the most favorable agreement possible (so can the union); he can use his bargaining power to get a better agreement as long as he intends to reach an agreement on the terms he has proposed, and end bargaining as soon as a party determines that further bargaining will not secure such agreement. Moreover, after bargaining to an impasse, the employer can implement his decisions even while a union grievance about the decision is pending (Section 8(d)).

(e) The law does not require that the bargaining process have even the pretense of joint decision making, by mandating common information and cooperation during bargaining. For one thing, the union is entitled to only a limited amount of information about the company, and that only during contract negotiations; the employer is not required to provide the union with investment commitments, or work reorganization plans. Labor's information rights are limited to information directly related to management's bargaining position. For example, labor has a right to information on corporate profitability during contract negotiations if, and only if, management bases its refusal to agree with the union's proposed wage increases on the corporation's inability (as opposed to unwillingness) to pay for them ("pleading poverty"). For another thing, during bargaining, before an impasse is reached, the employer (and the union) can deploy the ultimate weapon of the lock out (the strike) against the union (the employer). This provision was tested and confirmed in the Supreme Court's *NLRB v. Insurance Agents International Union*:

> "The parties . . . proceed from contrary and to an extent antagonistic viewpoints and concepts of self-interest. The system has not reached the ideal of the philosophic notion that perfect understanding among people would lead to perfect agreement among them on values. The presence of economic weapons in reserve, and their actual exercise on occasion by the parties, is part and parcel of the system that the Wagner and Taft-Hartley Acts have recognized . . . [A]t the present statutory stage of our national labor relations policy, the two factors—necessity for good-faith bargaining between parties, and the availability of economic pressure devices to each to make the other party inclined to agree on one's terms—exist side by side"[8].

(f) It provides that, while striking is a "concerted activity" protected under the Act (Sections 7, 8(a)(1), and 8(a)(3)), the protections given to strikers are seriously limited. As mentioned, the law prohibits an employer from "discharging" employees for striking[9] but allows an employer to "permanently replace" striking employees[10]. In other words, only if the employer has not found permanent replacements for strikers is he prohibited from discharging the strikers. Only strikers protesting an employer's unfair labor practices are entitled to reinstatement, if they offer to return to work unconditionally; "economic strikers", those protesting employment conditions, compensation levels, are not entitled to reinstatement[11]. The feeble nature of the existing legal protections to strikers became pertinent much later, in the 1980s, when employers showed their willingness and ability to use permanent replacements to break strikes.

In 1936 the Walsh-Healy Act was enacted. The Act stated that workers must be paid not less than the "prevailing minimum wage" normally paid in a locality; it restricted regular working hours to eight hours a day and 40 hours a week, with time-and-a-half pay for additional hours; it prohibited the employment of convicts and children under 18; and it established sanitation and safety standards.

Pro-labor legislation was dealt a major blow at the end of the decade. In 1939, in *NLRB v. Fansteel Metallurgical Corporation*, the Supreme Court effectively eliminated the sit-down strike as a legitimate labor weapon in influencing corporate decisions. Labor's legally protected rights at the workplace, the decision made clear, were rights pertinent to organizing labor's collective exit from the workplace. Labor could use the weapon of exit to gain degrees of control over the workplace, but labor's direct control over the means of production themselves or practices aimed at that, were not a protected right. The owners' interests in operating the means of production were given precedence over labor' interests therein[12].

Nonetheless, labor's influence in the production regime continued to grow during the Second World War. This was just another dimension of labor's growing influence in the production regime, that would be reversed after the end of the war. In 1941, the Supreme Court held that a union could picket businesses other than the one with which it had a direct dispute (secondary boycott), as long as the union did not combine with non-labor groups[13] The war years witnessed unions' further entrenchment in the production regime, as junior participants on the War Production Board, the inclusion of a maintenance of membership clause in virtually all wartime labor contracts (establishing, essentially, a union shop), and the acceptance by employers of the automatic dues check-off.[14] The emergency of the war had helped labor to reach gain unprecedented degrees of influence in corporate decisions, in exchange, however, for wage increase ceilings and a no-strike pledge[15].

Taft-Hartley and Landrum-Griffin

After the war, employer demands to curb "excessive" union power and to balance NLRA restrictions against employer unfair labor practices with union unfair labor practices resulted in the passage of the Taft-Hartley Amendments to the NLRA in 1947. The extensively revised legal framework for labor-management relations, renamed LMRA, faced the opposition of unions and was vetoed by President Harry Truman. However, Congress overrode the veto, and the unions soon agreed to abide by its most divisive provision, the signing of non-Communist affidavits as a condition for holding union office. The following LMRA amendments to the NLRA can be seen as indeed placing restrictions on unions similar to ones the NLRA had placed on employers:

- It prohibited unions from interfering with employee rights (Section 8(b)(1)), and from coercing or discriminating against employees because of their union activities (Section 8(b)(2))

- It prohibited unions from refusing to bargain collectively with an employer (Section 8(b)(3))

- It mandated a 60-day notification requirement before a strike, a lockout or changing or terminating the conditions of employment (Section 8(d))

- It authorized federal courts to enforce provisions of the Act by awarding financial and other damages for unfair labor practices against employers and unions (Sections 301, 302, 303)[16].

However, other LMRA amendments to the NLRA go further than restoring a balance in employer-union obligations, to undermine a key source of union power, labor solidarity:

- It prohibited secondary boycotts and picketing (sympathy strikes). This provision restricts labor's industrial actions and organization to the confines of "business" or "enterprise" unionism: by law, unions can organize and take industrial action on behalf only of the workers in a given company and against only an employer with which the bargaining unit has a contractual conflict. Employees in company A cannot strike against company B in solidarity with the strike of the employees in company B. Thus unions must form around and defend the (sectional) interests of business-defined groups of workers. (Sections 8(b)(4), and 8(b)(7))

- It prohibited a union from coercing an employer into entering into "hot cargo" agreements, under which the employer agreed to cease dealing with an employer whose employees were on strike (Section 8(b)(4)(A)).

- It explicitly permitted individual states to pass laws prohibiting union security ("union shop") agreements, i.e. agreements between an employer and a union requiring union membership as a condition of employment on or after the thirtieth day after the beginning of employment (Section 14(b))

- It prohibited another form of union security clause in labor contracts, the "closed shop." Prohibition of the closed shop meant that an employer and a union could no longer agree that an employee be a union member in order to be hired for a job (Section 8(a)(3)).

- It prohibited union officials from being members of the Communist Party, and required the signing of non-Communist affidavits by all union officials as a precondition for NLRB union certification and protection under the Act (Section 504 (a)). This provision was ruled unconstitutional as a bill of attainder, in 1965[17].

- It excluded supervisory employees from coverage of the Wagner Act (Section 2(11)). While this provision may have insulated unions from infiltration by management, it also strengthened the segregation between managerial and production employees. The Act did not merely withhold protection to supervisors wanting to join the same union as production employees; it withheld protection to supervisors wanting to join any union at all. Thus the Act impeded the development of a union consciousness by managerial employees.

The Landrum-Griffin Act of 1959, formally entitled the Labor Management Reporting and Disclosure Act, primarily regulated internal union matters. It established what became known as the Bill of Rights of union members in relation to their union: internal union election procedures, and reporting and disclosure requirements for unions, union officers, and employers. However, it also amended the LMRA with additional restrictions against strikes. The amendments put a blanket ban on any form of "hot cargo" contract clauses or practices[18], and sealed the fate of permanently replaced strikers by depriving them of the right to vote as members of their union, after twelve months on strike[19]. This provision, rightfully derided by unions as a "union-busting" provision, facilitates employer efforts to decertify the union during a lengthy strike. Clearly, if employees who did not join the strike and/or strike replacements file a petition to decertify the union a year after the strike began, there is high likelihood that the union will lose in the ensuing decertification election, particularly since striking employees would not be eligible to vote in the election.

Statutory Segregation, Exit and Voice

It is important to note that the above provisions of the NLRA, while clearly recognizing labor's rights to press for the inclusion of its interests in corporate decision making do not amount to a legal sanctioning of "labor's voice" in corporate decision making (beyond disciplinary decisions, where the grievance procedure provides for arbitration when labor's views are not reconciled with capital's). Thus the NLRA and the extensive unionization that followed did inaugurate a production regime of labor inclusion, which was predicated, however, on unions' potential to win strikes. Clearly, labor's only bargaining power in the negotiating table depended was its threat of a strike. The law guaranteed the right to organize for and to undertake collective exit for working conditions, i.e. to strike; it offered no guarantees for the right to a voice in the making of decisions affecting its fate, i.e. to participate in corporate decision making.

Medoff and Freeman have conceptualized labor's "voice" as an important facet of the role of United States unions in production[20]. They contrast "voice" to another facet of unions's role, "monopoly." While their work was path-breaking for using statistical methods to show a positive correlation between unionization and corporate productivity, it was nonetheless based on an over-broad conceptualization of "voice." Their conception of unions' "voice" function is unable to distinguish between substantial labor participation in top level decision making institutions, and other, indirect forms of labor influence on corporate decisions, from outside top level decision making institutions, such as the picket line. It would be more appropriate to reserve the term "labor's voice" to production regimes where labor's interests are included in decision making by virtue of labor's rights to be a voting representative in the corporate policy formulation forums.

Indeed, as we will see in the case of Germany, in "representation regimes" labor's influence over corporate decisions depends not only on its option to disrupt capital by exiting from any cooperation with it, but also, to a significant extent, on the rights to be represented on supervisory boards of directors and to be extensively consulted through works councils. Extensive information rights and parity voting at supervisory boards on the one hand, and the lengthy delays that works councils can impose to the implementation of decisions they deem inimical to their interests, give German labor a substantial discursive power in corporate decision making. American labor lacks such voice-based power; its influence over the board of directors depends not on the quality of its voice inside the board room where corporate decisions are taken, but on the magnitude of the noise it can create outside it.

2. THE INSTITUTIONALIZATION OF SEGREGATED INCLUSION

The nature of a (production) regime is delineated by a statutory framework, as well as by social practices/contracts that can circumvent, implement and supplement the laws. Thus, while the legal framework outlined in the previous section is a very important component of the formation of the production regime of segregated inclusion, our analysis would be incomplete without consideration of non-statutory developments that also shaped the production regime. We turn, then, to an examination of corporate policy making in order to assess the degree and quality of inclusion of labor's interests therein.

Whether the legislation of the 1930s was shaped by a restive labor movement or a federal initiative that fuelled the labor movement is subject to debate[21]. For the purposes of this section, however, it is not necessary to decide between different degrees of autonomy of the New Deal state from popular pressures. What matters, for our purposes, is the configuration of the regime that resulted from mass unionization, whether this configuration was initiated by the state or merely implemented it.

How did unionization spread during the New Deal? Was labor actually included in corporate decision making? Did a new production regime stabilize by the onset of World War II? When was the new regime consolidated? Does the nature of the new capital-labor relationship justify the characterization 'segregated inclusion'?

Rich secondary sources provide ample documentation for the following developments of this period: (a) the fast spread of industrial unions and of the UAW in particular in the auto industry, after the passage of the NLRA; (b) the close link between strike activity, union recognition by employers, and union growth.

The Inauguration of Labor's Inclusion

The passage of legislation sanctioning labor's inclusion in corporate decision making did not, in and of itself, bring about such an inclusion. For one thing, the legality of such legislation, such as the 1933 National Industrial Recovery Act, was challenged in court. Indeed, the NIRA was nullified by the Supreme Court in 1935 as unconstitutional. The National Labor Relations Act that was enacted several months later that year, was in part an attempt to protect labor legislation from constitutional challenges. Nonetheless, it was also immediately challenged in court, and most companies refused to recognize industrial unions. Second, even if employers accepted the legality of the NLRA and adhered to its provisions, making labor's rights of collective bargaining a reality still depended on the success of unions in organizing labor. Lastly, even if overcoming employer and judicial resistance to the NLRA was simply a matter of time (the Supreme Court upheld the constitutionality of the NLRA in 1937), the substantive, as opposed to the formal, dimension labor's inclusion would depend on the particular outcomes of intense labor-capital struggles within the boundaries of the law.

The significance of the New Deal labor legislation cannot be underestimated. While in the absence of intense labor mobilization it would have amounted to much less than it aspired to, it was nonetheless a powerful signal that, in the words of David Milton, " . . . the traditional united front against labor by business, the government, and the judiciary was broken"[22]

Attesting to the brewing worker revolt as the background for the labor legislation of the 1930s, the Henderson Report, written for the NIRA, lamented, among other things, the conditions of workers in the auto industry. Employment, the report found, was so sporadic, and earnings so low, that most workers depended upon relief for four to five months of the year. It concluded that:

> "Labor unrest exists to a degree higher than warranted by the Depression. The unrest flows from insecurity, low annual earnings, inequitable hiring and rehiring methods, espionage, speedups and displacement of workers at an extremely early age. Unless something is done soon, they [the workers] intend to take things into their own hands"[23].

Of course, labor's ability to assert itself was hardly obvious. During the previous decade, unions had witnessed a dramatic decline in membership, so that obituaries for the labor movement were drafted frequently. In 1933, the president of the American Economic Association emphasized structural, technology-related causes behind the unions' "irreversible" demise:

> . . . American trade unionism is slowly being limited in its influence by changes which destroy the basis on which it is erected. It is probable that changes in the law have adversely affected unionism.

Certainly the growth of large corporations has done so. But no one
who follows the fortunes of individual unions can doubt that over and
above these influences, the relative decline in the power of American
trade unionism is due to occupational changes and to technological
revolutions ... I see no reason to believe that American trade
unionism will so revolutionize itself within a short period of time so
as to become in the next decade a more potent social influence than it
has been in the last decade.[24]

FIGURE 1

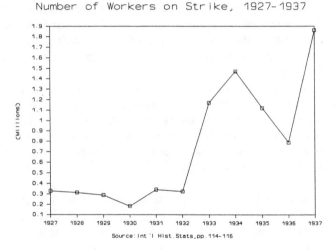

Number of Workers on Strike, 1927-1937

Source: Int 'l Hist.Stats,pp.114-116

Such dire prognoses were dramatically belied within the same year. The
passage of the NIRA was accompanied by an almost four-fold increase
in the annual number of workers on strike. The average number of
workers on strike annually, for the 1925-1932 period had been 300,000;
in 1933 the number of workers on strike jumped to 1,168,000. In 1934,
the year before the passage of the Wagner Act, the number of strikers
reached the record level of 1,500,000[25]. After dropping in 1935 and
1936, the number of strikers reached a new high in 1937, when
1,850,000 workers were on strike (see Figure 1).[26]

Acrimony between workers and employers was accompanied by acrimony within the labor movement over organizing principles and the orientation of the unions. In November 1935, a few months after the passage of the NLRA, John L. Lewis, head of the United Mine Workers, and other union leaders, formed the Committee for Industrial Organization, as a splinter group within the AFL, calling for the AFL to grant charters to industry-based, as opposed to only craft-based, union locals. The AFL was opposed to the idea of industry-based unions, and soon industrial locals that had been denied charters by the AFL were requesting affiliation with the CIO. By the first months of 1936, the CIO split completely from the AFL (until they two were rejoined in the AFL-CIO in 1955). In the spring of 1936 the UAW broke with the AFL, and in July it affiliated with the CIO. None of the major auto companies recognized the UAW as workers' representative, and they all refused to bargain with it.

In December 28, 1936 workers at GM's Fisher Body plant in Cleveland went on strike, the result of spontaneous rank and file action. Two days later, the strike spread to the Fisher Body plant at Flint, Michigan, only this time the workers went to occupy the plant, protesting the speed of the assembly line, wage cuts, unsafe and unsanitary working conditions, the lack of steady work, the capricious power of foremen, and the absence of any control over workplace conditions[27]. The UAW immediately announced its support of the strikers and claimed the sole representation of the strikers (a move strongly denounced by the AFL). The sit-down strike at Flint was only the most dramatic among a series of sit-down strikes and walk-outs at GM plants in Detroit, Anderson (Indiana), Morwood and Toledo (Ohio), Janesville (Wisconsin), St. Louis, (Kansas) and Atlanta (Georgia) that year.

The Flint sit-down strike that started in the last days of 1936, ended in February 11, 1937, with an agreement between GM and the UAW providing for a 6-month contract. The UAW was not recognized as the sole representative of auto workers, but as the bargaining agent at the striking plants; in the rest of the plants the UAW would be representing only its members. The company agreed not to interfere with unionization rights, not to discriminate against union workers, and to rehire discharged strikers. The UAW agreed not to strike during any contract it will sign consequent to that agreement, until all grievance procedures were exhausted. Lastly, GM, in a gesture of good will, unilaterally granted its employees a 5% wage increase[28].

The UAW's membership grew exponentially with the success of the sit-down strikes. In a nine-month period, from the beginning to the fall of 1937, the ranks of the UAW swelled from a mere 80,000 members to 400,000 in a total auto employment of 517,000, a union density of 77%[29]. GM's agreement to sign a contract with the UAW in 1937, was followed by more strikes and an eventual contract in Chrysler, in 1938.

FIGURE 2

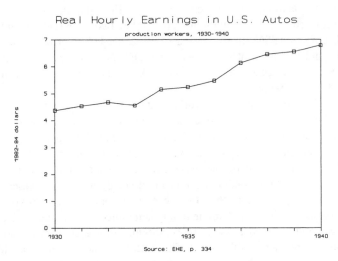

Real Hourly Earnings in U.S. Autos
production workers, 1930-1940

Source: EHE, p. 334

The redistributive policy of auto companies had began to change. Real earnings in the auto industry had reversed their post-1929 slump, as auto capitalists were succumbing to union pressure or were granting wage increases as a preemptive measure against unions (see Figure 2). Interestingly, changes in earnings during this period mirror developments in the inauguration of labor's inclusion. Earnings began to increase in 1933, with the onset of the nationwide strike wave, and this increase accelerated in 1936, with the onset of sit-down strikes in the auto industry.

Still, a sizable portion of auto workers were yet to be included in corporate decision making, as long as Ford, the second-largest auto company, refused to recognize and bargain with the UAW. Ford recognized the union in 1940, and as an exclusive agent of Ford employees in 1941—after the United States' entry into World War II, revelations about Henry Ford's sympathies for the Nazis, and a long strike had seriously weakened the company.

Between Segregation and Integration

The 1940s witnessed a series of victories and defeats for labor that shaped the mode of labor inclusion that ultimately prevailed as the postwar production regime. During this period, the labor movement in general, and the UAW in particular, energized by their newly gained strength, tested the limits of their influence in corporate (and also in federal) decision making.

With the United States' entry to the war, the government took an active role in pacifying industrial relations in face of military needs. It established the National Defense Mediation Board, the National War Production Board and the National War Labor Board. The unions agreed to a no-strike pledge and to a ceiling on wage increases in all labor contracts for the duration of the war. In return, unions got a minor role on the War Production Board, the inclusion of a maintenance-of-membership clause[30] in virtually all wartime contracts, along with a clause for automatic dues check-off[31]. The union shop agreements that spawned after the war grew from these pro-union provisions of the wartime contracts.[32] The unions' wartime no-strike pledge was often and flagrantly violated, mostly in wildcat strikes, unauthorized by the unions[33]. The apex of strike activity was 1944, when, in the auto industry alone, half of the workers were on strike at some time during the year[34]. With the exception of 1942, more man-days were lost to strikes during the war years than in ever before! Evidently, a lasting production regime had not yet been consolidated (see Figure 3).

Walter Reuther, the UAW's bold organizer of the sit-down strikes of the 1930s, rose to national prominence in the beginning of the 1940s by assaulting all the traditional prerogatives of the owners of auto (and aircraft) companies. In a direct attack on capital's monopoly in deciding what, how, and how much to produce, he issued the Reuther Plan for "500 planes a day" that would accelerate aircraft production by a government-sponsored rationalization of the production process throughout the auto and aircraft industries.

FIGURE 3

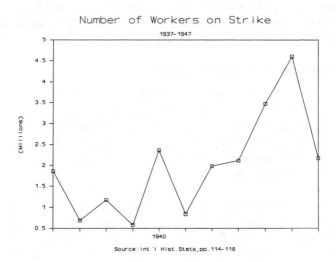

Number of Workers on Strike
1937-1947

Source: Int 'l Hist. Stats, pp. 114-118

The particular significance of the Reuther Plan, from the point of view of this section, lay in the explicit linkage it sought to establish between labor's redistributive and productivist interests. Labor was now openly challenging management's decision-making authority not only as unfair (in redistributive outcomes), but also as inefficient (in productivist outcomes). Certainly, labor's inclusion in the War Production Board had emboldened labor's claims over corporate decision making. However, concerted employer opposition sidelined Reuther's plan[35]. In fact, the 1945 GM-UAW contract, far from enacting the Reuther Plan, opened with the famous "managerial prerogatives" clause, that would reappear in every contract since then:

> "The right to hire, promote, discharge or discipline for cause, and to maintain discipline and efficiency of employees, is the **sole** responsibility of the Corporation except that union members shall not be discriminated against as such. In addition, the products to be manufactured, the location of plants, the schedules of production, the methods, processes and means of manufacturing are **solely and exclusively** the responsibility of the Corporation.[36]

At the end of the war, the union continued to press for labor's inclusion in productivist decisions. The UAW's new plan, which Gartman characterizes as an effort to "get labor's foot in the management door"[37], was a 16-point program for converting industry from military to civilian production. It included a 30-hour work week, pooling labor and technology from across corporate lines, fixing normal sales prices for some products, ending the seasonality of production, and setting up "technical commando units" composed of engineers, draughtsmen and tool and die workers that would eliminate production bottlenecks and increase efficiency in marginal firms. The entire conversion was to be managed by a Peace Production Board, composed of representatives of labor, government, and capital[38].

The UAW's peace conversion plan, just as Reuther's earlier 500-planes-a-day plan, was defeated under capitalists' protests. However, as the 1945 contract expired, the UAW, emboldened by a massive strike wave it was spearheading, tried to reverse the "managerial prerogatives" concessions of the previous contract. In its negotiations with GM, the UAW demanded (a) a 30% wage increase, to be accompanied by (b) a company commitment not to increase auto prices; (c) that labor participate in the determination of production standards (the speed of the assembly line, in particular); and (d) that the company "open its books" to an arbitration board inspection to let the latter decide the size of wage increase the company could afford without raising prices. In regard to the last demand, it must be noted that the LMRA and consequent decisions of the NLRB and the Supreme Court provided for only limited union information rights about the operation and finances of the corporation. In the area of wage bargaining, the corporation is required to provide the union with information about its profitability **only if** the corporation "pleads poverty": that it is **financially unable** to pay a requested wage increase. The union is not entitled to financial data just because it would assist it in preparing wage demands for bargaining. The Board is very strict in applying this doctrine[39]. Thus, if management indicates that it could afford a certain increase with difficulty but prefers to use its available funds for other purposes, the union would not be entitled to financial information because management did not specifically state that it could not afford the increase.

With its proposals the union was trying, simultaneously, to extend labor's influence to the area of work organization, investment and pricing decisions. At the same time, the UAW was stressing the stake the wider consuming public had in labor's success in controlling price increases. According to a GM official, these demands were "an opening wedge whereby the unions hope to pry their way into the whole field of management[40]". GM refused to discuss prices, to open its books, or to submit anything to arbitration, aware that the union was demanding fundamental, qualitative changes in the production regime. On December 30, 1945, GM took an ad in **The New York Times** stating:

> "America is at the crossroads! It must preserve the freedom of each economic unit of American business to determine its own destiny.. The idea of ability to pay, whatever its validity may be, is not applicable to an individual business within an industry as a basis for raising its wages beyond the going rate"[41].

That Reuther aimed at changing the production regime was not missed by auto capitalists. For GM the stakes were clear:

> "Is American business to be based on free competition or is it to become socialized, with all activities controlled and regimented?"[42]

The title of a contemporary article in a trade publication also makes clear that capital was aware of the strategic significance of erecting barriers around productivist decisions to keep labor out, and of keeping only redistributive decisions as subjects of collective bargaining: "With Collective Bargaining Established Union's Next Step is Management Control"[43].

Gartman summarizes the attitudes of auto capitalists towards labor's inclusion in decision making as follows:

> "Automotive manufacturers demanded from the union above all a stable, predictable, and compliant workforce to work their machines and valorize their capital. In return, they were willing to ensure the organization's survival, as well as make concessions in the areas of wages, benefits, hours of work, seniority, and other employment conditions. But manufacturers were adamant that collective bargaining be confined to these issues alone. They would not tolerate union interference in the sacred managerial rights of setting production standards, discipline, methods of production, hiring, pricing, and product determination"[44].

When General Motors rejected the UAW proposal, the union struck for
113 days, from the end of December 1945 to April 1946, in one of the
most bitter battles in the union's history, and in the midst of a nationwide strike wave that was numerically the most massive in United
States history[45].

FIGURE 4

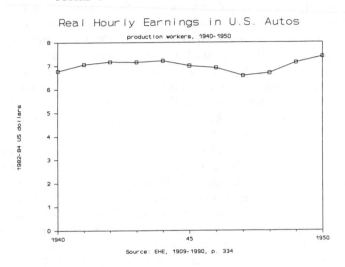

Source: EHE, 1909-1990, p. 334

In efforts to facilitate a settlement of the strike, a presidential fact-
finding board was appointed, which recommended a 19.5 cent an hour
increase. GM rejected the fact-finding board's recommendation. In fact,
the company had refused to open its books, discuss prices or submit
anything to arbitration. The strike ended with a two-year contract that
left managerial prerogatives intact, and increased the wage rate by 18.5
cents an hour, that corresponded to a 13% increase. The strike cost GM
nearly $90 million, but it recovered $53 million through tax credits[46].
While the wage rate increase was close to the one recommended by the
fact-finding board, it was far from the one demanded by the union.
Inflation wiped out most of the wage rate increase, when President
Truman abolished wartime price controls in August 1946. Indeed, as
Figure 4 shows, for the years 1945-1947 real average hourly earnings in
the auto industry declined, from $7.00 to $6.58.[47]

Meanwhile, however, Walter Reuther, even if not victorious against the auto companies, had gained the admiration of the auto workers, and the grudging respect of the industry and government. In March 1946, he was elected President of the UAW.

1946 was an impressive year for auto workers in terms of the strike they organized, but disappointing in terms of the contract they ended up signing. Why did Reuther end the strike before gaining better wages and participation in productivist decisions? The most often cited reasons are the following: Reuther's unwillingness to risk an even longer strike before solidifying his position in the UAW; his estimation of the negative political climate in the country (which was confirmed with the November sweep of Congressional elections by the Republican party); and the Cold War hysteria against anything resembling or associated with Communism[48].

The passage of the Taft-Hartley Act[49] was another major blow against the UAW's efforts to participate in productivist decision making at the corporate (and the federal) level. While the Act's requirement for union officials to sign non-Communist affidavits deprived the union of scores of activists and leaders, it also helped Reuther neutralize some of his strongest competitors for control of the union. Perhaps more important, however, was the Act's prohibition of sympathy strikes and its attribution of financial responsibility to the union for violations of the law by its members. These legal barriers, together with the formidable organizational and logistical difficulties of controlling a geographically dispersed and numerically vast labor constituency, sealed the fate of a national labor strategy based on industrial action for union participation in productivist decisions.

However, it would be a serious mistake to conclude from the postwar capitalist victory over labor on productivist decisions that labor's power over capital was obliterated. The price which capital had to pay for its victory was to grant labor unprecedented power over redistributive policy. Indeed, from mid-1930s to the end of 1940s, labor had been asserting its newly acquired power in the area of redistributive decision making. Real wages began rising steadily and at a faster rate than ever before. In the midst of the Depression, or of the War, or even after the War, real wages declined on only two years, 1945 and 1946 (Figure 4).

The 1948 and 1950 contracts between the UAW and auto capitalists represent a watershed in the consolidation of segregated inclusion. These contracts codify nearly all the terms of engagement and other basic features of labor-management relations that would prevail for the next thirty years.

In the 1948 round of GM-UAW negotiations, the company made some very generous offers on redistributive issues. These offers are attributed to GM's president and Secretary of Defense in the Eisenhower Administration, Charles E. Wilson. One was the Cost of Living Adjustment (COLA), and provided an automatic wage escalator for every increase in the national consumer price index. The other was the Annual Improvement Factor (AIF), and provided a formula for sharing with labor the benefits of productivity increases anticipated from the peaceful cooperation of labor and capital in a period of economic expansion and technological change. However, consistent with capital's intention to keep labor's redistributive interests segregated from productivist ones, the AIF was **not** tied up to the productivity of the auto company nor of the whole auto industry, but to the growth of the national economy (GDP). In the 1948 two-year contract, the AIF was set at 2%. In effect, workers would get, in addition to the wage rate increase agreed to for 1948, an increase in the wage rate of 2% in real terms the following year. The union, after some hesitation, accepted the proposal[50]. Two years later, a similar agreement solidified a labor-management regime that characterized the postwar United States production.

Another important issue pertaining to the scope of collective bargaining was settled by a 1949 decision of the Supreme Court: Are fringe benefits mandatory subjects of bargaining, if they were instituted by management? General Motors had strenuously refused to consider such fringe benefits as mandatory subjects of bargaining with labor. The Supreme Court's *Inland Steel v. NLRB* decision of 1949 let stand an NLRB ruling that fringe benefits are mandatory subjects of bargaining, even if they were initiated by employers[51].

The Consolidation of Segregated Inclusion

The 1950 contract between GM and the UAW (and reproduced in Ford and Chrysler), did not significantly depart from the provisions of the 1948 contract. Why, then, is the 1950 contract, and not the previous one, hailed as the Treaty of Detroit? The answer is that the 1948 contract was, in effect, the Truce of Detroit, paving the way for the consolidation of labor-capital relations into a lasting production regime in 1950 with the Treaty of Detroit. The 1950 contract confirmed, in effect, that the understanding reached between labor and capital in the 1948 contract was not a temporary, one-time agreement. The 1950 contract contained a no-strike pledge (a first in peacetime) for the five-year duration of the contract (the longest ever signed). Both provisions expressed labor's most concrete form of commitment to the particular labor-management relationship articulated in the contract, after years of aspiring to a more central role in corporate decision making. The 1950 contract was significant, not so much for its innovative provisions, but as a symbol of consolidation of a production regime that would last for more than three decades, what we call segregated inclusion.

The Treaty of Detroit represents the consolidation of a production regime, labor inclusion, into a more particular regime configuration, segregated inclusion. The regime of labor inclusion was **inaugurated** in 1933-35 with the New Deal labor legislation and the simultaneous explosion of unionization. In broad terms, the regime of labor exclusion from corporate decision making that had characterized the auto industry until then was being replaced by a regime where labor would exercise a definite influence over at least some corporate decisions affecting its vital interests. However, the precise configuration of labor's inclusion (the manner/basis and scope of inclusion) and perhaps even the very notion of labor's inclusion itself was not **consolidated** for another fifteen years: auto capitalists refused to recognize unions for many years after the Wagner Act and, when they did, after 1936-41, they did so only after prolonged strikes and, in the case of Ford Motor Co., under conditions of wartime emergency. Moreover, even as labor's inclusion was accepted, labor and capital continued to disagree on the appropriate scope and form of labor's inclusion, between 1941 and 1948. The UAW saw itself as a future partner of capital in organizing production, with a definite influence over the sharing of the fruits of production with capital as well as what, when, and how was produced. By 1950 capitalists were finally victorious in paring down labor's ambitions to a much more remote and narrow type of influence in corporate decision making. However, segregated inclusion was a Pyrrhic victory for capital. While it ensured labor's exclusion from productivist decision making, it did so at the price of accepting the legitimacy of labor's role in redistributive decision making. The Treaty of Detroit consolidated, at one and the same time, labor's inclusion in the regime and the particular form and scope of that inclusion. The regime entered a severe crisis in the 1970s, and underwent a fundamental transformation in the 1980s. Let us examine now the redistributive and productivist dimensions of the American auto production regime of segregated inclusion.

3. THE PERFORMANCE OF SEGREGATED INCLUSION

Redistributive decision making and outcomes under segregated inclusion

FIGURE 5

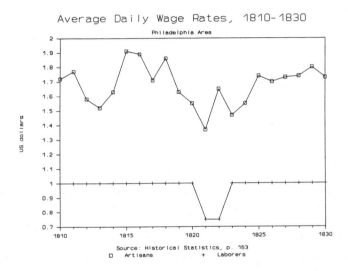

Average Daily Wage Rates, 1810-1830
Philadelphia Area

Source: Historical Statistics, p. 163
□ Artisans   + Laborers

Our framework of production politics anticipates that, before 1933, that is before the massive strikes precipitated by the onset of the Depression and the NIRA, when labor was still excluded from corporate decision making, labor's redistributive interests were not included in corporate decision making; at least not included strongly enough to result in rising wage rates. There are few reliable hourly earnings data from early years. However, available data on average daily wages for artisans and laborers from the previous century confirm our expectation, namely that in pre-1933 regimes of labor exclusion wage rates remained stagnant over long periods and even declined in absolute terms (Figure 5).

FIGURE 6

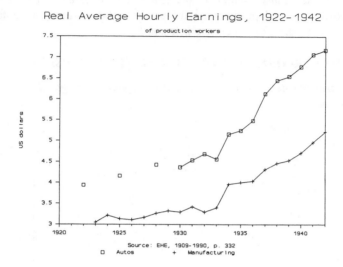

Real Average Hourly Earnings, 1922-1942
of production workers

Source: EHE, 1909-1990, p. 332
□ Autos   + Manufacturing

In the early part of the twentieth century things were not much different. As Figure 6 shows, real average hourly earnings from 1922 to 1929, a period of high economic growth dubbed the "roaring twenties", wage rates remained stagnant or rose marginally in manufacturing and in autos. While, as David Brody argues and Piore and Sabel echo,[52] "welfare capitalism" and the crushing of unions under the "American Plan" of the 1920s may have served some of labor's more intangible interests, the period certainly did not serve labor's redistributive interests particularly well.

Indeed, labor's real wages only began to rise regularly after 1933, when corporate decisions became the target of a tremendous strike wave over wages and union recognition. From 1925 to 1932 there were on the average 300,000 workers on strike annually; between 1933 and 1937 the average jumped to 2,318,800[53]. While the jump in wages was not analogous to the jump in strikes, it was closely related to labor's collective organization after 1933. Thus, as Figure 6 shows, in the manufacturing sector, average hourly earnings in the ten years between 1922 and 1932 had ranged from $0.45 to $0.57; between 1932 and 1942 they ranged from $0.44 to $0.85. These differences are not fundamentally distorted by inflation. Average hourly earnings in real terms (in 1984 dollars), for the 1922-1932 period ranged from $3.00 to $3.40; in the 1932-1942 period they ranged from $3.30 to $5.20. In the auto industry, during 1922-1932 real average hourly earnings ranged from $3.94 to $4.68, whereas from 1932 to 1942 they ranged from $4.55 to $7.17.

Soon after the end of World War II, the UAW had unionized all the hourly employees of the Big Three auto companies and a large portion of smaller auto firms. This remarkable feat was likely to have significant consequences on how the industry was to be run. Labor, as we have argued in the previous section argued, soon abandoned the strategic aim of sharing control of production with capital, in favor of focussing its energies and power on wage security. By the signing of the GM-UAW contract in 1950 (Treaty of Detroit), it was evident that labor, having been refused any rights over productivist decisions, would also be free of any financial responsibility for such decisions: labor's compensation would be protected from inflation but also from the year-to-year performance fluctuations of the company. Wages would be increasing irrespective of corporate profits.

More specifically, since the Treaty of Detroit, and until 1979, every labor contract in the auto industry between the Big Three and the UAW[54], included certain clauses that regulated labor's redistributive interests, a share of the wealth produced from the operation of the regime. Through these clauses, corporate decisions on the level of compensation would address labor's need in the following three ways (a) annual wage levels would rise analogously with the cost of living; (b) wage levels would also rise over and above the adjustment for the cost of living, along with the growth of the whole economy; and (c) capricious allocation of tasks, which altered the agreed upon reward/effort bargain, would be precluded. Rising compensation was transformed from an aspiration to an expectation, the determination of wage levels was transformed from a matter of the labor market and the employers to a matter mediated by labor's power; and seniority and work rules shielded labor from managerial arbitrariness in the allocation of the work effort. Although not owners of the means of production, workers had acquired a legitimate and effective influence in corporate decisions, at least in the area of wage determination. Corporate decisions, heretofore, were constrained to include labor's redistributive interests, through the following recurring provisions of multi-year labor contracts agreed upon by the UAW and the Big Three auto companies[55].

(1) The Cost of Living Adjustment (COLA), included in every contract until its suspension in 1982, meant that labor was not only included in wage bargaining, but that once the current level of wages was agreed upon by labor and management, it was also agreed that future wages would automatically rise along with the cost of living for the duration of the contract[56]. Still, the precise determination of the COLA remained a very contentious topic for collective bargaining. How often would the adjustment be made, annually, quarterly, or monthly? How sensitive should the adjustment be to changes in the general Consumer Price Index? These questions retained the COLA as a subject of collective bargaining, particularly when inflation exploded in the late-1960s. By 1976 the union and auto employers agreed to a quarterly COLA of 1 cent per hour for each 0.3 rise in the Consumer Price Index[57]. Thus the COLA all but ruled out corporate policies that grant only nominal or no wage increases and exposed real wages to the ravages of inflation.

(2) The Annual Improvement Factor (AIF) in multi-year contracts, another fixture of postwar contracts, provided an annual increase in wages, over and above the cost-of-living adjustment, for the duration of the contract. It was a flat cents-per-hour wage increase, determined by multiplying the rate of growth of the whole U.S. economy in the previous year by the average wage in the auto industry.

The AIFs reflected the inclusion of labor's interests in the redistribution of (anticipated) productivity increases. In other words, AIFs guaranteed labor an improvement in real wages, in light of possibly painful adjustment it had to undergo due to the introduction of labor-saving technologies and to related changes in the organization of work. With AIFs, capital could no longer make decisions about improving efficiency and profits without including in its calculations the provision of higher real wages for labor. The granting of AIFs was clearly linked to capital's perception that labor had grown to be too strong to withstand the anticipated negative effects of technological progress in production (elimination or transfer or devaluation of jobs) without sharing in any of its benefits. Alfred Sloan, the GM chairman, put his thinking behind the AIFs this way:

> "I think the fact that our workers benefit on a definite and prescribed basis, resulting in an increase in their standard of living, gives us a more sympathetic cooperation in the introduction of labor-saving devices and other improvements that flow from technological

progress,which on the whole have a healthy influence on the
efficiency of the corporation's operations."[58]

The AIF and multi-year contracts helped capital's search for
predictability of labor costs.

(3) Health and safety provisions and fringe benefits such as
pension plans, also introduced in 1950[59], were strengthened
significantly in the late-1960s and 1970s. Pensions, in fact, were
another embodiment of labor's stake in production; they signalled that
the means of production would be utilized to satisfy not only labor's
immediate but also post-retirement needs[60]. In 1950, pension payments
by the auto companies amounted to $100 a month for workers retiring
at age 65 with 25 years of service. Their consequent expansion, and
protection from inflation, has followed intensive collective bargaining.
In 1970, after a massive strike involving 355,000 workers, the Big
Three companies agreed to offer an optional early retirement plan to
workers with 30 years of service at $500 per month (less 8% for each
year under the age of 58). The expansion of pension funds both express
labor's rising power in redistributive decisions, but also ensure that
labor's interests are dependent on the well-being of the company. In the
1970s, issues of health and safety were addressed also through federal
legislation and the Occupational Safety and Health Administration
(OSHA). In 1976 a Paid Personal Holiday Plan granted workers 8 paid
days for personal holidays (in addition to the national or state
holidays)[61].

(4) Supplemental Unemployment Benefits (SUBs) were first
introduced in labor-management contracts in 1955. They provided an
employer-financed supplement to government-financed unemployment
compensation. SUBs entitled laid-off workers to 65% of their salary for
4 weeks and 60% for 22 weeks after the expiration of their
unemployment benefits. They addressed labor's right for protection
against cyclical and, more specifically, seasonal unemployment.
Seasonal unemployment results from the seasonal nature of the demand
for automobiles. From the early years of the industry, factories would
reduce production or shut down during low-demand months (in the
Summer), and reopen when demand picked up again (in the Fall).
While this was a rational profit-maximizing production practice from
the viewpoint of the employer, it caused serious disruption in the
lifestyles and the living standards of workers[62]. The inclusion of SUB
payments in corporate policy was a major victory for labor. The union's

efforts to end corporate policies that led to seasonal unemployment had been repeatedly frustrated[63]; SUBs expressed corporate recognition of the problem and concrete steps in addressing it. By 1967, SUBs were increased to a level that, together with unemployment payments, provided laid off workers with 95% of straight-time take-home pay, for 52 weeks of idleness. However, the funding of SUBs became problematic in the 1970s, and the subject of re-negotiations in the midst of strikes, as the number of workers on layoff was rising fast enough to deplete the companies' SUB funds. Moreover, as will be shown in the next section, SUBs did **not stop** seasonal, let alone cyclical unemployment, but ensured that auto workers would be compensated for having to bear such burden.

(5) Job classifications delineate the types of work to be done by each employee. In the U.S. auto industry job classifications have been very narrow, until the 1980s when, in a dramatic shift from established practices, job classifications were broadened. Thus a plant that had worked for decades with more than 100 classifications, was converted to operate with only 3 classifications in the 1980s. It has been argued that job classifications were management's way of controlling the workforce in the postwar period; an element of "bureaucratic control" whereby narrowly constructed job definitions, job and promotional ladder would increase workers' dependence on the corporate organization[64]. Job classifications have an inclusionary dimension inasmuch as they pose definite limits for management in deploying labor; the tasks each worker is asked to perform must be within the worker's class of proficiency, which is determined jointly by the union and management in contract negotiations. Labor has used job classifications as an impediment against work intensification; during "down time"[65] a welder, for example, cannot be asked to perform a maintenance or janitorial task. Labor has also used job classifications to protect union activists from being assigned punitive, degrading tasks. However, such limitations to managerial discretion do not amount to labor control of the content nor of the security of jobs; thus the term "job control unionism," often used to characterize American labor's relationship to production,[66] is a misnomer.

(6) Seniority has been a crucial institution for labor's inclusion in corporate decision-making. Its purpose, for labor, has been to ensure that management cannot capriciously lay off, recall, transfer, or promote workers on the basis of favoritism. Initially aimed at protecting workers who fall into management's disfavor because of

their union activism, seniority has also served to provide workers with a somewhat predictable career ladder based on their years of service in the same company. Thus a worker with more years of service can "bump" a less "senior" worker when a better position becomes available, will be laid off later, and will be recalled earlier.[67]

(7) Grievance procedures address primarily disciplinary measures taken by management against workers, although they may refer to any practice in violation of the contract. Workers have a right to be represented by a union official during a disciplinary hearing before management. If disciplinary action is then taken over the objection of the union official, the union can take the case to ("file a grievance with") the National Labor Relations Board, whose judgement, depending on the nature of the case, is binding for the parties involved or can be appealed to higher-level courts. Certain cases are resolved through third-party arbitration[68] Grievance procedures have been particularly important in enforcing certain contractual agreements dear to labor, such as that dismissals shall be made only "for cause." However, in recent years, an increasing number of state legislatures have enacted statutes that protect individual rights at the workplace. Some argue that the extension of individual rights may be undermining the relevance of organizations protecting collective rights.[69] Still, even if protective legislation originates in legislatures, unions continue to be crucial in implementing it at the shop floor.

While not contractually provided for, the standardinzation of wages and benefits and work rules across firms has also been a fixture of industrial relations in the auto industry. Beginning in 1945, the UAW developed the tactic of "pattern" or "connective bargaining"[70] in order to standardize wages and benefits across the auto industry. Accordingly, wages and benefits were negotiated with a selected company (one deemed most prosperous at the time), and then the resulting contract was duplicated in separate agreements with the other companies. Thus, although company-specific in form, labor-management relations in the auto industry were substantively determined at the national/industry level[71].

These negotiations also set certain work rules, such as seniority-based promotions and layoffs, overtime, intra-firm transfers, and job classifications on which pay scales were based. The details of these work rules (for example, the exact form of the seniority ladder, the specific job tasks for each job classification, job bidding and transfer rights) were negotiated by the union locals in supplementary bargaining agreements. However, local unions have had less autonomy in deviating from the industry-wide pattern than one might think, because these side agreements were subject to approval by the national UAW, which closely monitored local-level bargaining to ensure that individual plants would not be "whipsawed" against each other by either the local union or management[72]. The real autonomy local unions do have in determining working conditions derives from the fact that they are responsible for administering, and thus deviating informally from, the national and local contracts.

What were the outcomes of these contract provisions? Did they provide labor with the promised wage security? To answer these questions we now turn to an examination of redistributive outcomes under segregated inclusion.

FIGURE 7

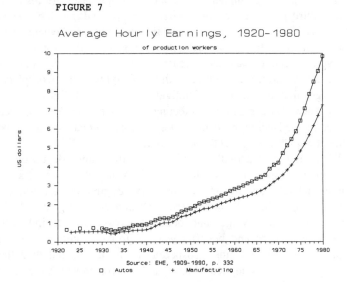

Average Hourly Earnings, 1920-1980

Source: EHE, 1909-1990, p. 332
□ Autos   + Manufacturing

Figure 7 shows the evolution of wages in American autos from 1922 to 1980. It can be seen that American auto workers experienced loss of nominal hourly earnings only during the first few years of the Depression. Beginning with the strike wave of 1933, nominal wage rates remain steady or are rising, through the war, and the whole postwar period. It is also interesting to note, in Figure 11, that the average wage of auto workers is higher than the average for workers in the whole manufacturing sector. Perhaps even more importantly, after 1950, the annual rate of change of auto wages becomes larger than for the wages of other manufacturing workers. These differences, it is worth noting, coincide with differences in redistributive decision making power between auto workers and other manufacturing workers—union density, the basis of labor's power in the U.S., is four times as high in autos than in manufacturing.

Of course, higher wages in autos could arguably result not from labor's higher power in autos, but from the ample wealth available in the auto industry for redistribution. However, a closer look at the evolution of wages lends support to the first explanation of inter-industry wage differentials, based on labor's power. The difference between average hourly earnings in autos and manufacturing increases at a faster rate after the year 1948. This is not a year marking a technological or marketing or organizational breakthrough in autos, as the second explanation would lead us to expect. It is the year of the historic GM-UAW contract that provided the basis for the signing of the Treaty of Detroit two years later, as the consolidation of the production regime of segregated inclusion, wherein labor's redistributive interests were unmistakably included in corporate policy making. The annual evolution of real wages (in 1982-84 US dollars) attests to auto workers' ability to protect their redistributive interests from the rising cost of living.

As Figure 8 shows, real wages continued to rise even during World War II, with labor as a participant in the War Production Board. Real wages declined somewhat at the end of the war, as a result of surging inflation. It can be seen how the 1948 contract marks an end to real wage losses, and how the effects of the 1948 and 1950 auto contracts ripple through the U.S. economy (the manufacturing sector in particular, and the non-agricultural private sector as a whole). Further, it is important to notice that uninterrupted real wage increases come to an end in 1969-1970. Is this the result of labor's loss of power in redistributive policy, or reflective of a learning curve in adapting to the much higher rates of inflation of the 1970s? Figure 7 above has shown that the increase in nominal wages did accelerate in the 1970s, presumably in order to catch up with inflation. Moreover, real wages in autos in the 1970s, despite the two oil shocks that restricted auto sales, and despite increasing import penetration, were still higher than in manufacturing as a whole. From 1970 to 1980 real average hourly earnings in autos moved from $10.87 to $11.95, a gain of 9.9%. In the same period, real average hourly earnings in manufacturing changed from $8.65 to $8.82, a gain of only 1.9%. In the non-agricultural private sector as a whole, real average hourly earnings even fell, from $8.29 to $8.00, a loss of 3.4%. If wages reflected not auto workers' power but simply their employers' "ability to pay", wages in autos would not have fared as favorably with those of less unionized sectors of the economy, particularly after the oil shock of 1973.

FIGURE 8

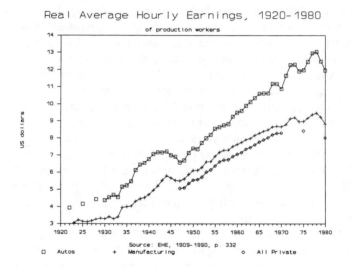

Real Average Hourly Earnings, 1920-1980

of production workers

Source: EHE, 1909-1990, p. 332

□ Autos   + Manufacturing   ◇ All Private

Next, we examine the relationship between wages and profits. Are wages' rise and fall in the auto industry related to the auto companies' profitability? Our framework and our analysis of the American auto regime suggest that wages and profits are not related, because of two defining characteristics of segregated inclusion: labor promotes its redistributive interests without regard for corporate productivist interests, such as profits; and the basis of labor's redistributive power is its ability to strike ("exit"), rather than a genuine forum in policy formulation based on full information and voting rights ("voice"). In other words, we expect little co-variance between auto profits and wages because labor's interests in a regime of segregated inclusion are segregated from capital's, and because labor pursues its interests on the basis of its power to strike, not on the basis of its information about and decision making power in the corporation. Let us first examine the relationship between wages and profits.

FIGURE 9

Corporate Profits After Tax, 1930-1980

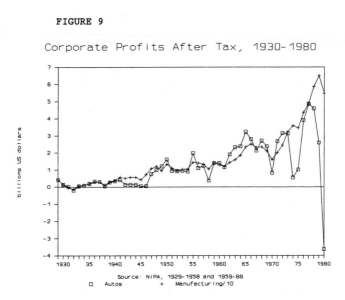

Source: NIPA, 1929-1958 and 1959-88
□   Autos   +   Manufacturing/10

Figure 9 charts the after-tax profits of American auto companies and of American manufacturing companies as a whole.[73] The profits of the manufacturing sector as a whole are, naturally, much larger than those of the auto industry alone. Thus, for easier comparison of changes over time, Figure 9 shows manufacturing profits divided by a factor of ten. Notice that until 1974 annual auto profits and manufacturing profits move in a parallel fashion. After 1974, the evolution of auto profits and manufacturing profits diverge sharply, with auto profits plunging while manufacturing profits retain their rise. Despite similar rates of growth in profitability between autos and manufacturing from 1944 to 1974, real wages in autos have grown at a faster rate than real wages in manufacturing (Figure 9)—a strong indication that higher wages in autos result from auto workers' superior power in redistributive decision making.

FIGURE 10

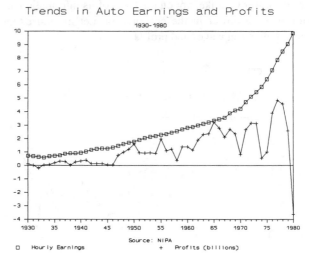

Figure 10 is more illuminating of the segregation between labor's and capital's interests in the American auto production regime. It charts nominal average earnings against corporate after-tax profits in the American auto industry (profits are shown in billions). It can be seen very clearly that annual wages are not at all linked to annual profits, strengthening our hypothesis about the segregation between productive and redistributive concerns being central of the American auto production regime. Most tellingly, even when the auto companies lost billions at the end of the 1970s, nominal wage rates continued to rise, in line with our expectation of segregation between capital's and labor's interests in this production regime.

Productivist decision making and outcomes under segregated inclusion

Central to our conceptualization of the postwar production regime of segregated inclusion is the observation that, while labor's redistributive interests are included in corporate decisions, labor's productivist interests are. In this section we will examine how the Treaty of Detroit consolidated this exclusion of labor from productivist decision making in the U.S. auto industry, an exclusion which is codified in labor-capital industrial agreements and reflected in unfavorable outcomes for labor's central productivist interest, employment.

Management Manages and the Union Grieves

Labor's exclusion from productivist decisions was conditioned by aforementioned omissions and commissions in the NLRA and the LMRA, but did not inevitably follow from the statutory framework. Economic expansion, society-wide and union-wide anti-Communism, the strategies pursued by capital and unions, as well as other historical contingencies, have all played their part in shaping the production regime of segregated inclusion. What interests us most, however, are the parameters that came to define the production regime, rather than how they were established. One such parameter is contractual language in labor-capital agreements that explicitly excludes labor from productivist decision making, despite labor's inclusion in redistributive decision making.

While American auto capitalists strenuously resisted labor's inclusion in any area of corporate decision making, their most determined and successful resistance centered on "sole managerial prerogatives" in productivist decisions. Allowing labor to exercise a concerted influence in the latter, for American auto capitalists was tantamount to surrendering their control over production. The 1935 and 1947 legislation of industrial relations, while clearly sanctioning the inclusion of labor's redistributive interests in corporate decision making, was too ambiguous with respect to labor's productivist interests. Section 8(d) of the NLRA refers to capital's obligation to bargain with the union over decisions pertaining to "wages, hours and other terms and conditions of employment", but does not specify what is meant by "other terms and conditions of employment".

Even after the major auto companies had accepted the legitimacy of collective bargaining, they strenuously objected to an expansive view of collective bargaining that would amount to codetermination: unions sharing with capital decision making powers over any corporate decision. The President of General Motors (and later Secretary of Defense) Charles Wilson presented the struggle around the scope of collective bargaining as a struggle between capitalism and socialism:

"If we consider the ultimate result of this tendency to stretch collective bargaining to comprehend any subject that a union leader may desire to bargain over, we come out with the union leaders really running the economy of the country . . . Only by defining and restricting collective bargaining to its proper sphere can we hope to save what we have come to know as our American system and keep it from evolving into **an alien form, imported from East of the Rhine**. Until this is done, the border area of collective bargaining will be a constant battleground between employers and unions, as the unions continuously attempt to press the boundary farther and farther into the area of managerial functions."[74]

With the Treaty of Detroit, managerial prerogatives in productivist decisions, first codified in contractual language in the 1945 GM-UAW agreement, were carved in stone. The significance of the Treaty of Detroit lies precisely in the unions' agreement to cede productivist decisions to management—in a tacit exchange for management's acceptance of unions' inclusion in redistributive decisions.

The influential *Fortune* magazine, heralded the signing of the 1950 GM-UAW contract as the Treaty of Detroit, precisely because it considered the union's ratification of the "sole prerogative" clause as a lasting settlement of the issue of productivist decision making; the high wages the industry would have to pay were well worth it:

"GM may have paid a billion for peace, but it got a bargain. GM has regained control over one of the crucial management functions in any line of manufacturing—long-range scheduling of production, model changes, and tool and plant investment."[75]

The unions' acceptance of managerial prerogatives in the area of productivist decisions provided a broadly-based legitimation to the regime of segregated inclusion which was incipient in the largest and most dynamic industrial production sites. By ceding productivist decision making to capital, labor was ceding control over its productivist interests; employment levels, skill formation, work organization and technological change were henceforth undisputed managerial concerns.

The Devil in the Formula

Besides managerial prerogatives, labor's exclusion from productivist decisions under the regime of segregated inclusion is also inscribed in the particular form of labor's redistributive claims. Since the Treaty of Detroit, annual changes in wages and benefits in multi-year contracts are determined on the basis of mathematical formulas to which both sides agree. This "formulaic determination of wages" brings desired predictability and stability for both labor and capital[76]. A closer look at these formulas, already discussed above, reveals that at the same time that they facilitate the inclusion of labor's redistributive interests in corporate decision making, they also reflect labor's exclusion from productivist decision making. This point will become clearer through the following considerations on the COLAs, AIFs, SUBs, seniority and job classifications, and the grievance procedure.

COLAs link wage rates to changes in the national Consumer Price Index. As such, they are a simple yet formidable mechanism that protects wages from the rising cost of living. Note, however, that COLAs protect labor's real wages (redistributive interest) without addressing corporate product pricing (productivist interest). Recall that COLAs were introduced in labor contracts in response to the UAW's 1945-46 campaign for a labor influence in product pricing. The union ended up losing the 1946 round (pricing and financial information remained a sole management prerogative), but only after 113 days of a debilitating strike. In the 1948 round, GM, unwilling to withstand another lengthy showdown with the union, offered COLAs as a preemptive move against labor's designs over productivist decision making. By providing for protection of real wages through COLAs, the company was undercutting one of the union's strongest arguments for the necessity of being included in productivist decision making. Labor's redistributive interests were protected at the expense of its productivist interests.

AIFs also express labor's segregation from productivist decisions. The wage increases they provide are only presumptively, not factually related to corporate productive performance. AIFs grant a wage increase in proportion to the Gross Domestic Product, which is an indicator of the performance of the national economy, not of the corporation or the auto industry. Thus, the worker's redistributive interests are segregated from his/her and the corporation's productivist interests (profitability, growth, etc): labor's annual wage rate changes occur **irrespective of** the corporation's performance and financial condition.

The elaborate system of numerous job classifications is another pillar of segregated inclusion[77]. Narrowly drawn job classifications

sought to "harmonize" management's insistence that the deployment of
labor and the redesigning production was its sole prerogative (it did not
have to even consult with labor on planned changes therein), with
labor's insistence on control over its working conditions. Job
classifications provided a compromise that kept labor out of production
decisions, with assurances that the content of work assigned to each
worker by management would not exceed or "fall beneath" the
qualifications of each worker. As we pointed out earlier, job
classifications provided labor with a degree of security against
managerial abuses of its power to organize production, (punitive job
assignments to union activists, speed-ups in lieu of hiring more
workers). However, contrary to what one may infer from some studies
on the issue[78],

> "[job classifications] were less the product of union power than a
> consequence of its defeat."[79]

The "job control unionism"[80] that resulted from the coupling of
seniority-based transfers and promotions and narrow job classification
was a poor substitute for a vigorous shop steward system which the
UAW had advocated as a way to instill shop floor "mutuality" among
workers and foremen, by making plastic the division of authority in the
shop[81].

Seniority "bumping" rights, like job classifications, provided a
minimum level of predictability for workers' career paths and
employment conditions[82], given their exclusion from a more substantial
and direct influence over their deployment. Segregated from the
process of rewarding good workers with better jobs or keeping good
workers on the job, and deprived from a direct influence over
employment levels, labor accepted (and then vigorously defended)
seniority rights as a safeguard against (potential) managerial abuses of
power. The Depression played an important role in introducing the
principle of seniority in personnel decisions. As David Montgomery
argues, during the high unemployment years of the late-1930s, the
union shied away from demanding direct control over personnel
decisions. With layoffs seeming inevitable, the union sought to avoid
the potentially divisive role of allocating the pain of layoffs among
workers. The principle of seniority-based layoffs seemed to both
absolve the union from direct responsibility for the layoff of individual

workers, while at the same time preventing managerial favoritism in the personnel decisions[83].

The grievance system, workers often complain, has bureaucratized the resolution of conflicts arising at the shop floor. However, more pertinent for the present context is the criticism that grievances do not suspend a managerial decision until they are resolved. The operating principle in workplace jurisprudence under segregated inclusion is "obey first, grieve later". Thus, particularly when needs arise to reorganize work, management decides on a new organization unilaterally. Then management action may be challenged by the union as adversely affecting workers, and, a grievance may be filed claiming that the action constitutes an "unfair labor practice."

Under the courts' interpretations of the LMRA, an employer does not have to bargain with the union before changing operations tantamount to the general direction of the business; but the employer is required to bargain with the union **over the effects** of such capital decisions after they are taken[84]. The management action, however, remains in effect until the grievance is processed, which may take many months. This is in contrast to practices in other production regimes, where the operating principle is that management should "consult first, decide later" (Japan) or "resolve grievance first, implement later" (Germany). Thus in the United States the union is ill-equipped to prevent, delay, or even anticipate an unpopular productivist decision. Management has the unilateral contractual right to organize and reorganize production, albeit without violating a detailed set of shop floor work rules. Thus,

> "management pays for the right to make unilateral decisions by constantly having to defend implementation in processes of grievance and arbitration and shop floor bickering"[85]

SUBs represented a compromise between labor's demands for ending seasonal and cyclical unemployment, on the one hand, and management's insistence on preserving its prerogative over productivist decisions, on the other. The compromise was labor's recognition of management's right to schedule production and employment as it saw fit, in exchange for monetary compensation for the adverse consequences of such policies. During the mid-1940s, labor had demanded the elimination of seasonal unemployment through a sliding scale in product prices that would lower car prices during the "slow" months from June to September and increase them subsequently; or through a reduction in the workweek to 30 hours; or through the GAW. Both proposals would have given labor some control in productivist decisions, and were both rejected. In 1955, moreover, SUBs were introduced as a counter-proposal to labor's proposal to reduce the workweek, which would have also granted labor entry into productivist decision making. Lastly, while SUBs probably curtailed the policies of hire-and-fire somewhat, it did not end them (see below).

After the signing of Treaty of Detroit, the UAW made one last attempt at including its interests in productive decision making, through the campaign for a Guaranteed Annual Wage (GAW). In the 1955 contract negotiations with Ford (the union's target for setting a industry-wide pattern), the union demanded a GAW as an assurance that sole managerial prerogatives in productivist decisions (which the union had already recognized) would not be used to undermine labor's productivist interests. Labor feared, in particular, that the rapid technological changes underway, "Detroit automation", might result in significant job losses.

> "With the widespread introduction of automation speeding up the potential output of goods and services, there is the possibility that markets may not grow fast enough to sustain high employment levels"[86].

Having to guarantee workers an annual wage would nullify the potential savings to capital from layoffs during slow demand months. Had capital agreed to a GAW, it would, in effect, be ceding away the policy option of hiring and firing labor as an adjustment to fluctuations in demand for autos. The Treaty of Detroit had recognized the legitimacy of unions' role in "taking wages out of competition", or "out of capitalists' hands", while the GAW would also take employment out of capitalists' exclusive domain. The GAW was labor's Trojan Horse: dressed as a redistributive demand for income stability, it was a productivist demand designed to ensure employment stability.

The idea of a GAW went down in defeat, as the 1955 Ford-UAW contract did not mention GAW. Instead, the 1955 included the innovation of Supplemental Unemployment Benefits (SUBs described above), aimed particularly at bringing an end to seasonal unemployment. The UAW declared victory, as though SUBs were a substitute for GAW. The idea was that the obligation to pay SUBs to laid off workers would serve as a strong financial disincentive against hire-and-fire policies, gradually bringing such policies to an end.

FIGURE 11

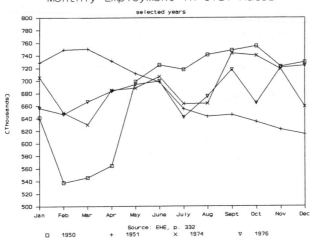

In reality, SUBs did not prevent seasonal (let alone cyclical) unemployment, even by the 1970s, when SUBs were increased to a level that, together with unemployment payments, provided laid off workers with 95% of straight-time take-home pay, for 52 weeks of idleness. Rather than ending seasonal unemployment, SUBs provided labor with a measure of monetary compensation for these ills[87], for as long as the company fund established to finance SUB payments remained solvent. In fact, in the 1970s SUB funds dried up, making SUB funding a hotly contested subject of collective bargaining.

Figure 11 charts the monthly employment of production workers in the auto industry during two years before the adoption of SUBs (1950, 1951) and during two years after the adoption of SUBs (1974, 1976). The years were selected because of their very similar annual average employment levels. Clearly, after 1955 there is a certain equalization of employment levels, but significant monthly fluctuations persist. Evidently, capital preferred to bear the cost of paying SUBs rather than ending its hire-and-fire policies.

At the same time, neither SUBs (instead of GAW), nor segregated inclusion in general (instead of integrated inclusion) seemed all that bad for labor, as the economy seemed poised for a lasting expansion. A rapidly expanding product market meant that managerial productivist decisions inimical to labor's productivist interests (layoffs), and labor-replacing technologies were likely to be accompanied by the creation of new jobs within the auto industry; the hurt would be of limited duration and would be compensated for with SUBs. Indeed, for the next two and a half decades, labor enjoyed rising wages and employment patterns characterized more by unsteadiness than by long-term insecurity.

Labor's Productivist Interest: Employment

Among productivist decisions, those pertaining to employment levels have an obvious, direct relationship to labor's self-interest, since they determine labor's very existence in the regime.

FIGURE 12

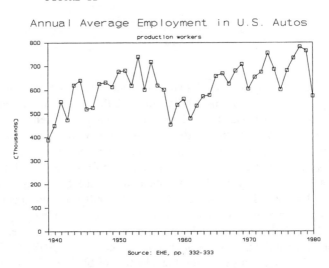

Employment levels are determined by a scope of productivist considerations that fall beyond labor's legitimate influence: investment, technology choice, training, work organization, overtime levels, line speed, quality control, product design. Thus, by being excluded from such "managerial prerogatives", labor was also excluded from any influence over its fundamental interest in employment stability. In the corporation's production strategy labor is but a variable input. Therefore, management is free to hire and fire labor according to the production strategy of the corporation. The wasteful dimension of hire-and-fire method of responding to variations in product demand—the idling of human capacity to produce, the disorientation and demoralization accompanying unemployment—is not included in management's cost-benefit calculus, simply because management does not bear the cost of such waste. Layoffs, in segregated inclusion, are an externality produced by firms whose costs are borne by the whole society.

Has labor's exclusion from productivist decision making described above actually resulted in wide annual fluctuations in employment levels? And have employment levels, as anticipated, fluctuated independently of changes in the level of earnings? Figure 12 summarizes annual changes in auto employment of production workers from 1939 to 1980. It is evident that the 1950 Treaty of Detroit did little to stabilize annual employment levels; before **and** after the Treaty significant employment losses regularly alternate with employment gains.

There is little evidence that the industry tried to stabilize annual employment levels. Clearly, if the Treaty of Detroit has consolidated the inclusion of labor's redistributive interests in corporate decisions, it has also consolidated the exclusion of labor's productivist interests. Further, the relationship between hourly earnings and employment levels in the auto industry, as charted in Figure 13, confirms the hypothesized segregation between labor's redistributive and productivist interest under the regime of segregated inclusion. The year of consolidation of segregated inclusion, 1950, coincides with a clear bifurcation between trends in annual changes in hourly earnings and annual changes in employment. After 1950, hourly earnings begin to rise at a faster rate than ever before, and irrespective of changes in employment levels. Interestingly, these inconsonant trends in the evolution of earnings and employment begin to dissipate in the 1970s, the decade we have characterized as the period of crisis of segregated inclusion.

FIGURE 13

Employment and Earnings in U.S. Autos

FIGURE 14

Employment, Earnings, Production

Even during the 1970s, however, earnings and employment levels begin to change in the same direction, but not consistently nor proportionately. Thus in the years of two consecutive significant drops in auto employment, 1974 and 1975, employment fell by 8.93% and 12.38% respectively, while hourly earnings in the same years dropped by 3.18% and rose by 0.53% respectively[88].

Figure 14 compares the evolution of employment, hourly earnings and output data in the American auto industry, from 1958 to 1980. It is evident that employment levels closely mirror production output levels.

Far from being controlled by labor, employment levels are reflective only of the level of output chosen by management.

As our earlier discussion of the 1930s and the war years pointed out, labor's original organizing efforts in the auto industry were not aimed only at collective bargaining over wages and hours. It was clear, especially to the leadership of the UAW, that the pursuit of wages was integrally related with the pursuit of employment security and the control of production. What needed to change was the whole production regime, the exclusion of labor from decision making—not simply an increase in wages for some workers at the expense of jobs for others. Walter Reuther told the convention that gave him full control of the UAW:

> "we are the vanguard in America . . . we are the architects of the future."[89]

The Basis of Labor's Power: Exit and Voice Revisited

Even when labor's inclusion in redistributive decisions was consolidated through successive multi-year contracts covering all non-managerial employees of the Big Three auto companies, labor's position in the corporation did not exceed that of contracted help; a more substantial position for labor was ruled out. Labor's exclusion from productivist decisions in segregated inclusion is suggestive, in and of itself, of labor's narrowly circumscribed position in the corporation. Equally telling of labor's position, however, is the **basis** of labor's power in the corporation. Even in the area of redistributive decision making, where labor has considerable power and interests are included, the **way** in which they are included is a defining characteristic of segregated inclusion. Frequent recourse to exit has been the basis on which American labor has been injecting its redistributive interests in corporate policy. Contrary to the evolutionary path of other labor movements, the American labor movement after the Second World War did not extend, in a fundamental way, the basis of its power beyond its capacity to bring production to a halt by striking.

The lack of legally sanctioned institutions where labor's voice would, in itself, constitute an influence in corporate decisions, is compounded by the absence of contractually sanctioned corporate decision making institutions of labor participation. Thus the inclusion of labor's interests in corporate decision making depends exclusively on labor's ability to organize and win strikes. Barring the threat of strikes, labor has no other venue through which to influence an unfavorable managerial decision, even in the narrow domain of redistributive policy making: there are no institutions of corporate policy formulation where labor is present even in an advisory (let alone voting) capacity. The existence of collective bargaining, often offered as evidence of the inclusion of labor's voice in the regime, does not, as we have argued, amount to an institutionalization of labor's voice. It is only an institution of bargaining, where there is no need for agreement to be reached, and wherein labor's influence is solely dependent on its capacity to back its demands by striking. Collective bargaining, by not requiring broad information sharing between the parties, lengthy and regular consultation, or any commitment to reach an agreement, is not an institution of labor's voice-based power, but a venue for labor's exit-based power. From the 1930s until 1979, the signing of **every** labor contract in the U.S. auto industry was preceded by a strike. The lack of institutions of genuine labor-management dialogue, moreover, by depriving labor from (timely) knowledge of management strategies, also limits the potency of the weapon of strikes.

FIGURE 15

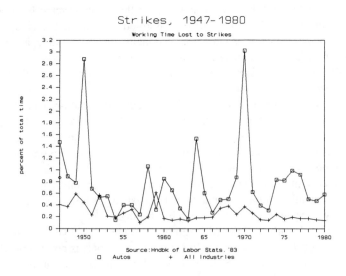

Strikes, 1947–1980

Working Time Lost to Strikes

Source: Hndbk of Labor Stats. '83
□ Autos   + All Industries

Labor's continued reliance on strikes as a means of furthering its interests in segregated inclusion is illustrated in Figure 15. Comparison of the pre-1950 with the post-1950 years indicate no significant decline in strikes. Had the 1950 Treaty of Detroit consolidated labor's "voice" as an alternative instrument of labor influence on management, there would have been an accompanying decline in strikes. What we find, instead, is that labor's recourse to strikes continues unabated after the Treaty.

Our hypothesis that exit, not voice, is the basis of labor's power in segregated inclusion, also finds support in another comparison offered in Figure 15. If labor's leverage in American labor-management relations were its (institutionalized) voice, we would expect to find that industries with long-established labor-management relations have fewer strikes, as more labor-management disputes therein would be resolved through voice. In fact, however, the opposite is the case. In the auto industry, where segregated inclusion is more extensively institutionalized than anywhere else, the percentage of the total work days that are lost to strikes is substantially larger than in the private sector as a whole.

Labor's power and industrial performance under segregated inclusion

Having confirmed the hypothesized relationship between labor's power in corporate decision making and the satisfaction of labor's interests, we now turn to an examination of the hypothesized relationship between labor's power and industrial performance.

As we stated at the outset, the hypothesis that labor's power in corporate decision making advances the regime's industrial performance will be tested through a cross-national comparison. Therefore, here we will not measure the auto industry's efficiency. Rather, we will analyze the ways in which labor-management relations particular to the regime of segregated inclusion have influenced the regime's efficiency.

Positive Consequences of Segregated Inclusion for Efficiency

Labor's motivation and capacity to contribute to productive efficiency is determined by the organization of interests of capital and labor. While labor's interests are formally excluded from productivist decision making under segregated inclusion, the inclusion of labor's interests in redistributive decision making contributes, in a limited and indirect manner, to productivist decision making and to the efficiency of the regime. This is accomplished because labor's redistributive power, while *de jure* segregated from corporate productivist policy, *de facto* affects the latter by making certain productivist policies too expensive to pursue.

Labor's inclusion in wage determination precludes, or at least makes less likely the feasibility of cost-cutting strategies that aim at lowering wages. Indeed, collective bargaining in the American auto industry effectively "took wages out of (inter-capitalist) competition". As profits at the direct expense of labor's compensation were precluded through COLAs and AIFs, management was compelled to focus with added rigor on more creative ways of improving profitability: improving product design and marketing to increase demand, expanding production to benefit from economies of scale, adopting new technologies to improve turnover rates. COLAs also put limits to how much management could simply pass the cost of agreed-upon wage increases to consumers through price increases. Since such price increases would result in higher COLAs, management was compelled to compensate for rising labor costs by relying ever more on product and process innovation that left labor's redistributive interests largely intact.

SUBs also contributed to innovations in production by operating as a penalty on management for production strategies that relied exclusively on layoffs as adjustment to demand fluctuations. As we have shown through employment data from the automobile industry, American management continued to rely on hire-and-fire methods to adjust to fluctuations in product demand[90]. However, the high cost of those methods to employers (paying laid off workers 95% of their regular compensation for one year), is likely to have deterred even wider fluctuations in employment.

Indirect yet positive effects on efficiency also derive from health and safety, unfair dismissal, seniority, and grievance administration provisions. At the same time as they express labor's influence on corporate policies, they facilitate the adoption of regime-wide efficiency-enhancing policies, by precluding or retarding policies that may reduce the cost-benefit ratio for employers by simply reducing the value of labor's compensation (the conditions as well as the hours of work may affect the level of compensation).

FIGURE 16

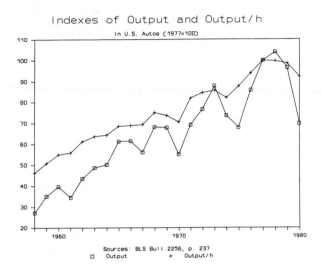

Indexes of Output and Output/h

In U.S. Autos (1977=100)

Sources: BLS Bull.2256, p. 237
□ Output   + Output/h

Such positive contributions to efficiency of labor's redistributive power, however indirect and limited, help explain the regime's effectiveness, and its acceptance by both labor and capital. The effectiveness of segregated inclusion in the auto industry is reflected in the volume of autos produced annually, in absolute terms as well as in relation to employee-hours worked, as charted in Figure 16. From 1958 to 1980, the regime's annual output has increased, although, beginning with the late-1950s, the regime's output is subject to ever-widening oscillations between sharp drops and sharp increases. The regime's hourly output has been increasing even more steadily than its output (Figure 16). Even during the turbulent 1970s, the regime's hourly output continued to increase. During the 1970s, the average annual increase in hourly output was 2.9%. This represents a slowing down in hourly output compared to the average increases of the 1960s (3.8%), but, nonetheless, a continuation of substantial improvements in regime effectiveness.

Major Innovations

Labor's inclusion in (the redistributive area of) corporate decision making in the U.S. auto industry does not seem to have stifled product and process innovation. Major turning points in auto manufacturing include the closed body (1910), automatic transmission (1943), power steering (1951), air conditioning (1955), alternator (1960), disc brakes (1968), catalytic converter (1974), all of which took a few years to be generalized[91]. Between 1950 and 1980 the process of auto production is further transformed through the gradual introduction of electronic computers, improved equipment for automatic assembly and inspection, widespread use of plastics and other light-weight material, widespread application of numerical control, and improvements in transfer lines.

Computers found their first applications in the auto industry in the area of business operations such as payroll and bookkeeping records. Subsequently, they found their way into an increasing number of research and production operations. Computers Aided Design systems (CAD), still in their infancy during this period, nonetheless enhanced auto styling and design. In CAD, mathematical information, representing auto body surfaces is stored in a computer memory system. A designer, working with a graphic display terminal, uses this information to design auto body parts. The computer translates the design into mathematical coordinates that can operate automatic drafting machines and numerically controlled (N/C) machine tools. Engineering, drafting work, and tool production operations are thus more closely connected, thereby speeding up the work flow. An auto parts manufacturer, for example, saved 9 to 12 months of development time by using CAD to perform preliminary design calculations on a new long-life piston ring[92].

In production operations, computers were introduced to keep track of parts and production materials and to forecast potential shortages that could disrupt production. Computer Control thus helped uniformity and quality control in machining. It also facilitated work scheduling and production line balancing (directing the proper materials to the workers at his/her place on the assembly line). Computer Aided Manufacturing is also introduced in the auto industry during this period, albeit only on an experimental basis. An auto plant used both a traditional, manual line and an automated, CAM line to assemble and test torque convertors used in automatic transmissions. In the automated line, a crew of 8 people per shift produced as much as 13 people on the manual line[93].

Another application of CAM, industrial robots, were introduced in autos in late-1960s. The number of robots in the U.S. jumped from 200 in 1970 to 3000 in 1979, but the auto industry lagged behind in the use of robots. In 1979 only 16% of the robots used in the U.S. were in this industry.[94] Robots found their most successful application in welding operations. While estimates of labor savings varied, there was agreement that the quality of the weld is more consistent in automated than in manual welding.

The use of plastic materials grew considerably as improvement in both the plastic material and the plastic-working technology became available. Advantages of plastics over steel (in those cases where plastics meet rigidity and strength requirements) included lower weight and generally lower tooling costs. Increased use of plastics reduced labor requirements because plastic parts required fewer finishing operations than comparable metal parts; large, one-piece molded plastic panels (such as dash panels or front-end body panels) began to replace an assemblage of sheet-metal parts, reducing assembly time. Plastics (especially fiber-reinforced composites using glass or other filaments) also seemed to address the new emphasis on lowering vehicle weight to improve fuel economy. Aluminum and special steels were also used for a growing number of auto components to reduce weight.

The industry's dynamism can also be gauged from its investments in plants and equipments. Between 1960 and 1975, expenditures for new plant and equipment, in current dollars, increased from $790 million in 1960 to $2.1 billion in 1975, an average of 7.4% per year. However, such expenditures grew at a slower pace in the 1970s than in the 1960s. This slowing down is mostly related to the construction of new plants; research and development expenditures as a percent of net sales was the same in the 1970s as in the previous decade, between 2.3 and 2.8 percent. Labor's contribution to the value of the good produced fell throughout the 1960s and 1970s. Payroll per unit of value-added fell at an average annual rate of 0.1%[95].

The Bitter Fruits of Segregation

Under segregated inclusion, labor finds itself in the unenviable position of having to bargain, so to speak, for slices of the pie, without any control over or knowledge of the size or quality of the pie itself. For example, labor's representatives may have to bargain for a 5% increase in hourly wage rates, without knowing how many workers will be employed when the contract goes into effect. Is a wage increase accompanied by layoffs a better deal for labor than no wage increase and no layoffs? Labor, in segregated inclusion, does not have to choose between the two options; employment is a productivist concern, outside labor's scope of bargaining.

Excluded from the making of productivist decisions, labor has no direct stake in their successful implementation; it can neither take credit for successes, nor does it necessarily benefit from them otherwise. In fact, it is even possible that the successful implementation of a productivist policy (such as a labor-saving process innovation) results in the layoff of some of the very workers that helped implement it, because fewer people are now needed to do that job. Consequently, labor single-mindedly pursues the highest wages it can get and provides the lowest work effort it can get away with. With management having the sole authority over organizing the work process and supervising the work effort, it also has the sole responsibility over those areas. Thus "adversarialism", the "arm's length relationship" between labor and management, and the lamented lack of labor-management cooperation in efforts to modernize production—they are all **consequences** of the organization of interests in the regime, rather than independent cultural variables.

More specifically, labor's exclusion from productivist decision making results in the segregation of labor's legitimate pursuits (higher wages) from capital's (higher profits) at the point of production. Capitalists, through management, have a central interest in the prompt and accurate performance of work, an interest which is not shared by workers: except for considerations of pride in one's work and one's work ethic, the American auto worker does not have a direct interest in the quality of work performed. Neither his/her pay nor his/her employment security are in any (direct) way linked to his/her performance at work. This segregation of pursuits is likely to hurt the regime's effectiveness and efficiency, for two reasons. First, even with improved systems of supervision, the work effort will be of lower quality than the work effort of a more motivated workforce (effectiveness undermined). Second, supervising an unmotivated workforce has considerable costs of its own (efficiency undermined even as effectiveness is restored).

Labor's exclusion from productivist decisions limits not only its motivation in productivity improvements, but also its ability to contribute to such improvements. In other words, labor, excluded from productivist decisions, loses its knowledge over productivist decisions, akin to the atrophy that sets in to an unused function. This has been most manifest in the area of skill formation and training. Unable to control decisions over employee training, reserved to management as a productivist issue, labor also loses the capacity to participate in productivist decisions, in case it were ever called to, has atrophied. Thus, even if adversarialism were eliminated as an attitude with a magic wand, cooperative labor-management relations would be thwarted by the narrowness of worker skills.

The ominous consequences of adversarialism for shop floor labor-management relations can be gauged through data on turnover rates, grievances filed for unfair labor practices and disciplinary layoffs. Between 1965 and 1969, turnover rates increased by 70%, grievances increased by 38%, disciplinary layoffs increased by 40%[96]. The hesitant introduction of quality circles in 1973 at Ford aimed precisely at correcting efficiency-impeding aspects of labor-management relations.

FIGURE 17

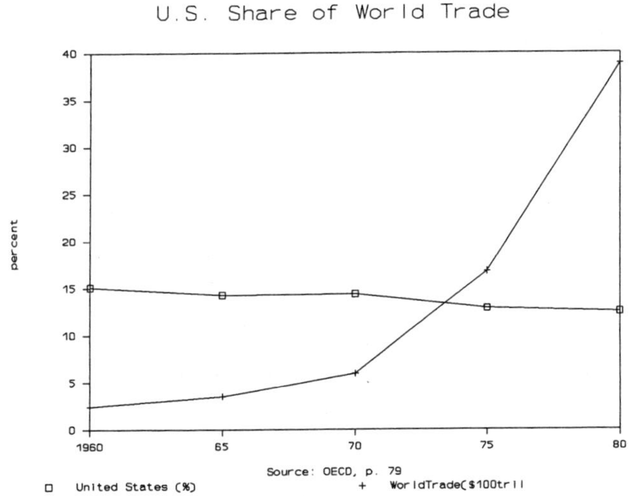

U.S. Share of World Trade

Source: OECD, p. 79
□ United States (%)   +   WorldTrade($100tril)

With no obvious deterioration in the regime's productive effectiveness until the late-1970s, why did the regime enter a crisis from the beginning of the 1970s, as evidenced by real wage declines and the end of employment-wage segregation?

A fundamental change in the context in which the regime operated, altered the benchmark for measuring its own success. In late-1960s or early-1970s, American companies began to compete with a range of world-class producers for the same markets, as foreign competitors completed their recovery from the devastation of the Second World War and consolidated their postwar production regimes. Indeed, in the 1970s, the total value of the world trade increased dramatically, from $250 billion in the beginning of the decade to $380 billion at the end. During the same period, the U.S. share of the world trade declined from 15.09% to 12.43% (Figure 17). Effective as the American auto production regime may have been, it was not effective enough. Efficiency was replacing effectiveness as an imperative in auto production. The U.S. auto industry was faced with a challenge it was slow to recognize and unwilling to take: transform thyself or perish.

FIGURE 18

US Share of World Auto Production

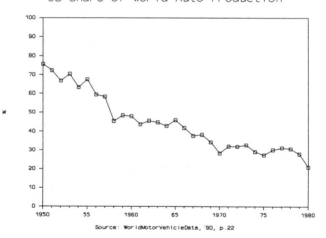

Source: WorldMotorVehicleData, '90, p.22

Was the U.S. auto industry spared the decline in the U.S. share of world production? No. As Figure 18 shows, the U.S. share of world auto production was in a steady decline since 1950. If the relative decline of the auto industry was due to a competitive disadvantage against foreign production regimes, such disadvantage was not new to the 1970s, but dated back to the 1950s, if not earlier. In fact, the 1970s, except for 1979, is the only decade since the Second World War when the U.S. share of world auto production did not decline.

FIGURE 19

US Share of the US Auto Market

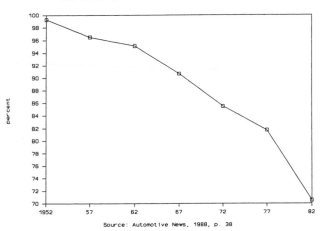

Source: Automotive News, 1988, p. 38

The shrinking U.S. share of world auto production would have been less alarming a signal of the performance of the U.S. auto industry, had its share of its domestic market remained intact. In fact, however, the U.S. auto industry's share of its domestic market was shrinking as well (Figure 19). In 1952 the U.S. share of the U.S. auto market stood at 99%; by 1982 it was down to 71%. If the American regime was still effective (in improving annual output, Figure 16), its efficiency (in optimizing production) was being put into question by the effectiveness of foreign producers and regimes. The penetration of the U.S. auto market by foreign producers was a particularly worrisome sign for the efficiency of the U.S. auto industry, given that it was not accompanied by increasing U.S. penetration of foreign auto markets. While the U.S. share of total world trade was shrinking (Figure 20 below), the U.S. was also experiencing a widening deficit in the automobile balance of trade. As Figure 20 shows, every year after 1955, the U.S. has had a negative balance of trade in autos. Worse still, the trend of the U.S. auto balance of trade was one of increasing deterioration.

FIGURE 20

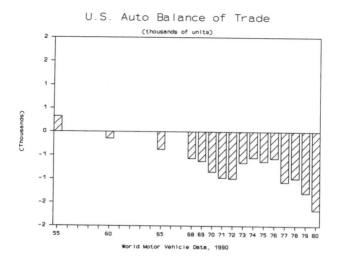

U.S. Auto Balance of Trade
(thousands of units)

World Motor Vehicle Data, 1990

4. CONCLUSION

The American production regime of segregated inclusion represented
an improvement both for labor (because of its remunerative and labor-
administrative benefits) and for capital (because of its predictability,
productivity and associated demand-stimulation benefits) over its
predecessor regime, which had excluded labor from redistributive and
productivist decision making. However, earlier labor demands for less
rigid demarcations between conception and execution and more worker
autonomy in the organization of work came to the surface again, when,
by the mid-1970s, it appeared that U.S. productivity growth was being
surpassed by foreign producers who had integrated such practices into
their production regimes. Why then, were American auto capitalists so
reluctant to integrate labor into the production regime? If the
integration of management's and labor's functions could improve
efficiency, why did the regime of segregated inclusion was maintained
largely intact until the 1980s?

   Part of the answer lies in social inertia against change. Capital was
likely to experiment with everything else before agreeing to share with
labor some of its hard-fought prerogatives to organize production.

Moreover, labor was also largely reluctant to change a production regime which, for two decades after the war, seemed to have maximized its power compared to what had preceded it. The unions had invested too much in fortifying their independence from capital's efforts to coopt them to readily risk a rapprochement.

However, the central difficulty with early attempts at functional integration (see QWL programs of the 1970s below) lay in the incompatibility of functional integration with interest segregation. The contradictions involved in giving workers autonomy and initiative in organizing production when they remain excluded from broader productivist decision making affecting work organization, productivity, and employment are encapsulated in General Motors' attempt at flexible work scheduling at one of its plants.

In a gesture of trust toward 500 unionized workers at a Flint, Michigan, factory that stamps out truck body panels, General Motors told them that they didn't have to punch a time clock when they left work. Managers allowed workers to leave once they finished banging out the day's quota of parts. The move sparked a startling jump in productivity. In fact, workers, many on the job for more than 20 years, suddenly found ways to do a full day's work before lunch. But management, dismayed at paying a full day's wage for a half day's work, unilaterally increased the quotas to the point that workers would have to put in eight hours even at the higher production levels they had achieved when they had the incentive to finish early.[97] The workers felt they had been tricked into a speedup. The old regime could not be fixed; it had to be changed.

NOTES

1. John Kenneth Galbraith, *The New Industrial State* (Boston: Houghton Mifflin, 3rd rev. ed., 1978).

2. James R. Green, *The World of the Worker:Labor in Twentieth Century America* (New York: Hill and Wag, 1980).

3. Section 8(d).

4. "Fibreboard Paper Products Corp. v. NLRB" (United States Reports, 1964, v. 379, pp. 203 ff., reprinted in BNA, Labor Relations Reference Manual, 1964, v. 57, pp. 2609 ff).

5. For a comprehensive list of NLRB and court decisions on the decision-versus effects-bargaining, see Philip A. Miscimarra, *The NLRB and Managerial*

Discretion: Plant Closings, Relocations, Subcontracting, and Automation (Philadelphia: University of Pennsylvania Press, 1983), p. 16-19.

6. "Fibreboard Paper Products v. NLRB," United States Reports, 1964, v. 379, pp. 203 ff. See also Bruce S. Feldacker, *Labor Guide to Labor Law*, 3rd ed. (Englewood Cliffs, N.J.: Prentice Hall, 1990), pp. 157-160.

7. *General Motors Corp.* (National Labor Relations Board Decisions and Orders, 1971, v. 191, Case 149, reprinted in BNA, Labor Relations Reference Manual, 1971 v. 77, pp. 1537 ff)

8. "NLRB v. Insurance Agents International Union," United States Reports, 1960, v. 361, pp. 477 ff., reprinted in BNA, 1960, Labor Relations Reference Manual, v. 45, pp. 2705 ff., cited in Feldacker, *op. cit.*, pp. 150-151.

9. The law prohibits the discharge of employees for striking, as long as the strike does not violate the statutory requirement to file a 60-day notice of the intention to strike (Sections 8(d) and 8(g)), or a contractual no-strike clause, or an illegal, sympathy strike (Section 8(b)(4)(B)).

10. See the Supreme Court's "NLRB v. Mackay Radio and Telegraph Co." decision of 1938, United States Reports, 1938, v. 304, pp. 333 ff.; reprinted in Labor Relations Reference Manual, 1938, v. 2, pp. 610 ff..

11. Since the NLRB's 1968 *Laidlaw* decision, permanently replaced "economic strikers" are placed on a list and are rehired as job openings (over and beyond those of replacements) become available. See National Labor Relations Board, 1968, v. 171, no. 175; reprinted in Labor Relations Reference Manual, 1968, v. 68, pp. 1252 ff.

12. Neimark (1992), p. 86.

13. "United States v. Hutcheson," United States Reports, 1941, v. 312, pp. 219 ff.; reprinted in BNA, Labor Relations Reference Manual, 1941, v. 7, pp. 267 ff.

14. With dues check-off the employer deducts union dues from the employees' paychecks and gives them to the union. This greatly facilitates the process of dues collection for the union.

15. The best account of labor-management relations in the war years is Nelson Lichtenstein, *Labor's War at Home: The CIO in World War II*, (Cambridge: Cambridge University Press, paperback ed. 1987).

16. Financial damages for breach of contract (for example, wildcat strikes) can be levied against the union's assets, not the union leaders.

17. "United States v. Brown," United States Reports, 1965, v. 381, pp 437 ff.

18. Section 8(e) added to the LMRA extends the prohibition against "hot cargo" clauses to include even voluntary agreements between an employer and a union, and voluntary, non-contractual compliance with such union request.

19. Section 9(c)(3).

20. Freeman and Medoff, *op. cit.*

21. Theda Skocpol makes a strong case for the autonomy of the state from class interests, including during the 1930s. See her "Bringing the State Back In: Strategies of Analysis in Current Research" in Evans et al., *op. cit.*

22. David Milton, *The Politics of U.S. Labor: From the Great Depression to the New Deal* (New York: Monthly Review Press, 1982, p. 73.

23. Quoted in William Serrin, *The Company and the Union: The 'Civilized Relationship' of General Motors Corporation and the United Auto Workers* (New York: Alfred Knopf, 1973), pp. 117-118.

24. George Barnett, "American Trade Unionism and Social Insurance," *American Economic Review* (March 1933).

25. From Roger Keeran, *The Communist Party and the Auto Workers Unions*, (Bloomington, IN: Indiana University Press, 1980), p. 184, and James R. Green, *The World of the Worker: Labor in Twentieth Century America* (New York: Hill and Wag, 1980.

26. Brian R. Mitchell, *International Historical Statistics: the Americas 1750-1988* (New York: Stockton Press, 2nd. ed., 1993), pp. 114-116.

27. David Milton, *The Politics of U.S. Labor: From the Great Depression to the New Deal* (New York: Monthly Review Press, 1982; Green, *op. cit.*

28. Keeran, *op. cit.*, p. 183.

29. Green, *op. cit.*, p. 158; and Neimark, *op. cit.*, p. 73.

30. A membership-maintenance clause prevents an employer from claiming that the union no longer represents a majority of the workforce (e.g. because new hires do not support the union) and thus calling for a decertification election.

31. Although Ford was the last of the auto companies to recognize the union, it was also the first company to grant the union shop (automatically recognizing UAW representation for all Ford employees) and the dues check-off, in the strike-settling 1941 contract.

32. A union-shop agreement requires that new hires join the union on or after thirty days of employment.

33. Not all of these strikes were directed at increasing labor's control over corporate decisions. Some strikes even had racist aims: in March-June 1943 over 100,000 man-days were lost in "hate strikes" over the hiring or upgrading of black workers in auto plants. See Mike Davis, *Prisoners of the American Dream: Politics and Economy in the History of the U.S. Working Class* (London: Verso, 1986), p. 81.

34. David Brody, *Workers in Industrial America: Essays on the 20th Century Struggle* (New York: Oxford University Press, 1980), p. 199.

35. David Brody, "The New Deal in World War II", in John Braema et al., *The New Deal: the National Level* (Columbus, OH., 1975, pp. 281-286.

36. General Motors Corporation, *History of the Movement to Organize Foremen in the Automobile Industry, December 1938-May 1945* (Detroit: General Motors Corporation, 1945, p. 9 (emphasis added).

37. Gartman, *op. cit.*, p. 267.

38. Victor Reuther, *The Brothers Reuther and the Story of the UAW* (Boston: Houghton Mifflin, 1976), pp. 247-248. See also Frank Cormier and William J. Eaton, *Reuther* (Englewood Cliffs, N.J.: Prentice-Hall, 1970), pp. 185-230; and a concurrent account by Irving Howe and B.J. Widick, *The UAW and Walter Reuther* (New York: Random House, 1949), esp. pp. 219-234.

39. Feldacker, *op. cit.*, pp. 163-4.

40. Brody, *op. cit.*, p. 176.

41. Nelson Lichtenstein, *Labor's War at Home: The CIO in World War II*, (Cambridge, MA: Cambridge University Press, paperback ed. 1987), p. 226.

42. GM ad quoted in Howe and Widick, *op. cit.*, p. 135.

43. The author of the article is Leonard Westrate. *Automotive Industries* 93 (December 1945), p. 17.

44. Gartman, *op. cit.*, p. 270.

45. Lichtenstein (1986), p. 123. See also Lichtenstein (1982), pp. 221-226; Cormier and Eaton (1970), pp. 185-230; and Howe and Widick, *op. cit.*, pp. 108-148.

46. Neimark, *op. cit.*, p. 80.

47. Nominal hourly earnings are from U.S. Bureau of Labor Statistics, *Employment, Hours, and Earnings, United States, 1909-1990, v. I*, Bulletin no. 2370, March 1991 (Washington, DC: GPO, 1991). Real wages, in 1982-84 dollars, were computed on the basis of the CPI from U.S. Bureau of the Census, *Statistical Abstracts of the United States*, 1962, (Washington, DC: GPO), p. 348 and Ibid, 1992, p. 46.

48. Lichtenstein (1986), p. 124.

49. See previous section.

50. The negotiations are aptly described by El-Messidi and Kathy Groehn, *The Bargain: The Story Behind the Thirty Year Honeymoon of GM and the UAW* (New York: Nellen Publishing Co., Inc., 1980). For a list of studies of GM's labor during this period see Howell Harris, *The Right to Manage: Industrial Relations Policies of American Business in the 1940s* (Madison, WI: University of Wisconsin Press, 1982), pp. 139-143.

51. Neimark, *op. cit.*, pp. 82-83.

52. Brody, *op. cit.*, pp. 48-81; Piore and Sabel, *op. cit.*, pp. 124-130.

53. Based on annual strike data compiled from Keeran, *op. cit.*, p. 184; Green, *op. cit.*; U.S. Bureau of the Census, *Statistical Abstracts of the United States, 1940* (Washington, DC: GPO, 1940), p. 355.

54. The Big Three companies comprised almost all of the auto industry. Even in 1930, GM, Ford and Chrysler together accounted for 90 percent of auto sales in the United States, Neimark, *op. cit.*, p. 186, note 95.

55. "Connective bargaining" ensures almost identical contracts in the Big Three: the union bargains a contract first with the most profitable company and then rallies demands from the other two companies to duplicate the terms of that contract. See Harry C. Katz, *Shifting Gears: Changing Labor Relations in the U.S. Automobile Industry* (Cambridge: MIT Press, 1985). Before the war, labor's position in the corporation and its compensation, varies significantly from one company to the other. See also Neimark, *op. cit.*; and Gartman, *op. cit.*

56. Originally, COLAs provided full cost-of-living protection, while in the 1970s they provided an 0.8 per cent increase for every 1 per cent increase in the national consumer price index.

57. Bureau of National Affairs, Inc., *Basic Patterns in Union Contracts* (Washington, D.C.: BNA Books, 1986). Notice that this COLA formula also serves to diminish pay differentials among workers; a 1 cent increase for a $8 hourly wage is proportionally a smaller increase than for a $6 hourly wage. For a good concise discussion of UAW-management conflict on inter-worker pay differentials see Gartman (1987), pp. 281-284.

58. Alfred P. Sloan, *My Years With General Motors* (Garden City, N.Y.: Doubleday, 1964), p. 402.

59. In 1950 pension payments amounted to $100 a month.

60. It has been argued that the inclusion of fringe benefits in bargaining was, in effect, detrimental to the development of the welfare state, by diffusing pressure for social benefits for all workers; the welfare state became more privatized and exclusionary than in Western Europe. See, for example, Nelson Lichtenstein "Reutherism on the Shop Floor: Union Strategy and Shop-Floor Conflict in the USA 1946-70," in Tolliday and Zeitlin, *op. cit.*, p. 240.

61. Bureau of National Affairs, Inc., *Basic Patterns in Union Contracts* (Washington, D.C.: BNA Books, 1986).

62. The 1935 Henderson Report to the President mentions seasonal unemployment in the auto industry as a major factor in the dire condition of the autoworker; cited in William Serrin, *The Company and the Union: The 'Civilized Relationship' of General Motors Corporation and the United Auto Workers* (New York: Alfred Knopf, 1973), pp. 117-118.

63. Ending the seasonality of employment was one of Reuther's 16-point program for converting the auto industry from military to civilian production, proposed (and rejected by the companies) in 1945.

64. The best exponent of "bureaucratic" control (as opposed to the "technical" and the "drive" types of control) is Edwards, *op. cit.*

65. "Down time" refers to periods during work when the assembly line stops (because of low demand for the product, slow delivery of requisite parts, or any other reason).

66. Katz, *op. cit.*; Turner, *op. cit.*, p. 37.

67. Seniority "bumping rights" did exist before the Treaty of Detroit, but only for certain skilled trades and based solely on tradition, particularly in the construction industry. They were institutionalized and generalized for the automobile industry and elsewhere with the Treaty of Detroit.

68. See Feldacker, *op. cit.*, especially chapters 1 and 9.

69. This point is well made by Katherine Van Wezel Stone, "The Post-War Paradigm in American Labor Law," *Yale Law Journal*, 90, 7, 1981, p. 1517.

70. "Pattern bargaining" is the term used by Michael Indegaard and Michael Cushion, "Conflict, Cooperation, and the Global Auto Factory," in Daniel B. Cornfield (ed), *Workers, Managers, and Technological Change: Emerging Patterns of Labor Relations* (New York: Plenum, 1987). "Connective bargaining" is used by Katz, *op. cit.*

71. The Swedish unions have used the tactic/method of pattern bargaining in order to reduce wage and benefits differential not only within an industry but across industries. The union federation LO has stressed that such wage equalization not only strengthens labor solidarity, but that it also forces productivity improvements across the economy by threatening industries that cannot afford the wages and benefits of the national pattern with economic extinction. Walter Korpi, *The Working Class in Welfare Capitalism: Work, Unions and Politics in Sweden* (London: Routledge, 1978). Gosta Esping-Andersen, *The Three Worlds of Welfare Capitalism* (Princeton: Princeton University Press, 1990).

72. Neimark, *op. cit.*, p. 83.

73. Based on data reported in the *National Income and Product Accounts* of the Bureau of Economic Analysis of the US Department of Commerce, various years.

74. Quoted in ibid., p. 83, emphasis added.

75. *Fortune*, July 1950, no. 42, p. 6.

76. Katz (1987).

77. One of the most comprehensive descriptions of job classifications in postwar industrial relations in the U.S. is Sumner H. Slichter, James J. Healy,

and E, Robert Livernash, *The Impact of Collective Bargaining on Management* (Washington, D.C.: The Brookings Institution, 1960). For a more synoptic account see Peter B. Doeringer and Michael J. Piore, *Internal Labor Markets and Manpower Analysis* (Lexington, MA.: D.C. Heath and Co., 1971), pp. 1-113.

78. See the contributions of Katz, Piore & Sabel, Tolliday & Zeitlin, in Tolliday and Zeitlin, *op. cit.*

79. Lichtenstein (1986), p. 130.

80. The term was first used by Katz (1985).

81. Lichtenstein (1986), pp. 130-31.

82. Edwards sees this as the ascendancy of "bureaucratic control" of management over labor, a method of diluting class consciousness through predictable material advancement. See Edwards (1979).

83. Montgomery, *op. cit.*, pp. 147-148.

84. See Philip A. Miscimarra, *The NLRB and Managerial Discretion: Plant Closings, Relocations, Subcontracting, and Automation* (Philadelphia: University of Pennsylvania Press, 1983), pp. 16-19; see also Feldacker, *op. cit.*, pp. 157-160.

85. Turner, *op. cit.*, p. 39.

86. Walter Reuther, quoted in Neil W. Chamberlain, *Sourcebook on Labor* (New York: McGraw-Hill Book Co., 1964), p. 281).

87. Lichtenstein (1986), pp. 128-129.

88. Calculations based on data from Figure 12.

89. *Proceedings of the Eleventh Constitutional Convention*, November 9-14 1947, p. 8.

90. Annual employment fluctuations become even wider if we consider monthly fluctuations.

91. Abernathy et al., *The Competitive Status of the U.S. Auto Industry: A Study of the Influences of Technology in Determining International Industrial Competitive Advantage* (Washington, D.C.: National Academy Press, 1982), pp. 45-56.

92. "Computer Speeds Design Production of Piston Rings," *Automotive Industries*, November 15, 1968, pp. 79-85.

93. U.S. Bureau of Labor Statistics, *A BLS Reader on Productivity*, Bulletin 2171 (June 1983), pp. 191-192.

94. Carl H.A. Dassbach, "Industrial Robots in the American Automobile Industry," *The Insurgent Sociologist*, (Summer 1986), p. 55.

95. U.S. Bureau of Labor Statistics, *A BLS Reader on Productivity*, Bulletin 2171 (June 1983) (Washington, D.C.: GPO, 1983), pp. 194-195.

96. Rosabeth Moss Kanter, *The Change Masters* (New York: Simon and Schuster, 1983), p. 217.

97. *Wall Street Journal* (August 29, 1990), p. 1, cited in Robert Buchele and Jens Christiansen, "Worker Rights Promote Productivity Growth," *Challenge*, September-October 1995, p. 36.

CHAPTER 4

Jointness: Reluctant Desegregation in U.S. Auto Production

This chapter reviews key developments in labor-management relations in the auto industry in the 1980s. Observed deviations from traditional patterns of labor-management relations were at once dramatic and flimsy. They were dramatic in that they signalled the embarkment of the U.S. auto industry toward practices which both labor and (especially) management had considered taboo for decades. They were flimsy in that they were adopted very hesitantly, and elicited only a partial commitment from either side. While, under the new arrangement, productivist decision making as such stopped being management's "sole prerogative," it is far from obvious that labor became more powerful than before. It will be seen that progress at including labor in productivist decision making came in a very truncated form, maintaining the exclusion of a substantial portion of productivist decisions from labor's domain: the increasingly important areas of foreign operations and assets, as well as the shifting of operations oversees, continue to be labor-proof. Moreover, while the new approach to industrial relations sought to improve efficiency by minimizing human waste (unemployment), efficiency improvements were undermined by reduced rates of investment at home. It is not, therefore, immediately clear whether in the 1980s labor gained new opportunities to control its future or gave legitimacy to its defeat. Whether Jointness is the last gasp of a bankrupt production regime or the first steps towards a new one; whether the "partial integration" of the 1980s is a contradiction in terms or the first steps towards a dynamic new regime, will be proven in the next century. What is already clear is that, by the end of the 1980s, the postwar regime of segregated inclusion was no more.

In order to assess labor's power in the production regime of Jointness, it is necessary to review the labor-management agreements of the 1980s, and analyze them against substantive indicators of auto workers' well-being, such as employment and earnings levels.

1. THE CRISIS OF THE 1970S: THE END OF THE LINE?

While the 1980s is the focus of our study and the decade when fundamental departures from the regime of segregated inclusion were undertaken, the roots of these departures were sown in the 1970s. Indeed, certain developments in labor-management relations during the 1970s, seen at the time as temporary and minor deviations from the dominant patterns of segregated inclusion, proved to be lasting and substantial, prefiguring the regime changes of the 1980s. These "aberrations" of the 1970s included the QWL programs, the co-variation of employment and wage fluctuations, the Southern compromise, and the invitation of the UAW president to sit on Chrysler's board of directors.

QWL: The Foot in the Door

In 1973 the UAW and General Motors agreed to introduce a new Quality of Working Life (QWL) program on a very limited scale. Ford followed suit with its own Employee Involvement program. Accordingly, small groups of workers and managers (sometimes referred to as "quality circles") would provide improved labor-management communication, in order to allow workers to quickly adjust their working environment according to their needs. Initially, at least, adopted measures aimed at simple shop floor issues, such as lighting, ventilation, cleanliness and noise levels; more complex issues such as work design, work allocation, choice of technology or investment, were left outside quality circles' domain.

QWL was the brainchild of Irving Bluestone, a retired social-democratic UAW official and later college professor[1]. It was intended to reverse the segregation between labor and management and, for the workers, the segregation between conception and execution. For Bluestone, the QWL was "labor's foot in the door" of corporate governance, the precursor of labor-capital codetermination. The QWL experience would give workers the knowledge and self-confidence necessary to demand their inclusion in a wide range of productivist decisions, while the demonstrated productivity improvements would alleviate management opposition to such inclusion.[2] However, QWL programs could also be seen as a golden opportunity for auto capitalists, as "capital's foot in the door" of unions, the precursor of a union-free or company-union environment. Indeed, the QWL experience could help workers identify with the concerns and interests of the company, and provide them with a substitute to the union as a venue of communication with management.

QWL was not very popular with labor nor with management: joint labor-management forums, however minuscule in their size, numbers or authority, were at odds with the strict division of labor between labor and management—a division that capital had vociferously insisted on in the years leading up to the Treaty of Detroit, and which labor had come to embrace as well. Why then was QWL introduced at all? The central reason was the inability of segregated inclusion to alleviate the rising problem of worker morale. Between 1965 and 1969, absenteeism increased 50%, turnover rates increased 70%, grievances increased 38%, disciplinary layoffs increased 40%[3]. At the same time, the U.S. auto industry, having long considered itself as the world paragon of manufacturing efficiency, was losing world market share to foreign producers with apparently more motivated and cooperative workforces. Between 1950 and 1970s the U.S. share of world auto production had fallen precipitously from 75.7% to 28.2%[4]. The possibility that imminent productivity improvement could be obtained by involving workers in daily worplace decisions could no longer be overlooked.

It was against such pressures in labor relations and competitiveness that QWL was introduced in the 1973 GM-UAW contract. It was a pilot program affecting a handful of auto plants. The parties were committing themselves to establishing formal mechanisms for exploring new ways of dealing with the quality of work, under the auspices of a National Joint Committee to Improve the Quality of Worklife. The parties agreed to set forth their general understanding on the subject and to urge their respective local managements and local unions to cooperate in quality-of-worklife experiments and projects. There were certain guidelines for implementing a quality-of-worklife program, such as no increase in production standards, no loss of jobs, voluntary participation, and union and management involvement in developing and setting up the program. Seven years after they were first introduced, there were about 50 quality-of-worklife programs in UAW-

GM bargaining units and an even smaller number of comparable programs at Ford and Chrysler, many of which still in their early stages of implementation[5].

In the immediate years after their introduction the effectiveness of these programs remained unclear, except for the area of absenteeism, which the introduction of QWL seemed to reduce significantly. However, the coincidence of layoffs and speed-ups with QWL programs reduced the atmosphere of trust between labor and management which the programs were intended to foster[6].

GM Abandons 'Southern Strategy'

Another important development of the 1970s that prefigured the evolution of labor-management relations in the 1980s was the agreement of General Motors, under pressure from the UAW, to abandon its Southern Strategy. At the end of the 1960s and in the early-1970s the union had been on the defensive against G.M.'s apparently coordinated effort to shut down plants in the North and the Midwest and open new ones in the South. Low wages, lack of union consciousness and "right-to-work" laws made the South difficult to organize. Thus the company, unable to break the union in the industrial states, saw in the South a tempting opportunity to dilute the union density of its workforce. The threat to the union was formidable, given that a dilution in union density directly undermined labor's only weapon, the ability to strike effecively.

The Southern Strategy, as a direct threat to the union, was at odds with the experiments at more harmonious labor-management relations heralded by QWL programs. It was also ill-suited to avert long labor disputes—a risk which the company might have well taken at another time. However, the auto industry entered a severe crisis in 1973-74, triggered by the oil shock and the first world recession since World War II. Thus, in 1976, after extended negotiations with the union, G.M. agreed to "observe a posture of neutrality" during union certification elections in its Southern plants[7]. The policy change came after meetings between UAW President Douglas A. Fraser and GM Chairman Thomas A. Murphy. Fears of strikes at key GM plants in the North during the critical model changeover period played strong roles in GM's policy-change decision[8]. In a tacit exchange, the union made some wage concessions: during the last years of the decade real hourly earnings for auto workers declined (see Chapter 3). In the 1979 negotiations, the union complained that the company had circumvented its promise of neutrality in the South by recruiting only workers who had no union background. The company relented. The final blow to the "southern strategy" was dealt when the company agreed to give unemployed union members preference in hiring at its Southern plants.

Although only about 2% of GM's production workers were to be employed in the 12 Southern plants[9]. The agreement's significance should not be underestimated. It marks a willingness on the part of the company to include in its investment strategy certain of labor's long-term interests, in exchange for labor's willingness to include corporate profitability in its bargaining strategy. Employers and the union began to focus their respective strategies on **avoiding** industrial conflicts rather than on **prevailing** in such conflicts.

Labor on Chrysler's Board

On October 25, a financially struggling Chrysler and the UAW reached a new agreement. The union agreed to an unprecedented separate agreement with Chrysler, deviating from those with GM and Ford. Equally unprecedented were negotiated wage concessions averaging $2,000 per worker per year, as a recognition of the company's financial dire straits. In return, the union won a seat on Chrysler's board for UAW President Douglas A. Fraser. Additionally, according to the agreement between the union and Chrysler, part of the company's pension contributions would be used to fund "socially desirable projects" rather than buy common stocks or government securities[10]. The UAW's sacrifices represented a $203 million savings for Chrysler. The company stood to save about $59 million in wages by delaying the effective date of the union's traditional 3% annual wage increase (AIF). Chrysler workers would not be paid for any personal holidays until 1981. An employee would have to miss 4 days before he could start collecting sick and accident pay[11].

While the presence of a single union leader as an observer on the Board of Directors was not likely to have any significant impact on policy making[12], it was a great symbolic blow against the wall dividing labor and capital under segregated inclusion. The top decision making institution of capital now included a representative of labor. It was a "breakthrough move," attacked by many corporate executives as a conflict of interest position for the labor leader; many American unions were also hostile[13].

Employment Meets Wages

FIGURE 1

While QWL may have signalled a departure from the **principle** of segregation in labor-capital relations, its very limited application resulted in only minimal deviation from the **practice** of segregation. However, another deviation from the principles of segregated inclusion had widespread consequences. For the first time since 1950, labor's productivist (employment) and redistributive interests (earnings) began to develop in tandem. As can be seen in Figure 1, beginning in 1969, uninterrupted annual wage increases, irrespective of changes in employment, come to an end. Unlike the two previous decades, during the 1970s annual wage and employment changes co-vary.

2. 1982: INTRODUCING JOINTNESS

In the 1980s the experimental innovations of the 1970s are extended and upgraded into pillars of labor-management relations in the U.S. auto industry (see Table 1 below). The regime of segregated inclusion, under severe competitive pressures by foreign regimes, begins to crumble: segregation between labor's and management's interests and functions, is now seen as a liability by both parties. However, measures to increase labor-management integration during the labor process (functional integration) are not matched by commensurate measures to increase the integration of labor's and management's interests (interest integration). In the emerging new labor-management relationship, which the parties refer to as "Jointness," labor's power is not diminished, increased or unchanged, but restructured: labor gains some authority over productivist decision making, in exchange for agreeing to subject its redistributive demands to productivist considerations. The following section reviews key innovations in labor-management relations in American autos as they are codified in three sets of labor contracts signed by the UAW and the Big Three auto companies in 1982, 1984, and 1987.

Table 1

INNOVATIONS IN THE 1980s
productivist decisions JC-MGF, QWL-EI, JOBS-GEN, closing moratoria
redistributive decisions givebacks (AIF, COLA), profit-sharing, GIS

In 1980, for the first time in its history, the entire industry was in the red: GM, Ford, Chrysler and American Motors lost $4.2 billion and more than $1 billion in the first nine months of 1981. Sales of North American cars during 1979-1980 dropped 32%, and capacity utilization in the motor vehicle and parts industry dropped from 91 to 52%. According to Department of Commerce estimates, during 1980 auto-related unemployment came close to one million: about 300,000 at the Big Four, and 700,000 at supplier, dealer, and other auto-related companies. At the worst point of the 1979-1980 slump, fully 32% of the Big Four's U.S. hourly workforce was on layoff[14].

The first auto contract of the 1980s was exceptional for its content but also for its timing. At the end of 1981, General Motors asked for the union's requisite consent for reopening the 1979s contract. The latter was due to expire in September 1982, but the company, citing the sharp downturns in the auto market and the severe recession, urged immediate revisions in key contract provisions. The UAW, despite its policy against reopening contracts, agreed: a growing number of plant closings, the specter of rising layoffs, and the consequent depletion of SUB funds had impressed on the union the urgency of revising the old contract. For the first time in its history, the union was settling two consecutive contracts without a strike.

The target company for 1982 was Ford, with the GM and Chrysler contracts following the pattern of the Ford-UAW provisions closely but with certain differences. Deviations from the Ford pattern in the Chrysler settlement were conditioned by the extraordinary circumstances of Chrysler's federal bailout from bankruptcy, but deviations in the GM contract point to a more general erosion of "connective bargaining" in favor of more company-specific arrangements[15]. Still, differences between the Ford-UAW and GM-UAW contracts were much fewer and less significant than their similarities.

In both the Ford-UAW and the GM-UAW contracts, the union agreed to significant monetary concessions to the companies in exchange for unprecedented commitments for job security and joint labor-management administration of programs to improve the quality of working life and of production. These path-breaking contracts included measure that mitigated the segregation of labor and capital's interests: wage concessions, profit sharing, and job security. And they also contained measures that moderated the segregation of labor's and management's functions in production.

Redistributive Decisions

The Ford-UAW contract covered 160,000 workers, of whom 55,000 were on indefinite layoff. The GM-UAW contract covered some 340,000 active and most of the 150,000 laid-off workers. Labor's **wage concessions** took three forms and were almost identical in Ford and in GM. First, the AIF for 1982, which was agreed upon in the previous contract, was suspended indefinitely, while the quarterly COLAs due in 1982 were deferred for eighteen months. Second, a **two-tier** system reversed the half-century old tradition of solidaristic and egalitarian intra-industry wage policies achieved by the union[16]. Under the new contract, new hires would be paid at 85 percent of the "normal" rate, with 5 percent increases following each six months over an 18-month span. Third, a Paid Personal Holiday Plan granting auto workers nine paid "personal" days off, first negotiated in 1976, was eliminated. All these concessions were justified as necessary for the survival of the industry, and as labor's acknowledgment that high American labor costs were undermining its competitiveness in a global market. As soon as competitiveness and/or past sales levels were restored, these concessions would be immediately renegotiated[17].

In what sense were such wage concessions a sign that the regime was moving toward interest integration? Why not view them, alternatively, as a sign of further interest segregation, given the losses suffered by labor? Before responding, it is necessary to review and evaluate the auto employers' concessions to labor, and other measures aimed at integrating labor's and capital's interests.

The 1982 contract introduced, for the first time in the history of the U.S. auto history a **profit-sharing plan**, to take effect January 1, 1983. Accordingly, Ford would provide its workers a share of the company's profits, whenever before-tax profits exceeded 2.3 percent of total U.S. sales. (Specifically, employees would receive 10 percent of that part of the profit between 2.3 percent and 4.6 percent of sales; 12.5 percent of the profit between 4.6 and 6.9 percent of sales; and 15 percent of profits in excess of 6.9 percent of sales.) Under GM's profit-sharing plan, employees would share 10 percent of the firm's before-tax U.S. profits, should the profits exceed a total of 10 percent of net worth and 5 percent of other assets[18]. These differences in the profit-sharing plans were meant to account for the more diversified nature of GM's operations and its larger size and lower profit rate.

The novelty and significance of the profit-sharing plan was unmistakable: until then, workers shared in corporate prosperity only inadvertently and not proportionately. Indeed, under the regime of segregated inclusion, labor had been pushing for raises irrespective of (and without formal knowledge of) corporate finances; and the raises granted were not calculated on a proportional basis to profits. Under the new profit sharing plan, labor's redistributive interests were integrated with those of capital's, **to the extent that** both parties's monetary welfare became a direct function of corporate earnings. It can readily be seen, however, that the extent to which wages became a direct function of profits was very small: only a tiny portion of a worker's annual earnings became a direct function of profits.

Equally significant was a new **"guaranteed income stream"** (GIS) program, under which a significant portion of the annual income of older Ford workers would be guaranteed against layoffs, until workers reached retirement age. The GIS, interestingly, was quite similar to the Guaranteed Annual Wage (GAW) that had been proposed proposed by the UAW in 1955 and rejected outright by the employers (see Chapter 3). The new plan had a dual character. As an income-protection plan it integrated labor's redistributive interests with capital's; as a disincentive to a policy of layoffs it integrated labor's productivist interests with capital's.

Under the new plan, workers with 15 years of service laid off after the contract took effect would be guaranteed an income stream equivalent to 50 percent of their hourly rate of pay until age 62 or retirement. The GIS for workers with more than 15 years of service would be 1 percentage point higher for each additional year to a maximum of 75 percent of the average weekly wage or 95 percent of take-home pay, whichever was less. Unlike Ford's, GM's agreement made GIS retroactive to March 1[19]. As in Ford, workers with 15 years of seniority were covered by the plan. But, in the event of a plant shutdown, it would be extended to workers with 10 (rather than 15) of seniority. In addition, all the workers at two closed plants in California became eligible for GIS payments.

Ford also agreed to inject $70 million to the **SUB** fund as a further commitment to labor's interest in employment. The fund, supplementing laid-off workers' government-financed unemployment benefits with corporate unemployment benefits, had been almost depleted because of the rising number of workers becoming eligible for SUBs; thus by 1982, SUB benefits were limited to workers with at least 10 years of service. Ford also agreed to increase its regular contributions to the fund by 3 cents for each paid hour of employee compensation. GM agreed to increase the SUB fund up to $200 million, if its assets fell below minimum levels; $163 of the advance would be recovered from future SUB contributions, once fund income exceeded payments.

Productivist Decisions

The contract's most innovative provisions opened up the area of productivist decision making to labor, if not all the way. Novel "job security" and "participatory" provisions appear, as both a victory and a defeat for labor. On the one hand, these measures, did little to offset the employment losses of the previous years and did not ensure the end of layoffs in the following years. On the other hand, however, these measures gave labor unprecedented powers in the area of productivist decision making. Labor's new powers took four forms: Joint Union-Management Councils (or Forums at Ford), teamwork and QWL (or EI at Ford), and moratoria on plant closings and JOBs (or GENs at Ford). The 1982 labor contract at Ford provided for the establishment of new joint labor-management committees, labeled Mutual Growth Forums,

> "for advance discussion of certain business developments of material interest and significance to the union, the employees, and the company."

In GM, similarly, a number of new committees were set up by the agreement. The long-winded yet tellingly named Joint Council for Enhancing Job Security and the Competitive Edge, was similar to Ford's Mutual Growth Forums, and was created out of

> "recognition of the mutual character of concerns previously considered the responsibility of only of party"[20].

Additionally, GM funded a Joint Skill Development and Training Committee with $120 million. Another joint committee was to study ways of containing health care costs[21]. While the precise composition, scope and authority of these forums remained quite vague, the readiness of both management and union to commit to regular discussions over a broad range of productivist and redistributive issues was, by all accounts, an unprecedented development in the arms-length labor-management relationship that had characterized industrial relations in the auto industry until then. If not substantially, at least symbolically, labor-management segregation in organizing production and promoting their respective interests was clearly receding.

More directly relevant to shop floor relations, the 1982 agreement extended the number of QWL programs dramatically. Thus, whereas from 1973 to 1980 there were 50 QWL programs in GM plants nationwide, by 1984 their number jumped to 3,000[22]. The original mandate and structure of these programs, introduced in the mid-1970s, remained essentially the same in 1982, but were now placed under the supervision of top-level union and management committees. Moreover, the expansion of QWL, from pilot programs to a mainstay of industrial relations, anticipated a qualitatively new relationship between labor and management on the shop floor of auto plants across the country.

"Management manages and labor grieves" was to be replaced by the principle of continuous communication, cooperation and consultation between labor and management on issues pertaining to the organization of work. A severe absenteeism control program, sought to elicit the parties' cooperation in addressing absenteeism in an expedited manner, outside adversarial grievance procedures. Those absent more than 20 percent of the time during a six-month period would receive benefits correspondingly reduced for the next six-month period, while counseling was to be provided for offenders. Symbols of labor-management segregation such as separate cafeterias and separate parking lots were abolished.

A **moratorium** on plant closings included in the 1982 Ford-UAW contract prevented management for two years from closing down a plant because of outsourcing (contracting out production that used to be done in-house). This provision addressed labor's increasing complaints that its interests in employment were directly undermined by management's unilateral decisions to eliminate jobs by purchasing auto parts (often from non-union suppliers) instead of producing them in-house, with union workers. GM also committed to the same moratorium; additionally, GM agreed to abandon plans to close four plants, that would have eliminated some 11,000 jobs.

The plant moratorium still left management free to close plants due to other reasons, such as declining demand for the product. However, even in the latter cases, management agreed to give the union six months' advance notice of impending plant closings, where possible[23]; alternatives to shutdown were to be discussed between labor and management upon such notification; and if closure could not be avoided, the company agreed to help workers find other jobs. Clearly, these measures brought issues such as capacity utilization and investment, heretofore the exclusive prerogative of management, onto the bargaining table, albeit in a truncated form: layoffs due to a fall in demand for American autos—the reason given for most layoffs—remained very much a management option.

The 1982 contracts also included two pilot programs of minimal impact but significant symbolic value. One was a joint training program for displaced workers, and the other a lifetime employment program in two Ford and four GM plants[24].

3. 1984: EXTENDING JOINTNESS

The pattern-setting contract of 1984 was negotiated with GM. Six days after the 1982 contract expired, and after the UAW began selective strikes around the country[25], the company and the union settled on a three-year contract, covering 380,000 active and laid-off workers. At Ford, a similar agreement covered 131,000 active and laid-off workers. The background for the agreement was the resumption of economic growth and the opening, for the first time ever, of two Japanese auto plants in the United States: Honda's plant in Marysville, Ohio, and Nissan's in Smyrna, Tennessee.

Redistributive Decisions

The contract did not include **wage concessions** such as those of 1982, or the kind wage increases which were norm before 1982. The GM agreement provided for an immediate raise averaging 2.5%[26]. That meant that labor would not recoup the suspended AIF of 1982. Moreover, an AIF would not be incorporated into base pay; rather, the contract also called for an immediate $180 bonus, and payments equal to 2.25% of annual pay in the second and third years of the contract. A COLA was incorporated into the contract, but in a truncated form. (Of $3.04 in COLAs generated over the past five years, only $2.99 was to be rolled into base rates. For purposes of benefit computation, even a smaller portion, $2.39 was to be considered.) Very similar redistributive policies were agreed between the UAW and Ford.

The **profit sharing** plans negotiated two years earlier remained in effect. According to the union's estimates, profit-sharing payments in 1985 would be around $1,000 per worker, up from $640 in 1984, according to the union's estimates.

The guaranteed income stream for high-seniority workers who were laid off was renewed. No significant changes were added to pension benefits. Little progress was made in medical benefits (choice of HMOs or traditional coverage).

Other provisions included two additional holidays (one to honor Martin Luther King, Jr. in the second and third years); and company payment for full time union work by presidents of locals with more than 600 workers.

Productivist Decisions

The key element of the new contract, and the union's first priority, was job security. GM agreed to establish a Job Opportunity Bank-Security (JOBS) program, with funding of $1 billion. Workers with one year of seniority losing their jobs **because of** new technology, outsourcing, negotiated productivity improvements, or transfer of work to other UAW plants, were to be placed in the job bank and receive full pay until a comparable job opening became available. The program was to continue for six years or until funding ran out. At Ford, the union secured a similar program, differing only in name (Protected Employee Program)[27].

The contract called for the establishment of several joint labor-management committees to address the quality of working life as a means of improving workers' skills, motivation and contribution to needed improvements in productivity. An "Executive Board-Joint Activities" committee, consisting of an equal number of labor and management representatives, would oversee a number of such joint committees:

- the National Committee to Improve the Quality of Work Life,

- National Joint Skill Development and Training Committee[28],

- the National Joint Committee on Health and Safety,

- the National Joint Committee on Attendance,

- the National Substance Abuse Recovery Program,

- the Tuition Assistance Program,

- the JOBS Program[29],

- the Growth and Opportunity Committee,

- and other joint activities that the two parties might agree upon[30].

Several points of the new contract were elaborated and clarified in a series of "memoranda of understanding" signed by General Motors Corporation and the International Union, UAW[31]. One such memorandum, titled "Joint Activities" is highly instructive of the concerns of the two parties in seeking Jointness and of the composition and role of the Executive Board-Joint Activities, and worth quoting at some length:

"During current negotiations, the parties discussed the **challenges in the marketplace** from both foreign and domestic competitors. There is mutual recognition that these challenges require a **fundamental change** to maximize the **potential of our human resources**. This change can occur only by building on our current joint efforts and by fostering a spirit of cooperation and mutual dedication that will permit the full development of the skill of our people and **meaningful involvement in the decision-making process**. Success in these endeavors benefits all of the parties. The UAW through a strong and viable membership; the employes through job satisfaction and job security; and the Corporation through achieving its goal of becoming a world class competitor.

The parties agree that in order to make constructive progress in this regard, there is a need to reach a common understanding of the concept of "jointness" and to establish a facilitating mechanism to assure that the various programs related to changes in the work environment are appropriately and effectively administered.

The term "jointness" is understood to mean that concepts for these activities be jointly developed, implemented, monitored, and evaluated. Furthermore, decisions must be arrived at in a setting which is characterized by the parties working together in an atmosphere of trust; **making mutual decisions at all levels which respect the concerns and interests of the parties involved; sharing responsibility for the problem solving; and sharing the rewards of achieving common goals.**

The parties agree that the appropriate facilitating mechanism for joint endeavors is the Executive Board-Joint Activities (Executive Board).

It is agreed that Co-Directors of the Executive Board will be the Vice President of Industrial Relations of General Motors Corporation and the Vice President and Director of the GM Department of the UAW. Each will appoint an **equal** number of persons from their respective organizations as members of the Executive Board. [. . .]

The duties and responsibilities of the Executive Board will include, but not be limited to, the following:

A. Setting policies and providing guidelines[32];

B. Allocating funds for projects and activities[33];

C. Monitoring expenditures for approved projects and activities;

D. Coordinating the efforts of the National Committees referred above;

E. Evaluating and auditing the ongoing performance and results of these committees;

F. Reviewing and approving proposals for National meetings, conferences, and workshops;

G. Integrating Joint Activities with Corporate structures and business decisions;

H. Keeping UAW leadership and Corporate management informed of joint Union-Management activities and the progress of the national committees in achieving their objectives, including encouraging regular meetings at the Group, Division, and Staff level to share appropriate business and joint activity information[34]."

A major failure for the union was its inability to stop, or at least restrict the companies from moving production from the U.S. to oversees facilities. Management maintained its exclusive right in that regard. However, GM promised to maintain the existing levels of small-car production in this country.

In its efforts to control employment levels by preventing outsourcing, the union made little progress. On the contrary, GM did not renew its last contract commitment not to close plants because of outsourcing. The only concession by the company was to give labor 60 days' notice of outsourcing plans affecting 25 workers or more, and to increase contributions to a SUB fund by 4 cents an hour. Ford, on the other hand, after a marathon 28-hour bargaining, reversed its announced plans to shut down 2 plants, and pledged not to close any plants during the next three years.

The companies refused to place limits on overtime, another union demand aimed at protecting employment levels; but they agreed to pay into a training fund a 50-cent-an-hour penalty for overtime hours exceeding 5% of straight time hours worked (calculated on a twelve month rolling average). GM also committed $100 million dollars for development of 'new business ventures' that could provide jobs for UAW members.

The absentee control program was extended, but was revised to grant awards for good attendance, in addition to the penalties for bad attendance that were in place. The plan provided for a $50 payment for each quarter of perfect attendance, and an additional $300 for a full year without absences. New safety and health provisions included a company-financed research fund, and company contributions of 4 cents per hour worked for a training program.

4. TWO IMPORTANT DETAILS: NUMMI AND SATURN

Two other auto contracts, negotiated between the 1984 and 1987 round, covered relatively few auto workers, yet were to pave the road for the future of American labor-management relations. One was the agreement between the UAW and New United Motor Manufacturing Inc. (NUMMI), a joint venture between General Motors and Toyota consisting of a single auto plant in Fremont, CA. The other was the agreement between the UAW and Saturn, GM's new independent division, consisting of a single auto plant in Spring Hill, TE. Both plants instituted labor-management relations that went the furthest in departing from the regime of segregated inclusion.

NUMMI was created in 1984, when a GM plant in Fremont, CA., that was shut down in 1982 as non-competitive, re-opened as a joint venture of Toyota and GM. The new plant opened with new management system, but with mostly the same UAW members[35], and essentially the same equipment, which was much less automated than in GM's most modern plants. One of the most important changes made at NUMMI was to guarantee the workers a high level of job security. Other changes included a reduction in job classifications, from about 100 to 4; the elimination of such management perks that had segregated it socially from labor as private dining rooms, parking lots, private offices, and separate dress codes; and the establishment of work teams of five to ten people who set their own work standards, laid out the work area, determined the work load distribution, and assigned workers to specific tasks (but team leaders were appointed by management). Emphasis was placed on a quality control system based on a modified just-in-time inventory system wherein defects were detected and corrected during production, not afterwards.

Saturn, General Motors' first independent division since 1918, was launched in 1985 as a joint GM-UAW effort to produce a small car by the end of the 1980s that would be able to meet the Japanese competition head on. Under the terms of the labor agreement for the project, 6,000 employees were to be recruited from GM's active and laid-off UAW members. Under the Saturn-UAW contract's language, the union and Saturn Corp. emphasized the need to "forge a new relationship" in which Saturn workers and their union were accepted as "full partners" in all decision making and under which the workers would enjoy unprecedented job security[36].

In Saturn, the union was included at every level of decision-making, not just on the shop floor as at NUMMI. The structure and decision-making process of Saturn reflected the importance and value of consensus decision, full participation of the workers and their union, and the free flow of information within the organization. The union was represented at all levels of the organization—work unit, work unit module, business unit, manufacturing complex and corporation—and participated in all decisions at all levels. Although consensus was emphasized and desired, it was stated that either party "may block a potential decision."[37]

In Saturn, labor's new status in corporate decision making was symbolically reflected in the abolition of hourly compensation. All workers were now on a salary, not hourly wages as in other plants. However, this new status came with a loss of pay: the new salaries were equivalent to 80% of average UAW wages at other American auto plants; the other 20% was pegged to factors such as productivity, profits, and quality. Also abolished were symbols of labor-management segregation such as separate cafeterias and parking areas, separate entrances and identification.

As in NUMMI, job classifications in the Saturn contract were reduced dramatically: there was only one classification for production workers and three to five for skilled workers. Work would be organized work on the basis of teams but, unlike NUMMI, Saturn provided for relief workers to each work team during expedited production schedules to fill surging orders for the product. Thus the work in Saturn is more self-paced (as opposed to market-paced) than in NUMMI. Moreover, the team leaders at Saturn are elected by members of their work units or through an election designed by the UAW.

Saturn also follows NUMMI's lead in giving workers job security, but it takes it one step further. It provides for no layoffs for 80% of workers, except for severe economic conditions or unforeseen catastrophic events. However in Saturn, in contrast to NUMMI, the contracts's provision for the union's representation on the company's Strategic Advisory Committee ensures that the union has a say in determining whether there are in fact "catastrophic" conditions that might warrant layoffs. GM's and UAW's Saturn teams participate on a parity basis at every level of decision-making, from the shop floor to the corporate board. Even the name "Saturn" was chosen jointly by labor and management.

UAW President Owen Bieber's assessment of the Saturn contract, as he introduced it at a press conference in the summer of 1985, was quite accurate. It features, he said, "a degree of codetermination never before achieved in American collective bargaining." He quickly added, however, that the contract represented a "special case" and should not be viewed as a precedent for other GM-UAW agreements[38]. By the 1990s, Saturn's distinctiveness in the U.S. context had become unmistakable, even for the casual observer. Print and television advertisements for Saturn featured UAW's logo very prominently, and they explicitly linked the quality of this "new kind of car" with the union-management cooperation on which the "new kind of company" was predicated.

5. 1987, 1990, 1993: AFFIRMING JOINTNESS

While there were no path-breaking innovations in the contracts of the late-1980s, they were extremely important in their affirmation of the innovations of the previous contracts. Jointness, far from being a temporary retreat from segregation, was being consolidated as the production regime of the auto industry.

The target company for the 1987 round of bargaining was Ford. The parties agreed without a strike to a three-year contract covering 170,000 employees. At GM a very similar agreement covered 335,000. Its key provisions entailed an expansion of labor's power in productivist issues such as employment levels in exchange for limited recovery of the wage concessions labor had made at the beginning of the decade, and a controversial provision for drastically reducing the number of job qualifications in favor of "teamwork." Don Ephlin, then

UAW Vice President and protege of Irving Bluestone, played a key role in the negotiations.

The new agreements at Ford and GM called for a wage increase of 3% immediately and lump-sum payments of 3% in the second and the third year. Additionally, the profit-sharing formula was enriched. Employees would share 7.5% of company profits in excess of 1.8% of sales, 10% in excess of 2.3% of sales, 13.5% above 4.6% of sales, and 16% above 6.9% of sales. Explaining the formula's improvement over the one negotiated in the previous contract, the UAW said that, had the 1987 formula been in effect under the 1984 agreement, workers's profit-sharing would have been $2,000 higher than they were. Another income protection measure was a negotiated rise in the maximum SUB from $135 to $150 per week.

The union hailed the agreement's job security measures as "historic." At Ford, a Guaranteed Employment Numbers program (GEN) required the company to maintain, for the duration of the contract a work force at specified levels at each unionized plant. GEN replaced the 1984 six-year Protected Employee Program PEP[39]. Jobs of employees with one year's seniority were covered; those on temporary layoff or short-term leave also were covered. Under GEN, employees who might otherwise have faced layoff were to be offered another job or the opportunity to enter a training program and suffer no loss in pay. The program's innovation over comparable 1984 programs (PEP at Ford; JOBS at GM) was that it banned, rather than compensating for) layoffs due to outsourcing, technological change, or negotiated productivity improvements. Layoffs were allowed only in response to sharp declines in sales or to "acts of god"—layoffs due to slow sales continued to be covered through the SUB plan. Additionally, the old contract's provision for a 60-days advance notice of outsourcing decisions when 25 or more jobs were affected was revised; the new contract required 90-days notice, even if one job were affected. The UAW-GM contract's language is indicative of the parties' intention to integrate their interests and activities. Consider, for example, the following excerpt from the opening paragraph of a Memorandum of Understanding on the JOBS program, signed by the UAW and General Motors:

> "As an outgrowth of these negotiations the Corporation and the Union expressed a mutual commitment that General Motors employes receive a full measure of job security, and mutual

recognition that this measure of job security can only be realized within a work environment which promotes operational effectiveness. The willingness of the parties to reach these understandings has led to the creation of the JOBS Program, through which **the Corporation and the Union jointly intend to enhance job security and operational effectiveness**"[40].

The 1987 contract called for major administrative innovations, including changes in the structure of the union and the companies, and grievance processing. One provision called for the Executive Board of Joint Activities "to integrate Joint Activities with corporate structure and business decisions." A National Skill Development and Training Committee was created to "promote the expansion of joint union-management efforts in our society." Newly established labor-management Quality Networks were assigned two priorities - first, "to secure GM's market position" and second, "the job security of its employees." Was the order of priorities telling or coincidental?

Teamwork was the other major innovation of 1987. Until then, only a handful of auto plants had changed their work rules dramatically enough to experiment with teamwork, in part because the national contract had allowed local unions only limited leeway in deviating from traditional work rules. Reportedly the union had been pressed to agree to the team concept[41]. Ironically, however, a proposal for organizing work on the basis of autonomous teams first came from the UAW in 1973, as a means to give workers more control. Now, however, the union was split on the concept. Would teams make work more fulfilling, the industry more competitive, and thus save jobs? Or was the team concept (at least in the context of American capitalism) a new-old company trick to get more work for the same pay, and to induce locals to compete for the highest work intensity? The answers were not self-evident, the stakes were high, but the union, and the rank and file who ratified the agreement overwhelmingly, showed a willingness to experiment.

However, the 1987 contracts also make it clear that productivist decision making under Jointness would ultimately be in the hands of management—labor's consultative role notwithstanding. Productivist decisions such as the determination of production standards, involving, most importantly, the speed of the assembly line, were to be set by management, within a certain range of "fairness." Thus, the GM-UAW contract of 1987 reads:

"Production standards shall be established on the basis of fairness and equity consistent with the quality of workmanship, efficiency of operation, and the reasonable working capacities of normal operators [. . .] The speed of such assembly lines will not be increase beyond the level for which they are manned for the purpose of gaining additional production or for the purpose of making up for loss of production due to breakdowns or unscheduled line gaps or stops [. . .] **The Local Management of each plant has full authority to settle such matters**[42].

The 1987 contract also had language making it a "living agreement." That meant that the contract could be reopened at any time during its life, as long as top UAW and company officials agreed; workers would not have to agree to the reopener, or vote on any modifications that result from one. Flexibility in union-management relations seemed to coincide, some feared, with decreasing accountability to union members.

The union was not any more successful than in the previous contracts in limiting overtime. However, it extracted a larger compensation for "excessive" overtime, namely for when overtime constituted more than 5% of straight-time hours (calculated on a twelve month rolling average). Corporate funding for jointly administered programs, such as the JOBS or the training programs would now increase by an additional $1.25 per hour of excessive overtime, compared to $0.50 under the previous contract. Additionally, Ford agreed to rehire workers laid off because of a sales slump instead of simply increasing overtime when sales picked up again. A moratorium on plant closings was extended for the life of the contract.

The 1990 agreement was negotiated by Stephen Yokich, the incoming UAW Vice President replacing retiring Ephlin. The opening statement of the contract is expressive of the integration of labor' and capital's interests that Jointness presupposes and, simultaneously seeks to accomplish:

"The management of General Motors recognizes that it cannot get along without labor any more than labor can get along without the management. Both are in the same business and the success of that business is vital to all concerned. This requires that both management and the employes work together to the end that the quality and cost of the product will prove increasingly satisfactory and attractive so that the business will be continuously successful. General Motors holds that **the basic interests of employers and employes are the same**"[43].

In the same contract, labor's productivist interest (in employment) was integrally linked to the corporation's ability to compete in the market. At least in words, labor's interest in employment is no longer seen as irrelevant for the corporation's operational effectiveness:

> "As an outgrowth of these negotiations the Corporation and the Union expressed a mutual commitment that General Motors employes receive a full measure of job security, and mutual recognition that this measure of job security can only be realized within a work environment which promotes operational effectiveness. The willingness of the parties to reach these understandings has led to the creation of the JOBS Program, through which **the Corporation and the Union jointly intend to enhance job security and operational effectiveness**"[44].

The GM-UAW agreement covered some 330,000 active and laid-off workers; very similar agreements were signed with Ford, covering some 100,000 workers, and Chrysler, covering some 60,000 workers. Highlighting the contracts was a provision designed to protect workers against the cyclical nature of the auto market by limiting layoffs to 36 weeks over three years; for the remaining 120 weeks work with full pay and benefits is guaranteed. The agreement called for an immediate 3 percent wage increase, 3 percent lump-sum payments in the second and the third years, and 1991 and 1992 $600 Christmas bonuses. A COLA providing for a 1 cent adjustment for each 0.26 rise in the Consumer Price Index was continued, and $1.68 of a $1.73 adjustment generated under the old contract was folded into the base rate. SUBs of up to 95 percent of take-home pay for laid-off workers with 10 year' service was extended from two years to three years; pay for those with less than ten year was extended from 26 weeks to 52 weeks. Advance notification from the company of plans to outsource was increased from 90 to 120 days.

Corporate funding for the JOBS program, which provides full pay and benefits for workers displaced by outsourcing or technological changes, was raised from $1 billion to $1.7 billion.

The profit-sharing plan was somewhat strengthened. A provision of the old contract, exempting the first 1.8 percent of sales and revenues from profit-sharing payment to workers, was dropped.

The companies were given more flexibility to reorganize work on the shop floor and authority to scrap expensive job classifications and rules.

By 1990, Mazda and Ford had been operating a joint venture plant in Flat Rock, Michigan; Mitsubishi and Chrysler had been operating their Diamond-Star joint division in Normal, Illinois; Toyota had a plant in Georgetown, Kentucky, Subaru-Isuzu had a plant in Lafayette, Indiana; and Honda had opened up its second U.S. plant in East Liberty, Ohio. Of these foreign-owned and partly-foreign-owned plants only NUMMI and Mazda-Ford were unionized.

The 1993 contract agreement followed the trends established in the previous two contracts. The contract was negotiated with Ford, and even though GM was saddled with large losses and excess capacity, the Ford pattern was repeated in GM (and Chrysler) with only minor deviations. The contract raised total labor costs by 5-7% per year, which was the smallest increase in a pattern contract in decades, and less than recent Big Three productivity gains.[45] The union's concession was that newly hired workers would start at 70% of full pay and take three years to catch up.[46] In the old contract, they began at 85% and took just 18 months to reach full pay.

Ford agreed to spend up to $ 1.8 billion in the next three years to maintain the income of laid-off workers. Because it didn't have many excess workers, and because industry sales were rebounding, Ford ended up keeping most of that money.[47] Both Ford and Chrysler hired more hourly workers. The more financially troubled GM was proceeding, meanwhile, with plans to trim 49,000 of its current 266,000 U.S. hourly jobs by 1996, through a combination of retirements, buyouts, layoffs, and plant closings or sales. Another 35,000 jobs seemed likely be trimmed by the end of the decade, especially if GM accelerated its efforts to sell or close parts plants. At Chrysler, a last-minute dispute on jobs sparked walkouts by 6000 workers in early October 1993, delaying production of 500 cars. The union successfully prodded Chrysler to create hundreds of new jobs to limit the use of outside construction and office workers, and to reverse some recent decisions to buy parts from outside companies.[48]

According to the profit-sharing formula, GM workers would get nothing the next year; Ford workers would get about $ 600; Chrysler workers will get about $ 2000.[49] Higher bonuses were anticipated for 1995—which turned out to be true: the 1995 profit-sharing checks for salaried and hourly workers were on average $ 550 at GM, $ 4,000 at Ford and $ 8,000 at Chrysler.[50]

Although it is clearly beyond the time frame of our analysis, it is noteworthy that the 1996 contract continued to extend Jointness and to integrate the industry's continuing restructuring needs with labor's fundamental interest in employment stability. The 1996 contracts with General Motors, Ford, and Chrysler set up mechanisms to maintain "minimum employment floors", extend protection to more workers, and make the company hire workers to make up for employment losses caused by outsourcing. In fact, with the 1996 contract U.A.W. seems to have advanced the pursuit of its productivist interests to a new level, seeking not only to protect the jobs of current workers but also to maintain the number of well-paying auto jobs for workers in the future.

Accordingly, the company has new obligations to prevent employment from dropping below 95% of the current number of jobs in a group. First, it would have to replace every worker who retires or otherwise leaves on a one-for-one basis, as long as new hires and other workers who haven't grown into eligibility, or laid-off members are available. Second, if no such workers are available and the company had outsourced more jobs than it had insourced since the beginning of the agreement, it would then have to hire a new worker for each one who leaves. The contract gives the company nine months to find new work to insource before the new hiring requirement is triggered.

6. JOINTNESS AT FORD, EDISON, N.J.

My visits to the Ford's Edison, New Jersey, plant during the Winter and Spring of 1991 provided me with a personal appreciation of the position of labor in an American auto company. Unsystematic yet very vivid evidence from this automobile plant of some 3,000 workers was consistent with the more systematic (see below) and aggregate forms of evidence I had been collecting on the nature of labor-management relations in the U.S. and abroad.

The Edison plant was not very representative of American automobile plants, in terms of commonly used criteria (plant size, plant age, technology use, product mix, level of labor-management conflict), but it was neither particularly atypical of many automobile plants. However, as my research strategy was based on comparison of aggregate data from the four countries and not on primary case studies, my research at Edison served a limited purpose, to get a hands-on "feel" for the working conditions and working relationship between labor and management. I was aware that I could not confirm or disconfirm the implications of the framework of production politics based on the data from Edison, yet I needed to go to Edison in order to assess whether my conceptualization of production politics, and particularly the conceptualization of a segregated inclusion regime in the U.S., seemed at all plausible in a concrete context.

My visits to Edison were facilitated by the UAW Local 980, on whose recommendation I gained access to the plant. I conducted open-ended interviews with production workers, union officials, and managers, mostly during work breaks in the plant, and several outside the plant. I took guided and unguided tours of the plant, observing the execution of tasks, the production set up, the dining areas, the medical office, the personnel assistance department.

Five things impressed me the most in Edison: the cleanliness of the plant; the highly repetitive nature of the work done by production workers; their apprehension at losing their jobs and at their laying the blame on Japanese trade barriers and low wages; the civil yet strictly formal character of all the exchanges between labor and management; and the lack of discernable concern about technology's impact on skills and employment, even among union activists and the union president himself.

The Ford plant was much cleaner than one might anticipate. Although it was one of Ford's oldest plants, the work areas were freshly painted, well-lit and rather orderly. Workers and managers credited this to a recent attempt to improve the quality of working life. On the other hand, the level of noise in work areas was almost unbearable. Still the plant was very impressive. Its size, the robots (which were made in Japan), and the mere fact that ready-to-drive Ford Escorts rolled out of a line that began with sheets of steel were enough to take one's breath away.

Relations between workers and managers were civil but tense. Posters in work areas and in the dining area extolled the virtues of labor-management cooperation and of quality-consciousness. As I was told, these were results of the "new relations" introduced four years ago, as part of Jointness. One could still tell managers from workers easily, although most managers were casually dressed, with only a few of them wearing ties. One worker expressed his resentment about a young supervisor. "He's fresh out of college, I've been working my ass here for twenty years, and he gets to tell me what to do. Not a bad guy, but he grades me." My presence on the assembly line, the paint shop, the inspection area, the loading section, seemed to touch on demarcation issues between labor and management. Was I there on behalf of the union? Was I sent there by management? What does the supervisor think? Is it o.k. with the union representative if I talk to workers during their work? Does the plant manager know about it? Can the section manager vouch for me?

A section manager walked me through the whole line, describing each phase of production. At one point he showed me a hydraulic system in the door-building section. He did not hide his pride when he said that the mechanism was installed at his suggestion three years ago and eliminated two workers. When I asked him whether he had any misgivings at workers thus losing their jobs, he somberly replied "that is not my business." Another manager showed me the newly arrived welding robots, their arms moving deliberately from one welding spot to another, with only two workers occasionally adjusting a pressure lever at each end of the line section. "The system now works like a clockwork," he said. "We can operate it using monkeys, if we wanted to."

The local union president was a burly man in his late forties. He told me how the plant was saved from closing several years ago, after a year-long shutdown. Most workers here had at least twenty years of seniority, but, he had to admit, were working under the constant fear that the plant would soon be closed for good. For the problems of Ford and the shutdowns he blamed "those damned Japanese" and their willingness to "work for a dollar an hour." He complained that Ford's management was "penny conscious" and that "sometimes they think they know everything." He (and other workers I talked to) expressed the hope that new technology would take the industry out of its slump. He was frustrated at the prospect of more job losses in the near future (1,000 workers were already laid off), but, he added, "that's the way it goes." When I asked him if the introduction of new technology is an issue in labor-management relations, he was genuinely baffled. "What about new technology?" he asked. "We have no problems with new technology. The more the better."

By everyone's account, Jointness had changed things at Ford, Edison. Most of the workers were old enough to remember "definitely worse" working conditions in the 1970s and early 1980s. Beyond this consensus, however, there was disagreement about how substantive the changes had been and the impact of the changes on workers' future. A significant majority considered the changes in worker-management communications and relations as substantive, while a minority saw them as merely decorative. A majority considered Jointness as effective in improving product quality. A marginal majority, however, believed that job losses were still a proximate threat. At least at Ford, Edison, neither interest nor functional integration had taken root; workers welcomed the steps taken in the direction of integration, but serious skepticism about their future remained.

Soon after my visits to Ford, Edison, I read a harrowing account of working conditions at a General Motors plant by an auto worker-turned-writer.[51] While working conditions have certainly improved from Ben Hamper's time as an auto worker, at a certain fundamental level a depressing similarity with the pre-Jointness, dehumanizing and humiliating working conditions lingers on. The passage that follows describes the job of an auto worker as witnessed by Hamper when he was seven, visiting his auto worker father's workplace at the old Fisher Body plant at Flint, during Family Night:

> "His job was to install windshields using this goofy apparatus with large suction cups that resembled an octopus being crucified. A car would nuzzle up to the old man's work area and he would be waiting for it, a cigarette dangling from his lip, his arms wrapped around the windshield contraption as if it might suddenly rebel and bold off for the ocean. Car, windshield. Car windshield. Car, windshield [. . .] We stood there fory minutes or so, a miniature lifetime, and the pattern never changed. Car windshield. Car, windshield. Drudgery pile atop drudgery. Cigarette to cigarette. Decades rolling through the rafters, bones turning to dust, stubborn clocks gagging down flesh, another windshield, another cigarette, wars blinking on and off, thunderstorms muttering the alphabet, crows on power lines asleep or dead, that mechanical octopus squirming against nothing, nothing, nothingness. I wanted to shout at my father "Do something else!" Do something else or come home with us or flee to the nearest watering hole. Do something else! Car, windshield. Car, windshield. Christ, no."[52]

7. LABOR'S POWER, DECISION MAKING AND SUBSTANTIVE OUTCOMES OF JOINTNESS

Having described the major changes which labor-management relations in the U.S. auto industry underwent since the early-1980s, we now turn to the examination of the actual significance of these changes for the industry's performance, and particularly for labor. Has labor in U.S. autos been granted more power over corporate decision making than before, as argued in the previous section, or have advances in that regard been only nominal/illusory? If labor's new powers in productivist decision making are not illusory, has labor acquired its new productivist power at the price of a diminished redistributive power (has it bought voice at the expense of exit, or merely added voice to exit)? Does Jointness amount to Integrated Inclusion? Has the regime's efficiency improved with Jointness? Are changes in efficiency related to changes in labor's power?

Labor's Power

The innovations in labor-management relations in the auto industry reviewed in the preceding section are highly suggestive, in and of themselves, that a significant restructuring of labor's power in corporate decision making took place during the 1980s. This restructuring entailed the delegation to labor—at one and the same time, but at different degrees—of (a) more authority over a broader range of corporate decisions; and (b) more responsibility for corporate performance. While the latter is widely accepted as fact (wage concessions were widely publicized), it is far from self-evident that during the 1980s labor's authority in corporate decisions increased.

Whether the new powers assigned to labor in corporate decision making in the 1980s are substantive or merely nominal, cannot be fully assessed through a content analysis of the labor contracts that encode those powers. Contractual language is ambiguous enough to allow for different kinds of outcomes for the parties involved, depending on the specific context in which it is applied. Thus it would be useful to supplement the above evidence of labor and capital's **stated intentions** and **institutional relationship** with empirical outcomes of the production regime for labor's interests. Specifically, we will examine whether the regime's outcomes for labor's key productivist and redistributive interests, employment and income security, respectively, correspond to hypothesized changes in labor's power.

Productivist Outcomes under Jointess: Employment

First, let us examine the evolution of employment in the 1980s. If labor's inclusion in the productivist area of corporate decision making in the 1980s was more than nominal, we should expect a correspondingly different evolution of annual employment levels in the 1980s than in the decades before it. In other words, if, auto workers begin to exercise considerable influence over corporate decisions affecting employment under the regime of Jointness, we expect to find that in the 1980s the wide annual fluctuations in employment[53] abate.

FIGURE 2

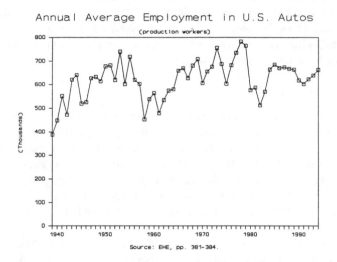

Annual Average Employment in U.S. Autos
(production workers)

Source: EHE, pp. 381-384.

Figure 2 lends strong support to our hypothesis. The formal decision making powers given to labor in the area of productivist decision making in the 1980s do in fact correspond with the end of the wide annual employment fluctuations characteristic of previous decades. Figure 2 charts the average annual employment of production workers in the U.S. auto industry, from 1930 to 1990.[54] It can be seen that there is a change in the pattern of annual employment changes between 1930-1982, on the one hand, and 1982-1990, on the other. During the first period, average annual employment of production workers is far from stable, increasing and decreasing significantly from year to year. By contrast, during the second period, which corresponds with the introduction and consolidation of Jointness, annual average employment levels for production workers increases or remains constant in seven of the eight observations. The drop in employment at the end of the decade, however, attests to the tenuous nature of labor's inclusion in productivist decision making under Jointness.

FIGURE 3

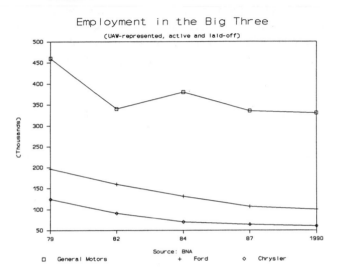

Employment in the Big Three
(UAW-represented, active and laid-off)

Source: BNA

□ General Motors   + Ford   ◇ Chrysler

Figure 3 charts the evolution of employment levels in the Big Three U.S. auto producers, where labor's power is most extensively institutionalized[55]. It can be seen that under the transitional regime of Jointness, labor's key productivist interest, employment, is far from safeguarded, even in companies where labor's influence in productivist decision is at its most extensive. It can also be seen in Figure 2 that not only have the employment losses of the late-1970s are not been recovered under Jointness, but employment losses continue into the 1980s. Thus, the productivist powers which labor was granted in the 1980s were limited, as the limited extent of their substantive impact on employment stability indicates. Under Jointness labor did not succeed in eliminating layoffs, but only in making them more gradual, more predictable, and better compensated.

Redistributive Outcomes under Jointness: Wages

Second, let us examine the evolution of wages in the 1980s. If our hypothesis of the end of segregated inclusion in the 1980s is correct, we expect to find that in that decade uninterrupted wage increases come to an end. In other words, if redistributive decisions are no longer the only ones on which labor has an influence, then there is more likelihood that labor will accept to trade off wage increases for non-redistributive benefits (such as employment security). Thus we expect to find that in the 1980s wages of auto workers no longer rise steadily, but that they decline, remain the same or increase, depending on corporate decisions.

FIGURE 4

Figure 4 charts the evolution of the hourly earnings of production workers in U.S. autos from 1930 to 1990, both in terms of current dollars (nominal compensation) and in terms of 1982-84 dollars (real compensation). It can be seen that, as expected, the pattern of real wage changes of the 1980s is distinct from previous decades. Real wages stop rising regularly; real wage declines are not only possible (as is also the case during the 1970s), but are also sustained over several years. What somewhat mitigates the loss of redistributive power of labor is that with the consolidation of Jointness we see an accompanying moderation in executive compensation increases. Officers and top executives of the General Motors Corporation suffered a 36 percent pay cut in **1991**, according to the auto maker's 1991 proxy statement, which also stated that the company had suffered a loss of $4.5 billion. The United Automobile Workers union, which has criticized G.M. in the past for raising executive salaries while workers were laid off, this year gave it grudging credit for having "tempered" executive compensation. But the union said in a statement that executive salaries were "still out of line— way out of line."[56]

Employment, Wages, and Production

FIGURE 5

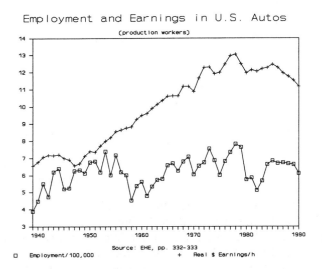

Figure 5 combines the earnings and employment data presented above. Annual employment figures are divided by 100,000 in order to facilitate the presentation; we can do so with no conceptual loss, since we are comparing trends, rather than absolute levels. It can be seen that the strict segregation of employment and earnings, shaken during the 1970s, is further diminished in the 1980s. But, to the extent to which labor has gained more influence in productivist decisions under Jointness, it has done so **at the expense of** its redistributive power:

employment stability in the 1980s coincides with real wage declines. In the 1980s, labor has given up on regular real wage increases for less than commensurate employment stability. And, as Figure 5 shows, during the 1980s, real wages drop not only in years of employment losses but even when employment rises.

FIGURE 6

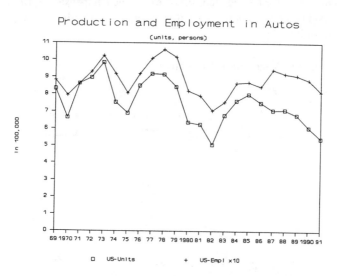

Next, we ascertain an alternative origin of the relative employment stability under Jointness. Although Jointness coincides with more employment stability than during the pre-Jointness period, most of that change may be attributable to the relative stability in output during the 1980s rather than to labor's ability to prevent layoffs. In other words, for most but not all of the years of Jointness, the relative employment stability enjoyed by auto workers (compared to the pre-1980 period of segregation) could be attributable to the relative stability of output, instead of labor's new decision making power under Jointness. Figure 6 combines the annual evolution of employment and output in the U.S. auto industry. Employment levels are shown multiplied by 10 in order to make comparison with output levels easier. It can be seen that employment and output in U.S. autos have evolved in tandem for most of the time. Apparently, American auto producers have been accustomed to liberally disposing of or hiring more labor to fulfill fluctuating orders for autos; shielding employment from the vagaries of fluctuations in demand does not seem to have been a consideration for U.S auto producers. Labor can be activated and idled according to the same considerations behind the activation of idling of machinery. This method of "adjustment" to demand through massive layoffs and hirings, characteristic of segregation regimes where labor has little authority in productivist decisions, does not end after 1980. Fluctuating employment levels persist under Jointness; if fluctuations become less dramatic, that seems to be related to less dramatic changes in output.

There is, however, some reason to consider the period of Jointness as distinct from the decades of segregation. For one thing, that employment stability in the 1980s is correlated with output stability in that decade is not a refutation of labor's new decision making powers in the area of employment under Jointness: output itself may have stabilized because of labor's effective pressures for employment stability. Moreover, as Figure 6 shows, between 1985 and 1986, for the first time ever, a decline in output is **not** accompanied by a decline in employment, but by an employment increase. Between 1987 and 1988, a further decline in output is also not accompanied by a drop in employment but by employment maintenance. These observations lend credence to the notion that labor's power **did** increase in the area of productivist decisions during the 1980s. However, if we consider the employment-output relationship during the whole decade, the increase in labor's power in productivist decisions during the 1980s, though actual, was very limited.

Lastly, Figure 7 allows us to examine the evolution of employment, real earnings and output (in units) in U.S. autos in tandem. It becomes clear that, as expected from a segregation regime, labor's power is considerable in the area of redistribution but limited in the area of productivist decisions. Thus, labor has protected real earnings from fluctuations in output (which, after all is beyond its sphere of influence), while employment has fluctuated as widely as production.

FIGURE 7

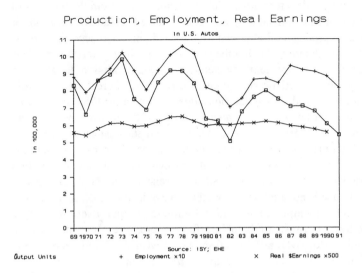

Production, Employment, Real Earnings

In U.S. Autos

Source: ISY; EHE

Output Units   +   Employment x10   x   Real $Earnings x500

Industrial Performance under Jointness

While there is a widespread impression that Japanese production is
more productive than American production, there is a lot of confusion
about what productivity means in the first place. There is a consensus
that, on an abstract level, the productivity of a unit of production is the
facility with which it can transform nature into useful products. In other
words, productivity is the ratio of its outputs to its inputs, or the ratio of
the value of what is produced over the cost of producing it: output/cost.
Cross-firm, cross-industry, or cross-national comparisons of
productivity are based on refinements of the output/cost ratio, which
usually entail certain simplifying assumptions aimed at "controlling
for" (holding as constant) either the numerator or the denominator of
the output/cost ratio. Depending on the particular interest of the analyst,
output as a ratio of cost is refined as cost-per-unit-of-output, which
assumes that the value of a unit of output (e.g. one car) is similar across
firms, industries, countries. If, moreover, it is assumed that capital and
raw material costs are constant, then productivity is measured as "unit
labor cost," as the labor cost of producing of one car. Alternatively,
productivity is measured as output-per-unit-of-input, called "labor

productivity" or "hourly productivity", which assumes that the value of a unit of input (e.g. hours of work) is similar across firms, industries, countries.

The problems with measuring productivity begin when "cost" is operationalized. (A parallel argument can be made for the difficulties in operationalizing "output", which could entail not only the value of the item produced but also of the value of the intangible but valuable satisfaction generated from being a productive member of society). What costs are germane? Whose costs must be measured? Widely used measures of productivity, including the one used by the U.S. Bureau of Labor Statistics, measure output over costs for capital, ignoring costs borne by labor. Thus "productivity" refers to the cost-benefit ratio for the firm, without considering labor as part of the firm (any more than machinery is considered as part of the firm).

According to this common measure of productivity, the United States still has the most productive firms in the world. Its only worry should be that the productivity gap with other countries is diminishing. But this leaves unanswered significant questions: if the American production regime has been so productive, why has the productivity gap been narrowing by regimes that are most dissimilar to the U.S.'s? Why has the U.S. been moving in the direction of German and Japanese regimes rather than the other way around? Is it plausible, as such productivity measures suggest, that Canada is more productive than Japan and Germany? Lastly, according to the standard measure of productivity, ancient Egypt's slavery-based regime would score as one of the most productive regime ever invented by humans. Indeed, labor costs in ancient Egypt were close to nil (for the Pharaohs), boosting the output/cost ratio to near-infinity. Nonetheless, it is less plausible to characterize such a production regime as very productive than to call it as very wasteful of human lives.

These considerations point to the woeful inadequacies of the standard measures of productivity in living up to the concept's meaning. We need to devise a measure of "regime productivity" that reflects the **total** cost of producing a unit of output to the participants of the regime, mainly, capital and labor. Unfortunately, the task of operationalizing the costs of production borne by labor that are not reflected in the standard measurement of productivity—layoffs, exploitation—is an overwhelming one. How do we operationalize the cost to labor of a production process that renders a sizable portion of the labor force idle? What is the numerical value of the feeling of uselessness and of other social malaise associated with unemployment? Is the numerical value of the cost of unemployment to the worker the same in the United States as in Japan? If such a measurement were to be devised at all, very advanced mathematical skills would be required, which I lack. But even if such skills were available, the resulting measurements of regime productivity would be too parochially-based to allow meaningful cross-national comparisons.

Other, more sophisticated measures of productivity, such as "multi-factor productivity" (MFP) do not alleviate the problems of the standard measure of productivity identified above. MFP, for example, is capable of isolating the distinct contributions to the firm's productivity of each factor of production: capital's, labor's and raw materials'. Still, however, as the previous sentence states, MFP measures the productivity of the firm from the vantage point of capital; costs of production borne by labor are ignored.

In order to assess the productivity of the American auto production regime without having to rely on untenable assumptions about the real, total costs and benefits of production, we have proposed an indirect strategy. Given long periods of time, a regime's productivity is analogous to its industrial performance, its ability to produce higher-"value" goods (better quality for the money) than its competitors. We can trace the evolution of the American auto production regime's industrial performance as a proxy for the evolution of the regime's efficiency relative to its competitors. The evolution of the American auto production regime's performance since the 1950s can be traced through (a) market-based indicators of regime performance, namely the evolution of the U.S. world auto market share and the U.S. balance of auto trade, checked against possible systemic distortions in trade (protectionism); and (b) non-market indicators of performance, namely product quality and product reliability surveys, checked against survey reliability.

(a) market indicators of industrial performance

An important market-based indicator of relative regime performance is the world market share. The more competitive a regime's products are, the larger the share of the world market its products will comprise, holding other influences on market share constant. While we cannot accomplish the latter directly, we can minimize the effect of exogenous influences on market share by looking at **trends** in market share, over many decades. Indeed, on a given moment in time, a certain production regime's competitiveness in the world market in a given good depends not only on its productivity, but also on the size of its economy, the success of its marketing strategy, the extent of protectionism its products confront, and others. Thus that a regime has a high share of the world market on a given year is not very telling about the regime's competitiveness; its high market share could be the result of the lack or the nascent state of competing regimes. A **rising** market share is a little more telling of the intrinsic superiority of the regime's products, although the possibility remains that the rise is attributable to a rise in a factor unrelated to productivity, such as the lowering of tariff barriers against the products of that regime. However, the longer a regime's market share continues to rise, the more confident we can be that the regime is more productive than others.

FIGURE 8

US Share of World Auto Production

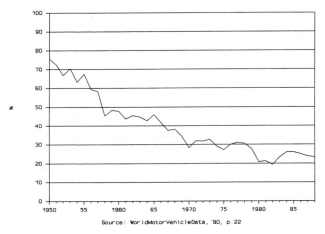

Source: WorldMotorVehicleData, '90, p.22

Figure 8 charts the U.S. share of world automobile production, from 1950 through the 1980s. The U.S. share of world auto production, measured in units or vehicles, fell from 75.7% in 1950 to 23.3% in 1988. The drop in the U.S. market share was more precipitous during the 1950s than in following decades. This, however, is probably due to the fact that at the end of the Second World War, auto production in countries other than the U.S. had come to a standstill; that along with the postwar reconstruction of their economies they would capture some of the world auto market was to be expected, even if the U.S. had the most productive regime. What was not anticipated was that the 1950s decline in the U.S. share of world auto market would continue unabated in the decades to come.

Another striking fact in Figure 8 is that there is a certain improvement in the U.S. position in the world auto market during the 1980s. On the one hand, from 1982 to 1984 the U.S. share registers its largest two-year increase ever. On the other hand, while we cannot dismiss the significance of the fact that the U.S. share declined in the next four years, there was a net increase of the U.S.'s share of world auto market over the 1980s: the U.S. share grew from 20.8% in 1980 to 23.3% in 1988. The 1980s, indeed, is the only decade since the Second World War over which the U.S. share of the world market registered a net increase. We must guard against overly optimistic conclusions that may stem from the latter observation, however, by considering that during the 1970s, a few consecutive years of relative U.S. market-share stability were followed by a significant decline. Thus, while Jointness cannot be said to coincide with a dramatic or lasting reversal in the declining U.S. world market share, it does seem to be associated with a marginal improvement for the U.S. in that regard.

Another indicator of regime performance is the balance of trade in automobiles. Figure 9 charts the evolution of the dollar value of the U.S. balance of trade in automobiles (exports f.o.b. minus imports c.i.f.). The following observations are of central importance: (a) for about two decades after the end of World War II the U.S. balance of trade in autos was positive; (b) the decline in American auto competitiveness, or at least in its balance of trade in autos, begins in the second half of the 1960s; (c) the American regime's decline bottoms out in the mid-1980s; (d) the differences in the evolution of U.S. world market share and balance of trade reflect the fact that market share is measured on the basis of units of autos, whereas the balance of trade measures the dollar value of auto exports and imports.

FIGURE 9

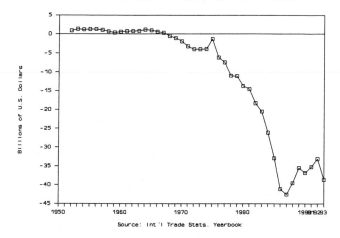

U.S. Automobile Balance of Trade

Source: Int'l Trade Stats. Yearbook

Figure 10 presents the constituent elements of the auto balance of trade presented in Figure 9, exports and imports. The following observations are critical. First, clearly, the deterioration in the U.S. auto balance of trade is not the result of declining exports (except for the dramatic one-year drop in 1975-76), but of very rapidly increasing imports, since the second half of the 1960s (except for the one-year drop in 1975-76). Second, after dropping precipitously in 1975-76, and remaining stagnant from 1976 to 1982, exports begin to increase every year since then. Third, in 1987-88 and 1988-99 auto exports rise while imports are falling, for the first time since the 1960s.

FIGURE 10

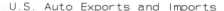

U.S. Auto Exports and Imports

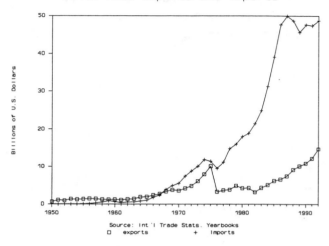

Source: Int'l Trade Stats. Yearbooks
  □   exports   +   Imports

(b) non-market indicators of industrial performance

Lest our assessment of the productivity of the American auto
production regime is too dependent on sales data, we must examine
whether similar conclusions are warranted from more direct evaluations
of industrial performance, namely product reliability and product
quality surveys. It should be noted that there are no appropriate auto
reliability and quality surveys before 1973, and that surveys rate
individual car models which are often discontinued after several years,
making it difficult to trace the evolution of quality of the same model
over time. Thus we provide the evolution of the reliability of U.S. made
autos from 1973 to 1994, based on the annual frequency-of-repair
records of *Consumer Reports*. In the next two chapters we also provide
reliability data comparing American, German, and Japanese autos by
J.D. Power and Associates.

Figure 11 below presents the annual reliability rating of all
American models compared to the reliability of all models sold in the
U.S.. Clearly, the annual reliability rating of American models is
inversely related to that of foreign ones. Thus, for example, a drop in
American reliability in a given year indicates an increase in the

frequency-of-repair of American models **relative to** the frequency-of-repair of foreign models in the same year.

FIGURE 11

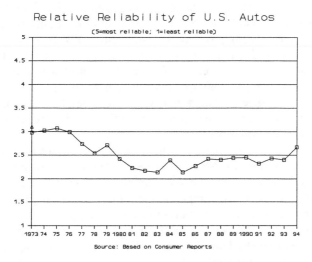

Relative Reliability of U.S. Autos
(5=most reliable; 1=least reliable)

Source: Based on Consumer Reports

The evolution of the reliability of American autos relative to foreign models sold in the U.S. lends support to the implications of the auto balance of trade presented in Figure 9 above for the evolution of American auto quality. Indeed, the deterioration in the U.S. auto balance of trade since the mid-1970s, corresponds to a contemporaneous deterioration in the reliability of American autos compared to foreign ones sold in the U.S. Clearly, the auto trade deficit cannot be attributed solely to market distortions such as protectionism. Moreover, in line with the improvement in the U.S. auto trade after the mid-1980s presented in Figures 9 and 10, Figure 11 indicates clearly that American auto reliability improved steadily after the mid-1980s. (It will be noted that the deterioration in the U.S. auto trade since the late-1970s is much more dramatic than the corresponding deterioration in reliability. The discrepancy may be attributed to markets' tendency to move en masse away from demonstrably inferior products.

8. CONCLUSION

The American production regime of segregated inclusion was under-performing, compared to its German and Japanese competitors, in the post-1960 environment of international competition. The reconstruction of the German and Japanese economies along with the micro-electronic revolution have aggravated the competitive disadvantage of the American production regime, forcing it, by the early-1980s, to transform itself in the direction of labor-management integration.

Intensified cross-national competition has acted as a motive force behind the changes in American industrial relations, by rewarding, as it were, the most productive (least wasteful) production regimes while punishing the least productive ones.

Technological changes may have further exposed the inferiority of segregation regimes. Micro-electronic technology with its infinite malleability and communicative ability likely rewards functional integration. Increased competition and rapidly changing patterns of demand add to the attractiveness of functional integration.

In the hybrid new auto production regime of Jointness, established in the mid-1980s, labor's functional integration is attempted with limited interest integration. This is due to the fact that capital is strong enough to resist the integration of its interests with labor's, while labor is not committed or strong enough to impose such integration over capital's resistance. However limited, progress towards integration has been substantive, and accompanied by limited yet vital improvements both in the auto industry's performance and in labor's productivist interests, as hypothesized.

Having so far established (a) that in the U.S. auto industry labor's power has been actual but limited, especially in the area of productivist decision making; and (b) that the U.S. auto industry has been, until the mid-1980s, under-performing compared to its rivals—we can now turn to testing our hypothesis that the mode of labor's inclusion greatly influences industrial performance. We will do so by showing, first, that labor's power in the world's other two leading automobile producing countries is in fact broader than in the U.S., and that alternative explanations of those countries' performance are unable to account for, especially, the relationship between industrial performance and labor's fortunes therein.

NOTES

1. Irving Bluestone was vice-president of the UAW and director of the union G.M. department. He is currently teaching at Wayne State College.

2. For the evolution of the QWL, and its place in labor strategy see Barry Bluestone and Irving Bluestone, *Negotiating the future: a labor perspective on American business* (New York: Basic Books, 1992).

3. Indegaard, Michael and Michael Cushion, "Conflict, Cooperation,and the Global Auto Factory," in Daniel B. Cornfield (ed), *Workers, Managers, and Technological Change: Emerging Patterns of Labor Relations* (New York: Plenum, 1987), p. 217. See also Rosabeth Moss Kanter, *The Change Masters* (New York: Simon and Schuster, 1983).

4. Motor Vehicles Manufacturers Association, *World Motor Vehicle Data, 1990*, p. 22.

5. Irving Bluestone, "How Quality-of-Worklife Projects Work for the United Auto Workers," *Monthly Labor Review*, v. 103 no. 7 (July 1980), pp. 39-41.

6. For an assessment of QWL programs during the 1970s, see Robert H. Guest, "Quality of Work Life—Learning from Tarrytown," *Harvard Business Review*, v.57 no. 4 (July/August 1979), pp. 76-87. See also, from that period, Albert Cherns, "Perspectives on the Quality of Working Life," *International Studies of Management & Organization*, v. 8 no. 1-2 (Spring/Summer 1978), pp. 38-58. For a review of contemporary interdisciplinary literature on QWL see Keith Newton, Norman Leckie, and Barrie O. Pettman, "The Quality of Working Life," *International Journal of Social Economics*, v. 6 no. 4 (Winter 1979), pp. 199-234.

7. Bureau of National Affairs, Inc., *Basic Patterns in Union Contracts* (Washington, D.C.: BNA Books, 1993), p. 18:43.

8. "Why GM Abandoned Its "Southern Strategy," *Business Week*, October 16, 1978, p. 50.

9. Ibid., p. 51.

10. Bureau of National Affairs, Inc., *Basic Patterns in Union Contracts* (Washington, D.C.: BNA Books, 1993), p. 18:45.

11. "The Price of Peace at Chrysler," *Business Week*, no. 2611, November 12, 1979, pp. 93 and 96.

12. For business reactions to Fraser's seat see "More Unions Knocking at Boardroom Doors?" *Industry Week*, v. 203 no. 4, November 12, 1979. pp. 19-21. When Fraser retired in 1983 his vacated seat was abolished. For Fraser's own assessment of that experience see "My Years on the Chrysler Board," *Across the Board*, June 1986, pp. 33-43.

13. "The Risk of Putting a Union Chief on the Board," *Business Week,* no. 2637 (Industrial Edition), May 19, 1980, pp. 149-150.

14. Lydia Fischer, "Auto Crisis and Union Response," in D. Kennedy, C. Craypo and M. Lehman (eds), *Labor and Technology: Union Response to Changing Environments* (Pennsylvania State University, 1982), p. 172.

15. For connective bargaining and its erosion in the 1980s auto industry see Harry C. Katz, *Shifting Gears: Changing Labor Relations in the U.S. Automobile Industry* (Cambridge: MIT Press, 1985). For a cogent analysis of the French experience with enterprise-level determination of labor-management relations during the 1980s, see Chris Howell, *Regulating Labor: The State and Industrial Relations Reform in Postwar France* (Princeton: Princeton University Press, 1992).

16. For the UAW's solidaristic wage policy see David Gartman, *Auto Slavery: The Labor Process in the American Automobile Industry, 1897-1950* (New Brunswick: Rutgers University Press, 1986), pp. 280-284.

17. Indeed, a provision of the 1982 Ford-UAW contract explicitly authorized a reopener of the contract, if retail deliveries in the U.S. of new cars and trucks produced or imported by the automaker exceeded 1,925,000 units in any six-month period. The GM-UAW contract's reopener threshold was 3,850,000 units, reflecting the generally much larger size of the company.

18. In addition, one-tenth on 1 percent of "other assets" would be diverted to the "guaranteed income stream" plan (see below) with the rest distributed among GM employees.

19. It covered those already laid off, not only the workers laid off in the future as in Ford.

20. The quote is attributed to a UAW negotiator, in Bureau of National Affairs, Inc., *Basic Patterns in Union Contracts* (Washington, D.C.: BNA Books, 1986).

21. General Motors expected to pay more than $2 billion for health care insurance coverage in 1983, or $250 per employee per month. These figures indicate a 50% increase in health care cost over the past five years. Reported by G.M.'s David C. Collier in *Employee Benefit Plan Review,* Feb 1984, pp. 40-41.

22. For the number of QWL programs at General Motors in the beginning of the decade see Irving Bluestone, "How Quality-of-Worklife Projects Work for the United Auto Workers," *Monthly Labor Review,* v. 103 no. 7 (July 1980), pp. 39-41; for QWL's expansion after 1982 see Mike Parker, *Inside the Circle: A Union Guide to QWL* (Boston: South End Press, 1985).

23. The pledge was not applicable to plant closings in response to floods, earthquakes, dramatic slump in sales and other "acts of God."

24. While the number of GM plants covered by these programs double than that of Ford, so is the total number of plants of GM compared to Ford's.

25. 91,000 workers walked out at 17 GM plants.

26. The raise corresponded to 9 cents per hour for janitors and 50 cents for the highest-paid skilled workers.

27. There were also some differences in funding. Ford funded its PEP program with $280 million, compared with the $1 billion GM gave to its JOB fund. The smaller funding level at Ford (3.5 times less than at GM) was **not** proportional to its smaller workforce (2 times smaller than GM's). In 1987 Ford agreed to close its "funding gap."

28. This committee also controls the funds used by QWL.

29. This committee evaluates the cause of each layoff and assigns each laid-off worker to an appropriate status in the Job Bank, oversees training programs, oversees use of workers in areas of "nontraditional work," makes proposals for changes in the local contract to make the plant more competitive, and makes proposals for beginning new businesses to the New Business Development Group set up by the Growth and Opportunity Committee.

30. *Memorandum of Understanding: Joint Activities*, UAW-GM Contract, 1984.

31. Several of these clarifications for the provisions of the 1984 contract were issued at the 1987 round of negotiations.

32. For the Joint Committees mentioned above, not for the corporation in general.

33. The Corporation agreed to provide funding at five cents per hour worked. "Memorandum of Understanding: Joint Activities" in Bureau of National Affairs, Inc., *Collective Bargaining Negotiations and Contracts* (Washington, D.C.: BNA, Inc., 1990), p. 21:84.

34. "Memorandum of Understanding: Joint Activities" in Bureau of National Affairs, Inc., *Collective Bargaining Negotiations and Contracts* (Washington, D.C.: BNA, Inc., 1990), pp. 21:83-21:84, emph. added.

35. The union was recognized by NUMMI without contest.

36. Saturn-UAW Agreement, in Bureau of National Affairs, Inc., *Collective Bargaining Negotiations and Contracts* (Washington, D.C.: BNA, Inc., 1993), p. 16:911.

37. Saturn-UAW Agreement, in Bureau of National Affairs, Inc., *Collective Bargaining Negotiations and Contracts* (Washington, D.C.: BNA, Inc., 1993), p. 16:911.

38. Owen Bieber cited in Bureau of National Affairs, Inc., *Collective Bargaining Negotiations and Contracts* (Washington, D.C.: BNA, Inc., 1993), p. 16:911.

39. Ford agreed to spend up to $500 million to fund the program, thus closing the "funding gap" between that program and GM's corresponding JOB program.

40. Bureau of National Affairs, Inc., *Collective Bargaining Negotiations and Contracts* (Washington, D.C.: BNA, Inc., 1993), p. 21:74 (emph. added).

41. Aaron Bernstein and Wendy Zellner, "Detroit vs. the UAW: At Odds over Teamwork" *Business Week*, August 24, 1987 (Industrial/Technology Edition), pp. 54-55.

42. Bureau of National Affairs, Inc., (1993), p. 21:31 (emph. added).

43. From the 1987 GM-UAW Contract Settlement Agreement, Introduction, in idem., pp. 21:7-21:8 (emph. added).

44. Ibid., p. 21:74, emphasis added.

45. By designing cars that are easier to build, GM was planning a 28% increase in its car plant productivity between 1993 and 1996. *Automotive Industries* November 1993, p. 40.

46. The concession was intended as a trade-off that successfully blocked the company's bid to saddle current workers with co-payments and deductibles on health care.

47. Even at the more troubled GM, payments to jobless workers dropped by 50% to less than $ 2 billion.

48. By designing cars that are easier to build, GM was planning a 28% increase in its car plant productivity between 1993 and 1996. *Automotive Industries* November 1993, p. 41.

49. *Automotive Industries* (November 1993), p. 40.

50. *Ward's Auto World, 1995* (Nexis: Ward's Communications Inc., 1995).

51. Ben Hamper, *Rivethead: Tales from the Assembly Line* (New York: Warner Books, 1991).

52. Ibid, p. 2.

53. It will be remembered that we have attributed the wild annual employment fluctuations in the U.S. auto industry before the 1980s to the nature of labor's inclusion in corporate decision making under segregated inclusion: while labor was included in redistributive areas of decision making (wages, hours), it was still excluded from productivist areas of decision making (employment, work organization)

54. Source: U.S. Bureau of Labor Statistics, *Employment, Hours, and Earnings: United States, 1909-1994, v. I*, Bulletin no. 2370 (Washington, DC: GPO, 1994).

55. Employment levels in Figure 2 appear inflated, because they include active and laid-off workers. At any given year during the 1980s one-third to one-half of the workers covered by a contract were on layoff.

56. *The New York Times*, April 14, 1992, p. D1.

CHAPTER 5

Integration Through Representation in German Auto Production

This chapter presents the central parameters of the German auto production regime, and analyzes the relationship between labor's power and industrial performance therein. It is argued that auto production in Germany fits well within our typology of production regimes, as a regime of labor integration, further specified as a regime of representative integration. German labor's impressive formal powers in corporate decision making are matched by impressive substantive outcomes of the production regime for labor's key interests. Moreover, far from undermining industrial performance, German labor's power is at least consonant with it.

1. THE PRODUCTION REGIME: LABOR INTEGRATION THROUGH REPRESENTATION

The defining characteristic of the German auto production regime is labor's ability to integrate its productivist as well its redistributive interests in corporate decision making. This results in labor's "integrated inclusion" in corporate decision making, and thus in significant degrees of integration between capital's and labor's fundamental interests in production. The basis/source of labor's power is two-fold: its ability to (credibly threaten to) organize collective **exit** from any cooperation with capital and thus bring production to a standstill (strikes); and its much more frequently utilized ability to make its **voice** heard during the process of corporate policy making. The modality through which labor's voice is institutionalized in the

German auto production regime is **representation**. Accordingly, the formulation and implementation of a broad array of corporate decisions takes place in institutions where labor and capital are represented in equal proportion, which in turn puts a premium on consensus-based corporate strategies and decisions rather than on decisions that are taken by the dominant party at the expense of the other.

Industrial relations in Germany display a morphological dualism, in the sense that labor's inclusion in corporate decision making is achieved through two distinct "points of entry": **codetermination** at the firm/plant level (board representation, works council), and **collective bargaining** at the regional/sectoral level (union). Region- or sector-wide norms for wages and working conditions are settled by collective agreements between unions and employers, while workplace- or company-specific issues not covered by collective agreements, such as work rules and work organization, are settled between the works council and management.[1]

Wolfgang Streeck sees this dualism as having served labor well: the region-wide and bureaucratic organization of unions has counteracted the danger of atomization inherent in plant-level bargaining that circumvents union representation.[2] More recently, however, he sees a trend toward more decentralization of industrial relations that he attributes, primarily, to a "liberal offensive" initiated by employers and governments that cultivate "plant egoism."[3] Others see this trend as the consequence, primarily, of a market-driven crisis of the mass production paradigm.[4] Thelen sees this dualism as contributing to German labor **and** competitive success,[5] and as an instance of the broader German economy's ability to experiment within stable institutions.[6]

At the codetermination level labor specializes in the pursuit of its productivist interests, such as working conditions, technology and, most crucially, employment. At the level of collective bargaining, labor pursues mostly redistributive interests, such as wage levels and hours-of-work standards. However, this division of labor between the two levels does not amount to a strict separation between the pursuit of productivist and redistributive interests characteristic of other production regimes. A sizable number of labor seats on supervisory boards are reserved for trade union representatives (see Table 1 below), while almost all works councilors in the auto industry are also trade unionists.[7] The diffusion of the union federation IG Metall's influence beyond collective bargaining into the level of codetermination enables labor (through the union) to integrate the pursuit of its redistributive and productivist interests.[8]

Codetermination in the German Auto Industry

Codetermination in the auto industry is codified in the Codetermination Act of 1951 ("Act on the codetermination of workers in the supervisory and management boards of undertakings in the mining industry and the iron and steel production industry").[9] Historical analysis indicates that the particular constellation of forces at the end of World War II played a critical role in the enactment of such pro-labor legislation by the conservative postwar governments: two key factors were the employers' teetering economic position and political weakness under the occupation authorities,[10] and the newly legalized unions' aggressive pursuit of control over the means of production.[11] The 1948 Allied Law Number 75 "merely formalized" labor's *de facto* parity representation on company supervisory boards. Meanwhile, at the plant level, works councils, which had been eradicated by Nazism, resurfaced with a vengeance. In the first weeks after Germany's defeat, in many instances, works councils even took over the running of plants under their authority. Thus,

> "as early as 1945, works councils were already a political fact in search of a legal identity.[12]

In 1951, codetermination in the coal, iron and steel industries was embodied into the laws of the Federal Republic. The passage of the Codetermination Act of 1951, it must be stressed, did not reflect any cultural predisposition of Germans towards it. In fact, the Act was passed only

> "[a]t the insistence of the workers and their trade unions and after violent disputes and quarrels in and outside Parliament."[13]

German unions' monumental success of 1951 was followed by disappointment and defeats, beginning in the following year. In 1952, the legislative framework for codetermination in the coal, iron and steel industries was expanded to include all companies with more than 500 employees that were not in the coal, iron and steel industries—but with an important difference. The Works Constitution Act of 1952 gave labor representatives in such companies only one-third of the seats on supervisory boards, while mining and metal workers enjoyed parity representation. Still, it granted those German workers more power over corporate decisions than found in most other parts of the world. The employers' victory of 1952 was a Pyrrhic one, inasmuch as it imparted lasting legitimacy to labor's right to participate as a partner (albeit of junior status in non-metal industries) in the process of directing the means of production.

German auto companies are directed by two boards of directors, as are their American counterparts, except that in Germany labor is formally represented in both (Table 1).

Table 1: The Codetermination Model in Autos (Coal, Iron and Steel)

	SUPERVISORY BOARD	
Works → Council	2 company employee reps	
	4 shareholder reps	← Shareholders
Trade → Unions	2 outside employee reps	
	1 other 1 other 1 neutral chair	
	↓	
	Management Board (incl. labor director)	

The supervisory board of German companies may be said to correspond to the Outside board of directors of American companies, meeting a couple of times a year and overseeing the long-term direction of the company. The management board of German companies corresponds to the American executive board, and serves as the acting director of all company operations. However, the role of labor on those boards in the two countries cannot be exaggerated. While in the U.S. the Outside board is elected by the shareholders and the executive board, in Germany labor elects its own representatives on both boards.

The supervisory board consists, typically, of eleven members,[14] and the management board of three. The management or managing board is responsible for the day-to-day management and operation of the company, and acts like an American executive board, while the supervisory board has the principal oversight responsibility, or a reinforced version of the power of the shareholders' meetings in an American corporation. By law, the supervisory board has the sole power to appoint members of the managing board, to review the performance of managers on the managing board and determine whether or not to renew their (four-year) contracts. The supervisory board also participates in decisions concerning plant closings and other matters that significantly affect employment and the strategic orientation of the company. Thus, decisions particularly consequential for labor during periods of restructuring, such as foreign acquisitions and plans to set up foreign manufacturing operations, must be approved by the supervisory board.

A related venue of labor involvement in company decision-making in large German companies, particularly in the auto industry, is the authority of the labor directors on the managing board. Labor directors are appointed in the same way as all the members of the management board, i.e. are subject to approval by the employees' as well as the shareholders' representatives on the supervisory board. Labor directors are usually highly qualified and experienced union members (but not officials). They are responsible for matters such as personnel management, organization of work in accordance with human needs, performance and remuneration, matters concerning collective agreements, training and further training, labor and social law, industrial safety and housing.

The labor director's specific responsibilities require a close cooperation with the works councils. This illustrates the intimate link between codetermination on the shop floor level and the board level.[15] While their special concern is with personnel policy, labor managers also participate fully in the shaping of general company policy, which is subject to the *joint* approval of the members of the managing board, which decides by consensus.

While German labor's scope of authority in corporate decision making is already apparent from its rights to be represented on supervisory boards on a parity basis, the effectiveness of labor's influence on more practical, day-to-day operations is far from evident. As noted, only a third of the management board members are labor's representatives. The works council plays an important role in promoting labor's interests in the day-to-day running of the company, based on its rights of information, consultation and codetermination (consent/veto) on corresponding distinct sets of issues, specified in the Codetermination and Works Constitution Acts. While the works council's information and consultation rights may be seen as a reinforced version of shop steward rights in the U.S., Germany's workplace codetermination rights are unparalleled in the U.S..

The works council has information rights on matters connected with the "fulfillment of its general duties" and on matters relating to manpower planning and the introduction of new technology and working processes.[16] Moreover, the council's elected "economic committee" must be informed on a full range of economic and financial matters, including production level, sales, investment, profits, rationalization plans, plant closings, and changes in work organization. Reductions in operation, transfers, and the introduction of new working methods also have to be communicated (in "good time") to the works council.

Labor's consultation rights extend the right to be informed of a planned change a step further: the right to be heard before a consequential change is undertaken. Clearly, after listening, management is free to ignore labor's proposals and proceed with its original plans. These consultation rights do not give labor a real "voice," inasmuch as the latter does not have to be really "heard" by capital. Nonetheless, in conjunction with other, codetermination rights, consultation rights do have an indirect impact on decision making, to the extent that they impose on the implementation of unpopular managerial decisions the added cost of significant delays in consultation sessions.

Labor's consultation rights pertain to issues such as the closing or scaling down of operations of a department or a plant, mergers of departments, significant changes in plant organization or equipment, and the introduction of new working methods or production techniques. In all such matters management must consult labor prior to taking any action. Moreover, when the mentioned changes are expected to have a "large-scale" impact on the workforce[17], the works council has codetermination rights for a "social plan" or compensation for those adversely affected by the proposed changes. In cases labor and management cannot agree on the specifics of a social plan, an independent conciliation board steps in and formulates a binding compromise plan.

The works council's "full codetermination" or consent/veto rights apply to the following areas: the organization of working time; pay procedures; the scheduling of holidays and individual leave arrangements; the introduction and deployment of techniques to monitor employee performance; health and safety measures; social services specific to the establishment or company; principles, methods, and changes of remuneration; the fixing of bonus rates and other forms of performance-related pay; and training and retraining.[18]

Thus the works council is limited to only consultation rights over such issues as the introduction of new technology and job design, which means that management is only obligated to inform the works council and listen to comments and suggestions prior to implementation. On the other hand, the works council can exercise significant influence even on such decisions, through its codetermination rights on decisions that are related to technology choice and job design: work schedules, piecework rates and bonuses, monitoring worker performance, hiring, firing, transfers, job classifications, training and retraining, and social compensation plans in case of changes in the company such as mass layoffs. In case of a deadlock between the works council and management over a issue over which labor has codetermination rights, the decision is submitted to binding arbitration.[19]

While employers have long accepted (parity) codetermination in the coal, iron, and steel industries, they were strongly opposed to the Codetermination Act of 1976 which extended parity codetermination to all companies with more than 2,000 employees (until then, in such companies, labor had one-third of the seats on supervisory boards). In the new version, labor in all such large companies would have a near-parity representation, except that the chair, in case no candidate receives two-thirds approval by all members of the board, is elected by the shareholders. However, "in practice this has made less of a difference than was often feared, or hoped. In a considerable number of cases, the middle management representative cooperates closely with the other members of the "labor bank" and casts his vote with them."[20]

In 1977 employers challenged the constitutionality of the 1976 codetermination law, claiming that it would overly curtail property rights. The suit was filed by nine companies and was supported by the Federal Union of German Employers' Associations (BDA) and the

Federal Association of German Industry (BDI). In their suit, employers argued that the Codetermination Act infringes the property guarantee contained in Article 14 of the federal constitution, the Basic Law. Shareholders' property, they claimed, is fundamentally affected both in the substance of members' rights as well as in that of their pecuniary rights. In 1979 the Federal Constitutional Court rejected the suit, ruling that the act is compatible with the Basic Law. The Court ruled that not all property is equal in the eyes of the Basic Law. Property enjoys a particularly marked degree of protection wherever, as personal property, it forms an element for the safeguarding of individual freedom. On the other hand, the protection of property is becoming less and less firm—the more that the item of property in question has "a social relationship and a social function," e.g. the shareholdings in companies. The Court also pointed out that the company's interests observed by the management are not necessarily identical with those of the shareholders. Thus it was reaffirmed that legislators (such as those that initiated codetermination) do have the broad authority to regulate and limit the influence of shareholders on large concerns.[21]

Collective Bargaining in the German Auto Industry

A distinctive characteristic of the German unions and collective bargaining is that the latter results in contracts that cover many more workers than the members of the union that signed them. In sharp contrast to the U.S., German workers do not have to join a union in order to receive the benefits of collective bargaining. While this poses a free-rider problem for German unions, it also elevates their social standing, and ensures them a membership loyal to the whole union's (as opposed to their sectional) interests. Union density in Germany is estimated to be around 39-45%, while collective bargaining coverage is around 90%.[22]

Most German unions, representing 85% of total union membership, belong to the German Trade Union Federation (*Deutscher Gewerkschaftsbund*, DGB), a peak association of sixteen affiliated unions. In 1992-93 DGB membership stood at 11,016,000 workers.[23]

Almost all workers in big assembly plants are members of IG Metall, a union representing workers in the broader steel and metalworking industry (steel, machine-tool, ship-building, aerospace, electrical engineering, autos). Roughly 70% of all workers in the auto industry (including half of the white collar workers) are members of IG

Metall—a union density that has remained constant over the last few decades, while its contracts cover almost all of auto workers.[24] IG Metall, with 3,394,000 members in 1992-93 is the largest single union in the world. It is the most influential union in the DGB. Some consider IG Metall as the most important political force in the German union movement, more important even than its peak organization, the DGB.[25]

Like other unions in DGB, IG Metall organizes workers regardless of skill and occupational status. It is "an extreme case of industrial unionism," its organizing slogan being "all plants in an industry—one union."[26] IG Metall is widely regarded as the "wage leader" of the other German unions' yearly wage negotiations.

The union has a "strike monopoly" in its area of jurisdiction; by law, works councils cannot call a strike. However IG Metall, like other German unions, uses its exit power rarely and deliberately. Labor's institutional position on supervisory boards, management boards and the works councils provide it with alternative, discursive means of persuasion—voice.

FIGURE 1

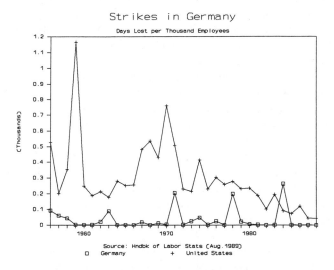

Figure 1 compares the incidence of strikes in Germany and the U.S. as the number of days lost to strikes per thousand employees in non-agricultural industries. The incidence of strikes in Germany

confirms our hypothesis that labor's power in Germany's integration
regime is less based on exit than on voice. As Figure 1 shows, there
have been hardly any "small" strikes in Germany. When strikes do
occur, they are well-coordinated and massive, organized around an
issue critical for the direction of the labor movement as a whole—as
was the 1984 strike that established the gradual reduction of the
workweek to 35 hours. In the 1980s, while on average there are many
fewer strikes in Germany than in the U.S., German strike activity in a
year of mobilization can even surpass American strike levels. In a
regime of integrated inclusion, in order to ensure that its interests are
included in corporate decisions, labor is not expected to take recourse
in striking (exit) as much as in a regime of segregated inclusion.

Except for the steel production industry and metal artisan firms that
constitute separate industrial bargaining units, IG Metall negotiates one
encompassing collective bargaining agreement for the entire
manufacturing sector (which includes, of course, autos).[27] Formally,
negotiations for the industry are conducted, and separate agreements
are signed, by regional officials in 11 territorially-defined (not
employer- or even trade-defined) "bargaining districts". However, all
important decisions by the IG Metall negotiators require approval by
the national executive, and the differences between separate agreements
as are thus very minor. "[W]age rounds affect incomes and conditions
in all regions in about the same way."[28]

Interestingly, while before the Second World War, centralization
was imposed on unions by their employers' associations, after the war
it was the unions that pressed for the re-establishment of a centralized
bargaining system. The employers' association that covers the auto
industry, the Federation of Employers' Associations of the
Metalworking Industry, or *Gesamtmetall*, formed in 1960.

Solidaristic wage policy is the basis for the centralized and
integrated pattern of collective bargaining. Centralization of bargaining
is organizationally supported and protected by the dominant position of
professional union officers:

> " . . . the dominant role of the full-time officials in the actual
> negotiations, the composition of the pay committees, their close
> involvement in the bargaining process, the right of the national
> executive to reject demands by pay committees for a strike vote or a
> strike, and the need for comparable agreements to be reached in all
> regions ensure that the **national executive always gets its way**. In

this sense, rank-and-file participation in collective bargaining in IGM[etall] has aptly been characterized a **'quasi-participation'**, serving important functions for internal consensus-building while leaving the discretion of the professional leadership unimpaired."[29]

However, union officials are not seen as serving the special interests of a bureaucratic organization. Rather, they help insulate the union's political processes against the pressures from the sectional interests of the membership ["plant egoism"]).[30]

The territorial organization of bargaining units is supplemented by the territorial, as opposed to functional, constitution of organizational units in union decision-making: there are no "auto representatives" in IG Metall's decision-making hierarchy: divisions among members by production units are **not** represented in internal decision-making structures.

In the 1980s there was a trend toward devolution of capital-labor arrangements to the plant level. In an insightful earlier analysis, Streeck (1984b:306) identified centrifugal tendencies in the German industrial relations system signaling "emergent enterprise unionism."[31] Streeck and others claim that "qualitative demands" have increased in their importance and that these demands are being settled through "productivity coalitions" being formed at the plant or work group level.[32] Thus, often, local solutions within nationally negotiated parameters are sought to questions such as the consequences for workers of the introduction of new technology, the adjustments policies introduced to respond to displacement, and the form and procedures through which team-work is introduced.[33]

This decentralization of German industrial relations, while certainly posing the perennial challenge of adaptation for German labor, has not altered its power in the production regime. After all, whatever transfer of authority has taken place from the level of IG Metall to the works councils in recent years, has been from the union to the union-dominated works councils.[34]

2. LABOR'S POWER AND REDISTRIBUTIVE AND PRODUCTIVIST OUTCOMES

In the previous section we argued that German labor, at least in the auto industry, is powerful enough against capital, so as to have institutionalized the insertion of its productivist and redistributive interests in corporate decision making. Collective bargaining (exit) and codetermination (voice) complement each other as labor's weapons in defending labor's extensive claims over the means of production. In this section we examine whether the institutions of labor inclusion described above have operated in labor's interests as hypothesized. More specifically, we will examine the evolution of certain key indicators of labor's power in corporate decisions, its ability to extract high wages and to enjoy employment security.

labor's power and redistributive outcomes

FIGURE 2

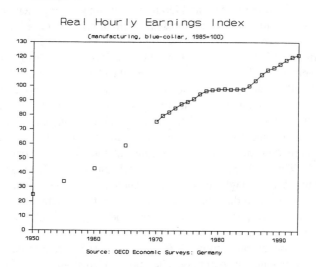

Real Hourly Earnings Index
(manufacturing, blue-collar, 1985=100)

Source: OECD Economic Surveys: Germany

The evolution of real wages in Germany since 1950 indicates that labor has had considerable power in securing and improving its living standards every year. Figure 2 charts the evolution of hourly wages of blue-collar workers in manufacturing from 1950 to 1993, against the 1985 level (=100) and adjusted for changes in the Consumer Price Index. We have chosen manufacturing earnings instead of auto earnings because there are no reliable auto earnings data for over four decades. We expect that the **index** of auto earnings will be nearly identical to the index of manufacturing earnings because, at least at least during 1978-

1987 German auto earnings were on the average 115% higher than manufacturing earnings, varying annually between only 114% and 116%[35]. The relatively small and stable difference in German auto-manufacturing earnings can be attributed to the high level of unionization throughout the manufacturing sector[36], the even higher degree of non-union employee coverage of union wage contracts,[37] and the regional basis and high degree of centralization of collective bargaining.

Perhaps the most important finding that emerges from Figure 2 is that, since 1950, German manufacturing and auto workers have never experienced real wage declines, whether in times of economic growth or during cyclical recessions. Moreover, while real wages have for the first time stagnated (though not declined) for five years during the competitive crisis of the 1980s, they took off consequently. Thus from 1980 to 1993 real wages increased by 20%, all of the increase coming after 1985.

FIGURE 3

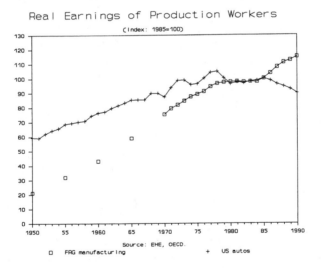

Figure 3 compares the evolution of German real hourly earnings of production workers in autos and that of American earnings in relation to their respective 1985 levels. Three observations are most pertinent. First, compared to their respective 1985 levels, German wages in 1950

were much lower than their American counterparts, probably due to the
low starting level of wages in war-torn Germany. Secondly, even if the
faster rate of growth of German real wages compared to the U.S. from
1950 to 1980 is attributable to their lower starting point, their post-1980
evolution is not. Whether the German-American wage differential is a
reflection of the hypothesized German-American differential in labor's
power or the result of some other differential, cannot be conclusively
decided at this point. Suffice it here that we demonstrated that the
German auto production regime has compensated labor at rates that
surpass those of any other auto production regime. Thirdly, the
robustness of German wages and their overtaking of the highest
American manufacturing wage levels in the 1980s should be
particularly impressive for those who might have expected that in
"social democratic" or "neo-corporatist" regimes such as Germany's
labor trades-off wage militancy for (employment and social) security.[38]

Focusing on hourly earnings as proxy for the regime's outcomes in
redistributive benefits for labor, however, is not entirely appropriate.
Hourly earnings constitute a major but hardly all the (monetary)
benefits labor receives at work. Moreover, hourly earnings do not
constitute the same portion of the total monetary benefits of labor
across countries. As Table 2 shows, in 1992 the earnings of production
workers in the German auto industry constitute 63% of their total
compensation, while the earnings of American auto workers constitute
53% of their total compensation.[39]

Table 2

	Hourly Earnings	Additional Monetary Benefits	Total Compensation
GERMANY	25.06 DM	22.53 DM	47.59 DM
U.S.A.	15.19 US$	9.02 US$	24.21 US$

A more meaningful assessment of labor's redistributive interests
requires an analysis of labor's total hourly compensation. The latter
measure is more representative of the compensation workers receive
from employers than hourly earnings, because it includes bonus
payments, employer contributions to social security, health insurance,
paid vacations, and other such benefits.[40]

FIGURE 4

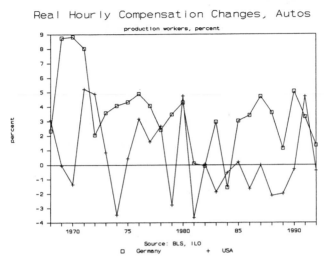

Real Hourly Compensation Changes, Autos
production workers, percent

Source: BLS, ILO
□ Germany   + USA

Thus Figure 4 charts the evolution of real annual changes in hourly compensation costs for production workers in the German and American auto industries, measured in the national currency of each country, from 1966 to 1992. Each series in Figure 4 is the difference between the annual compensation increase for auto workers and the annual increase in the Consumer Price Index. Thus Figure 4 allows us to examine the annual rate of real compensation increases.

It must be mentioned here that the rise in German workers' hourly wages in the 1980s is closely related to IG Metall's aggressive campaign to reduce the weekly working time (from 40 in 1984 to 35 by 1994) without a loss in pay. It will be noted, in Figure 4, that in 1984 German auto workers may not have had a loss in nominal pay, but they did have a loss in pay in real terms. What is most remarkable, of course, is labor's ability, as 35-hour campaign vividly illustrates, to closely integrate its redistributive and productivist interests: While improving workers' hourly wages (though not necessarily annual wages as well), the policy also helped preempt significant losses in employment stability in a period of intense international competition—when meanwhile, the American production regime was responding with mass layoffs.[41]

FIGURE 5

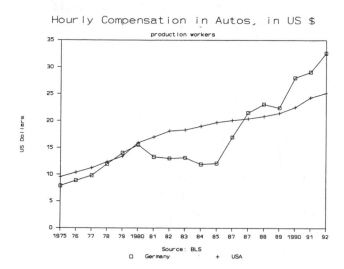

Hourly Compensation in Autos, in US $

Source: BLS

Let us finally examine the evolution of total hourly compensation of German auto workers in U.S. dollars, in order to compare the purchasing power of German and American auto workers in the world market. Figure 5 charts precisely that, without any adjustments for inflation. As can be seen, fluctuations in the exchange rate can certainly affect the relative compensation of German and American workers in dollar terms. However, even in this respect, the trend is in favor of German workers. By 1992, German auto production workers' hourly compensation stood at $32.61 to $25.12 for American auto production workers, a difference of 23%, making German auto workers clearly the best paid in the world since 1987.[42]

labor's power and productivist outcomes

Labor's productivist interests are manifold, most of which are related to the quality of the working experience. Labor has an interest in "productivist" decisions such as those that relate to less stressful and less monotonous working conditions. Thus labor has a direct stake in which form of product design and work organization will be adopted. Labor also has a stake in the "product market strategy" adopted, to the extent that the quality of labor inputs required in production depends on the quality of goods that are to be produced. Wolfgang Streeck was one of the first to argue that the stability of German industrial relations in the auto industry is largely due to a fortunate confluence of a rich engineering tradition with a conscious union effort to commit management to an up-market product strategy. An up-market product strategy, accordingly, has an "elective affinity" for highly-skilled (and thus better-paid) labor inputs, as well as employment stability.[43]

There is a broad consensus that German auto workers have more influence over corporate productivist decision making than American auto workers, with disagreements arising about the extent and sources of the difference. Recent analyses point out that much more than in other countries, IG Metall and the works councils have been engaged in debate about work organization and job design in relation to new technologies, considering such issues critical to labor's interests.[44]

Employment security is both a fundamental productivist interest of labor, and, unlike other productivist interests, amenable to operationalization (through employment stability) for comparative purposes. Employment security is a fundamental labor interest for quite obvious reasons. Whatever degree of influence labor may have over the utilization of the means of production (i.e. over the production and redistribution of surplus) becomes almost meaningless as soon as labor is "separated" from them (is laid off). Thus employment security, it could be argued, is both a precondition for and the purpose behind labor's efforts to influence other productivist decisions, such as product-market strategy, technology, work organization.

Thus, if we accept that employment security is a fundamental labor interest, and that providing employment security is not a fundamental interest of capitalists or a "natural" outcome of capitalist production, it follows that the incidence of employment stability over prolonged time periods (so as to control for extra-ordinary factors' possible contribution to employment patterns) is a reflection of labor's power in corporate decision making.

Case studies have indeed pointed out that German workers enjoy more employment security than workers in the U.S., U.K. or France. It has been argued that codetermination and works councils contribute, in effect, to "unofficial lifetime employment,"[45] through extensive reliance on internal labor markets,[46] and through a "highly elaborate system of layoff and dismissal restraints."[47] Job tenure is "significantly higher in Germany than in the U.S.."[48] In what follows we compare the

degree of employment stability in Germany and in the U.S. over several
decades.

FIGURE 6

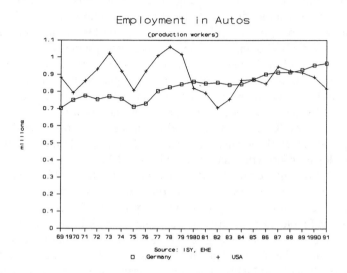

Employment in Autos
(production workers)

Source: ISY, EHE

□ Germany   + USA

Figure 6 charts the evolution of annual employment for production
workers in German autos and juxtaposes it to the corresponding
evolution in the U.S.. It can be seen that there is a qualitative difference
between the employment outcomes of the two regimes. The comparison
of German-American employment data confirm our expectations.
German auto workers enjoyed a markedly higher level of employment
security than their American counterparts throughout the postwar
period. Employment reductions have been very few, and small enough
to be accomplished through attrition rather than layoffs. By contrast,
the U.S. auto industry has been using the more "traditional" hire-and-
fire approach to adjusting to demand fluctuation.

Figure 7 juxtaposes auto employment and output data for Germany
and the U.S. It can be seen that the two countries' qualitatively distinct
patterns of employment are closely related to their distinct patterns of
output. This fact, however, can be interpreted not as evidence of labor's
power in corporate decision making, but as evidence of distinct
employer strategies of adjusting production volume to demand
fluctuations. According to such an interpretation, German auto

workers' impressive employment security is merely a fortunate side-effect of strategic choices made by their employers, independently of labor's demands for employment stability.

FIGURE 7

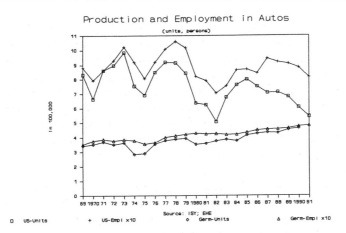

Production and Employment in Autos

However, the objection raised above, that employment stability may be unrelated to labor's power but to an independently formed employer strategy of output adjustment begs the question: what explains such employer strategies of adapting to fluctuations in demand? Besides, demonstrating that employment and output co-vary is not a refutation of our hypothesis, since employment and output stability is bound to co-vary, whether employment policy is subject to unilateral employer decisions or subject to labor pressures. While at this point we cannot prove that German employment stability is caused by labor's power in productivist decision making, it should suffice that we have shown that the German production regime has operated in a manner consistent with a labor's-power interpretation of its dynamic.

It does not detract from the above observations and conclusions to add that one important mechanism through which the German production regime adjusts to fluctuations in demand without disturbing employment stability is the adjustment of total working hours through short-time work.[49] This is the conclusion reached in a recent

econometric study of employment, hours, and output in German and
U.S industries, including autos:

> "German companies rely much more on the adjustment of average
> hours, including the use of short-time work, to reduce labor input
> during downturns; American companies make greater use of layoffs,
> including temporary layoffs."[50]

Consistent with our hypothesis that corporate employment policies
reflect labor's power therein, the authors of the above study agree that,
while the distinct adjustment mechanisms adopted in Germany and the
U.S. may be functionally equivalent from the employers' perspective,
they have significantly different impact on workers' lives. In fact,
Abraham and Houseman document the less disruptive and more
equitable character for the workforce of the short-time mechanism
compared to the layoff mechanism (the latter concentrating the pain of
adjustment on the laid-off workers), and refer to the broader social
costs that result from unemployment.[51]

Statutory regulations of dismissals are based on the 1951 Dismissal
Protection Act (amended in 1969), and the 1985 Employment
Protection Act. Statutory regulations of employment, however, must be
seen as extensions rather than substitutes of labor's power in corporate
decision making. Moreover, the effectiveness of statutory regulations
on corporate employment policy is doubtful, particularly in the absence
of labor's own organization around corporate employment policy. Firm
surveys and company case studies indicate that personnel managers
have been able to realize almost all intended layoffs and dismissals
without incurring major financial and/or legal difficulties. In fact, the
majority of personnel managers do not perceive statutory employment
security regulations to be major obstacles to necessary employment
terminations.[52] The Employment Promotion Act of 1985 "has made a
minimal impact on employment levels."[53]

3. IN SEARCH OF INDUSTRIAL EFFICIENCY

Has the relative generosity of the German auto production regime's
outcomes for labor's productivist and redistributive interests
documented above, undermined the German auto industry's productive
performance?[54] Here we explore the relationship between labor's
power in corporate decision making and industrial performance in two

steps. First, we briefly illustrate how labor's power is actually applied in productivist decisions, such as employment and overseas investment, and how industrial performance is affected by labor's representation in corporate decision making institutions. Second, we review alternative sources of German production's performance to labor's integration in decision making, such as Germany's venerable vocational training system, the close supervision of finance capital over industrial capital, and the centralized structure of German labor organizations and employer associations.

illustrations

The influence of German labor's representation has been tested sharply in the past twenty years in the automobile industry, without, however, resulting to its curtailment. Wildcat strikes and widespread unrest among the rank-and-file from 1969 to 1973 expressed not only complaints about wages but a growing dissatisfaction, especially among younger workers, with traditional assembly-line working conditions.[55] Under the threat of the breakdown of shop floor discipline, labor was successful in pushing the SPD government to amend the Works Constitution Act in 1972 so as to include expanded rights of works councils and union presence in the plants, and in developing "humanization of work" programs in the 1970s. In these programs, researchers in conjunction with unionists and managers developed alternatives for work organization, such as job rotation job enrichment, and work teams—almost a decade before they were developed in the U.S..

In 1973, automobile workers spearheaded IG Metall's campaign for a new Wage Framework Agreement with a strike at Daimler-Benz. The new framework contract, covering all metalworkers in the North Baden-North Wurttermberg region, placed limits on the division of labor; no work unit could be less than 1.5 minutes (contrasted to usual auto plant cycle times in the U.S. of one minute or less).[56] In 1978, another strike in the same region, also spearheaded by automobile workers, resulted in an improved "rationalization protection" agreement.[57]

The processes underway in the German automobile industry in the 1970s and early 1980s, also amounted to a shift in labor's orientation in corporate decision-making. Until that point, German unions's productivist orientation was still of a reactive nature. The dominant union attitude with respect to work organization was "let management manage"—similar, in a way, to American labor's tradition of "management manages and labor grieves." However, unlike American labor, German unions would defer to management on work organization issues in exchange of both rising wages and the effective preclusion of management decisions that resulted in job loss. Beginning in the mid-1970s, German labor has moved away from that reactive posture in decision-making, and has put forward proactive proposals and strategies for work organization, called group work (**Gruppenarbeit**), at the center of which is the coupling of teamwork with higher levels of training and works council supervision of its design and operation.[58]

Even with the influence of American management traditions at American subsidiary automobile companies in Germany (GM's Opel, and Ford-Werke), industrial relations in foreign-owned companies are quite similar to those in German-owned companies. This similarity reflects the fact that

"management in the West German auto industry simply has less independent discretion than do its counterparts in the United states. This limited discretion results directly from institutional constraints: the integration of the union and works council into managerial decision-making processes; the legal framework (codetermination laws) that regulates this integration from outside the firm; and the relatively cohesive labor movement led by the IG Metall."[59]

Works councils in the large auto assembly firms generally have more influence on more subjects than given to them by the Works Constitution Acts. Their influence differs among firms, the opposite extremes being, perhaps Volkswagen and Ford. However, even in foreign-owned firms such as Adam Opel (GM) and Ford, eliciting the works council's support before almost any corporate decision is considered an imperative of corporate decision making. In the words of a manager at Opel's Russelsheim plant, "Without the work council nothing goes; with the works council everything goes."[60]

Volkswagen

In Volkswagen, the state government owns 19.7% of the shares and has 2 of the 10 shareholder seats in the 21-seat Supervisory Board (employees have 10 seats, one of which is reserved for a representative of managerial employees and another for a salaried employee). Traditionally, the state representatives are in coalition with employee representatives. Thus, even in times of intense pressures to cut production costs to restore profit margins, proposals by capital to cut the workforce founder on the labor coalition on the board. Thus in the crisis years of 1973-1981, Volkswagen workers' representatives refused to allow layoffs or make any wage concessions.[61] The head of Volkswagen's supervisory board Ferdinand Piech, said of the labor-cutting efforts of his predecessor Carl Hahn at the end of the 1980s:

> "Hahn's team realized Volkswagen's German costs were well out of control. But they could not crack the labor coalition on the board."[62]

However, employment reductions are not completely precluded in a representation regime as in an incorporation regime such as Japan's. The labor coalition on the board has the power to block employment cuts, but can also approve such cuts if it deems them necessary. Thus in Volkswagen, faced with a dramatic slump in profitability and market share, the labor coalition finally approved cuts of 36,000 of its 276,000 workforce over four years. Labor's chief representative on the board Klaus Volkert had said at an employees' meeting before approving the cuts that the company's situation was the most severe test faced since the 1974-75[63]. The layoffs would be complemented by a shift in its method of quality control. Moreover, instead of the practice of testing and fixing any defects after a car rolls off the assembly line, Volkswagen would adopt the "Japanese" method of weeding out defects during production, thereby keeping production costs low while improving quality. The new quality control method would be integrated to a new just-in-time inventory system.[64]

Volkswagen's decision highlights the realization in Germany of a shortcoming in its representation regime. While the regime integrates labor and capital in decision-making, the **mode** of labor integration (representation) leaves certain aspects of labor-capital relations segregated. While (or because) labor is integrated into decision-making through (formal) representation in pertinent decision-making bodies and processes of companies, there is little integration of labor in less formal bodies and processes. Thus, while workers' representatives are involved in all major corporate (and plant-level) decisions, there has been little direct involvement by rank-and-file workers in shop floor decisions. The involvement of rank-and-file in decision-making has been limited to determining who among them will be involved.

One habituated to American business practices may question the efficiency of Volkswagen's participatory system of decision making. Even if good decisions are reached as a result, one may wonder how speedily such decision can be taken. In a recent interview, Carl Hahn, the chairman of Volkswagen's board of managers was asked whether he considers codetermination in decision-making processes as efficient:

> "Emphatically yes. The velocity of our decision making is second to none. It has been my experience that when labor representatives, who are highly accomplished in their own jobs, come on the supervisory boards, they can come to agreement with boards of management over complex and painful business decisions, as long as they know all of the facts . . . The important thing is to maintain the spirit of understanding with open communication and continuous information."[65]

Another "wonder," from an American perspective, is how German automobile managers, who have been moving operations to low-wage areas outside Germany, can elicit the requisite approval of labor representative for such activities that would appear to result in fewer German jobs. The answer lies in that certain types of foreign ventures may, indeed, even help job creation at home. For example, Volkswagen's recent acquisition of Spanish Seat resulted in job creation in German transmission plants, engine plants, and axle plants. German auto workers will approve a foreign venture if, and only if, the proposals for such a venture demonstrate that it will not lead to job losses at home.

Audi

Similarly, employee representatives at the supervisory board of Audi gave their conditional approval to a plan to open a new components plant in Hungary, where labor costs were 50% lower than in Germany. In exchange for labor's allowing the implementation of the plan, Audi guaranteed that it would funnel 33% of the saving to worker retraining and other benefits for employees at its main plant in Bavaria. Audi also had to convince its workers that low-cost production of components might be the only way for the auto maker to survive in the intensely competitive market.

BMW

Even after the decision to open a plant abroad is taken, German auto workers exercise certain influence over the working conditions in the new site. When BMW management wanted to ban unions from representing workers at its first overseas plant, in South Carolina, U.S.A.,[66] labor's representatives on the company's board voiced their opposition. In a terse letter to BMW's chairman, Klaus Zwickel, workers' representative on BMW's supervisory board and current deputy president of IG Metall, said that the union would fight to ensure that employees at the American plant would be allowed to organize themselves under union protection. More recently, Freightliner, the heavy truck division of Daimler-Benz attempted to circumvent unionization when it opened a factory two years ago in North Carolina. But the UAW, with the help of the trade union at Mercedes, eventually won the right to represent the workers and negotiated "an excellent contract" with the German owner, according to the UAW.[67]

> "We have a history of forcing German firms who set up abroad to work with local unions and we do not intend to make an exception here. If BMW was allowed to get away with it in South Carolina, they would try it on everywhere."[68]

BMW appeared determined to press ahead with plans to go without union representation at its plant to be built in South Carolina, despite fierce protests from IG Metall, Germany's largest trade union. Werner Rothfuss, a BMW spokesman, said that local conditions in South Carolina were "not suited" to trade union activity and that the company wanted to deal directly with the workforce there. In a terse letter to Eberhard von Kunheim, BMW's chairman, Klaus Zwickel, IG Metall's deputy president, said that the union would fight to ensure that employees at the plant would be allowed to organize themselves under union protection.[69]

4. TRAINING, FINANCING, NETWORKS, AND CORPORATISM AS INTERMEDIATE VARIABLES

A very broad range of perspectives on the requisites of economic success in a global economy converge on one factor: flexibility or adaptability of the organization of work to ever-changing signals from technological capabilities, product markets, trade and environmental policies. There is also a near-consensus that cooperative labor-management relations is a requisite of such flexibility. After this point, disagreements arise about the requisites of cooperative labor-management relations. There are two broad perspectives on the requisites of cooperative labor-management relations, the "neo-liberal" and the "neo-radical" perspectives.

The "neo-liberal" perspective of the MIT's International Motor Vehicle Program envisions cooperative labor-management relations stemming from the weakening of one or a combination of three types of institutions: unions, state-level regulations, vertical corporate integration.[70] The breaking down of such "rigidities" will make the system more flexible and thus more efficient. The breaking down of such rigidities might leave the system vulnerable to conflict, but its efficiency endows it with enough resources (revenue) to "buy" labor's cooperation. The evidence from this perspective highlights the relative efficiency of "lean" production: Japan is the most flexible and efficient, the United States comes second, "Europe" comes third. Germany is lumped together with a very heterogeneous set of European countries, thus obfuscating the possibility that a certain "rigid" system might be much more efficient than others.

The "neo-radical" perspective advocates the strengthening of unions and/or state-level regulations. Streeck, Turner, Thelen (to a progressively less extent) focus on the importance of strengthening neo-corporatist institutions as a means of securing labor's cooperation, which is requisite for flexibility and adaptability. The problem with this perspective is that, while it considers "cooperation on labor's terms" as compatible with flexibility and efficiency, its analytic framework is too constrained by a social-democratic or neo-corporatist (or perhaps even an ethno-centric) institutionalism. "Labor's terms" should instead be understood broadly enough to enable us to include the widely different forms they take in different settings.

Our analysis relies heavily on many of the findings, insights and problematiques of both of the above perspectives, but rejects, as well, many of their central premises and conclusions. The "neo-liberal" perspective puts the cart (flexible deployment of labor, integration of design, engineering and manufacturing functions) before the horse (labor's active cooperation in the above). While correctly pointing out the efficiency of alternatives to mass, "rigid" production, and while it stresses that without labor' active cooperation such alternatives would crumble, it provides little evidence for how efficient systems elicit the requisite cooperation from labor in the first place. Why would labor be willing to be used flexibly and work creatively, in the absence of guarantees that it is cooperating in an endeavor over which it has a meaningful degree of control? And why would labor be granted such control if it does not have the power to require it in the first place?

The "neo-radical" perspective, on the other hand, is also not entirely satisfactory. It correctly stresses how cooperative industrial relations in Germany are predicated on intense class conflict; and it identifies the usually neglected positive consequences for industrial efficiency of a balance of power between capital and labor. However, its understanding of labor's power prevents it from taking these observations to their logical conclusion. By conceiving labor's power only in its social-democratic or corporatist Western renditions, it is forced to treat it as one among several factors on which industrial cooperation may depend. Accordingly, labor's power is neither a necessary nor a sufficient condition for a production regime to be cooperative: the Japanese regime is cooperative despite labor's presumed weakness; the German regime is cooperative because of labor's strength.

Thus Streeck, while suggesting that labor's power is central to Germany's (and Sweden's) cooperative and thus flexible and efficient industrial relations, concedes that in the case of Japan labor's subjugation may well be central to that country's cooperative and thus flexible and efficient industrial relations. Labor's power and subjugation are viewed as "functional equivalents" for flexible mass production.[71] Our analysis submits that labor's power is central to the success of **all** advanced capitalist countries' cooperative and thus flexible and efficient industrial relations. Our analysis propounds a functional equivalence between labor's power as expressed in Japan's incorporation regime (lifetime employment) and Germany's representation regime. In what follows we review the organizational-structural variables which the "neo-radical" school treats as independent variables; we argue that these variables are only some among other possible regime responses to labor's significant decision making power, particularly in the area of employment.

The Vocational Training System

In Germany, a high-school graduate does not have to read classified ads to find a job in his/her chosen field. He/she can enter an apprentice program in a company that will teach him/her a profession and virtually guarantee a job. Typically, he/she will spend three years as an apprentice working at a large company and following specialized classes, thus receiving theoretical and practical experience at the same time. At the end of three years he/she will take an examination, and if he/she does well, he/she will probably be offered a job at the company where he/she had trained. During training, the trainee will receive a "training wage" of about $650 a month for the work performed for the company. However, when finished training, he/she will earn three to five times his/her apprentice salary. A recent survey of 10,000 apprentices showed that 95% were learning careers they found interesting, and that only 3% were pessimistic about job prospects.[72]

While one could trace the roots of training in Germany to the century-old guild apprentice system, it is only in the postwar era that it has been institutionalized in such a wide-reaching career training and placement center.[73]

Principal responsibility for overseeing the German system lies with the Federal Labor Agency, a nonprofit corporation run by representatives of capital, labor and government. It employs close to 100,000 people at its headquarters in Nuremberg and at two hundred branches around the country. The labor agency has a legal monopoly on career counseling in Germany, but it does more than channel people into vocations. It supports a research institute at which 120 specialists analyze long-term trends affecting the German economy. They predict which industries are likely to grow, which new ones are likely to emerge, and what sorts of skills future German workers will need.

In Germany, the cost of vocational training is borne, in descending order, by capital, the state, and organized labor, and it is supervised jointly by capital and labor.[74] Budget figures indicate that local and federal government spends close to $10 billion a year, and industry supports around 1.5 million apprentices annually. One research agency has estimated that business invests about $8,400 a year in each apprentice.[75] Companies also assign many of their experienced workers to part-time teaching posts at vocational schools, picking up most of the costs themselves. Margaret Hilton, on the basis of a major Office of Technology Assessment report, estimates that in 1987 German employers were spending an average of at least $633 per worker annually on training; the corresponding U.S. figure was $263.[76]

> "Employers in what was formerly West Germany spend twice as much as U.S. firms on worker training. The key to this investment is that German employers can pool the costs and benefits of training through strong industry and trade associations."[77]

Despite these heavy costs, however, most capital leaders are pleased by the results. One administrator of vocational programs in Berlin said:

> "Our German economy lives from the high quality of its workers. Business recognizes this, and pays a great deal of money to guarantee a steady flow of highly trained workers It's an investment in human quality."[78]

While Germany's vocational training system is an important ingredient of its industrial relations system, particularly in providing employment security and efficiency, it must be seen as the regime's solution to the problem of surplus labor: if you cannot simply discard labor made "redundant" by process innovations, maximize its productive potential by training it in multivalent skills and problem-solving.[79] What is critical for the cooperative culture, flexibility and efficiency of the German system is labor's power to integrate its interests in corporate decisions. Inasmuch as a company's workforce is not easily disposable when demand for the product falls or the design of the product changes, employers are likely to opt to invest in training for a skilled and adaptable workforce. Once they are committed to training, employers are then likely to socialize the costs of training through strong employer associations, government agencies, and labor's associations—or, alternatively, through company-provided training in a context of a strongly tenure-based employee compensation system.

The close relationship between the training system, the efficiency to which it contributes, and employment stability is borne out clearly in the following statement of Joachim Drechsler, a Siemens executive:

"We have a [training] system that has provided us with great prosperity and stability. The American hire-and-fire system would definitely not be accepted here."[80]

While Streeck sees the German training system as a source of labor-capital cooperation,[81] we see it, primarily, as a consequence of the necessity for cooperation deriving from the near-parity of labor's and capital's power in corporate decision making.

David Soskice uses both the financial and the industrial relations factors to explain the existence of the German training system and Germany's industrial success: "the operation of the German financial system, allowing companies to adopt a long-term financial perspective, combined with the industrial relations system, making low-cost labor strategies difficult, pushes companies in competitive markets toward high-quality production using highly skilled labor in internal labor markets."[82]

Organizational-structural variables

Peter Hall has attempted to explain patterns of socio-economic outcomes among advanced capitalist countries through an "organizational approach."[83] Accordingly, the **way** in which each of the three pillars of the political economy (the state, capital, labor) are organized is what determines, which type of policy will prevail; the state's, capital's and labor's organization determine what policy makers are pressed to do and what they can do.[84] In terms of labor's organization, Hall looks at the degree of centralization of the union movement. Union centralization, particularly if accompanied by centralization of employers' associations, is critical for generating the necessary pressures for and the necessary discipline to implement a state incomes policy of wage restraint in exchange for labor-friendly social programs. In a way, Hall lays out the organizational preconditions for what Pizzorno characterized as the "political exchange" between unions and labor-based parties.[85]

It has also been pointed out that the legal framework for and structure of German banks allows the Bundesbank close supervision of the German industry, and the German banks an ability to steer companies towards long-term strategies.[86] The venue through which German financial institutions influence corporate strategy is their voting power as shareholders of borrowing companies.[87] While this is an important ingredient of its political economy (and thus of more employment stability and more efficiency), it is not "necessary" inasmuch as it has its functional equivalents in Japan's MITI or in Sweden's Social Democracy.

While its centralization and its close relationship to a powerful political party are two central ingredients of labor's power in Germany as well as in Sweden, the significance of these factors for labor's power tends to be overstated. That labor's access to the government or the State enhances labor's power is, after all a truism; it begs the question of how labor gained such access in the first place. The degree of union centralization (or corporatism) enhances labor's exit-based power, but it does not determine its voice-based power. Thus Lowell Turner's emphasis on centralization in his German-American auto industrial relations is particularly unfortunate, because it steers his otherwise germane observations into another truism, that more centralized unions will result into more homogeneous industrial relations across plants (see Chapter 2). He fails to notice that the critical difference in German-American auto industrial relations does not lie, primarily, in German unions' more thorough organization (the significance of the latter notwithstanding), but in their more productivist orientation and voice-based power. As the next chapter will demonstrate, Japanese labor has achieved remarkable employment and income security without the "cohesiveness" of German labor or its close articulation to the State.

5. LABOR'S POWER AND INDUSTRIAL PERFORMANCE

We have argued that several popular ways of assessing industrial performance, such as profitability and various calculations of "productivity" (based on an output-per-employee definition), are potentially very misleading. They assess productive performance as a cost-benefit analysis from the perspective of the employers only. Profitability and "productivity" say more about how well the employers are doing than how well the production regime (which includes labor too!) is performing. In fact, it is quite possible that profitability and "productivity" thrive **at the expense of** labor's wages and employment. Moreover, the popular measure of "productivity" not only abstracts from the conditions in which labor produces, but is also of little use as an indicator of an industry's ability to compete.

Based on the mis-conceptualization of "productivity" as output per employee, the "productivity" of the German auto industry has been lagging that of the U.S. seriously, for decades, albeit to a diminishing degree: in 1961, German productivity was only 20% of American productivity; in 1971 32%; in 1981 51%.[88] Even highly sophisticated data collection methods by respected consulting firms lead to similar results about "productivity". According to the McKinsey Global Institute's detailed report *Manufacturing Productivity*, which analyzes selected industries in the U.S., Germany, and Japan, the productivity of the German auto industry should be more the object of pity than of envy. Based on the output-per-employee definition of productivity (adjusted for capacity utilization, cost of materials and other factors), the McKinsey study concludes that in 1991, productivity in the German auto industry was only 66% of the American auto productivity! In face of such chronic productivity deficits, the German auto industry's ability to survive (and, as we show below, to have a positive trade balance) would have to be considered as nothing short of miraculous![89]

A somewhat different conceptualization of industrial performance informs the seminal M.I.T. International Motor Vehicle Program that culminated in the publication of the influential *The Machine That Changed The World*.[90] The authors of that study use two indicators of industrial efficiency/performance: productivity and quality. They define quality production as the inverse of "assembly defects per 100 vehicles," while productivity is defined as the number of employee-hours it takes to produce a vehicle. The latter definition represents a certain refinement of the same concept of productivity: it is sensitive to the variability of hours worked by each employee in different production systems.[91] Moreover, their analysis, by accounting for defects in the product, is sensitive to the fact that the "output" in "output/hour" does not always denote the same value or quality of output.

Nonetheless, while enviable in its scope and influence,[92] the measurements of the M.I.T. study are problematic, from our perspective, for three main reasons. First, the definition of productivity being used is based on the output/hour concept, which we have found misleading (the "hour" may be of different intensity and cost in different regimes). Second, while the authors stress the difference which different systems of production can make for efficiency, they furnish evidence of productivity differentials based more on the geography, rather than on the nature of different production units. In particular, they lump together very dissimilar systems of production, such as the German and the British, under the category of a "European" system.[93] Thus, while Womack et al. conclude that the productivity and the quality of the average auto plant in Europe is lower than in the U.S.,[94] they leave us in the dark on the comparison of German-American productivity or quality. Third, the authors' assessment of production quality as the number of defects per vehicle, while somewhat indicative of quality, says little about the number of defects that may appear three months later or five years later.

We now turn to an analysis of the comparative evolution of industrial performance of the German and American auto industries, based on the indicators of regime efficiency developed in Chapter 2, the balance of trade in autos and on auto reliability surveys. We expect to confirm our hypothesis that labor's power in a regime and industrial performance co-vary. In the concluding chapter we will address directly whether the co-variance of productive performance and of relatively favorable outcomes for labor documented in the present chapter is the result, primarily, of labor's power or of other factors.

Market-based indicators of industrial performance

FIGURE 8

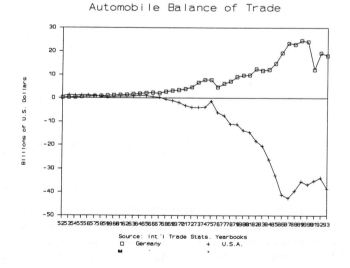

Automobile Balance of Trade

Source: Int'l Trade Stats. Yearbooks
☐ Germany   +   U.S.A.

Figure 8 charts the balance of trade of the German and U.S. auto industries. Several observations are pertinent. First, the German balance of trade in autos is very similar to that of the U.S. during the 1950s and early-1960s. This is to be expected, even though the basic features of the two production regimes were already in place. While the German regime may have been already more efficient that the American regime, the difficulties of reconstructing a war-ravaged industry are likely to have retarded German performance for a certain number of years. Secondly, Germany begins to outperform the U.S. in the mid-1960s, and, at an ever-increasing extent in the mid-1970s. Thirdly, during the 1980s, Germany's auto balance of trade continues to improve, despite the intensified international competition, restructuring, etc, while that of the U.S. is on a nose-dive.[95]

FIGURE 9

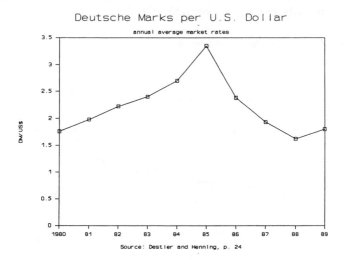

In anticipation of monetarist arguments that the difference between the German and the U.S. auto balance of trade is the result, primarily, of changes in the exchange rate, we provide data on the evolution of the DM/US$ exchange rate in the 1980s. As Figure 9 shows, the German currency began and ended the decade at the rate of approximately 1.7 marks per dollar, peaking at 3.3 marks per dollar.[96] Had movements in balance of trade been largely exchange-rate-driven, the German currency's marked depreciation with respect to the US dollar in the first half of the 1980s would have resulted in a corresponding deterioration in balance of trade.

FIGURE 10

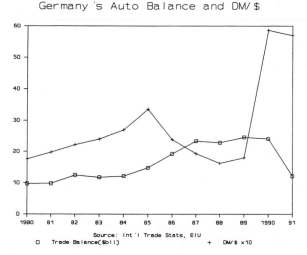

Germany 's Auto Balance and DM/ $

Source: Int 'l Trade Stats, EIU
□ Trade Balance($bll) + DM/$ x10

Figure 10 compares the evolution of exchange rates (Figure 9) and auto balance of trade (Figure 8) during the 1980s. The juxtaposition of the two trends severely undermines the explanatory power of exchange-rate changes for the fluctuations in the auto balance of trade. While the German currency's depreciation against the US dollar from 1980 to 1985 is paralleled by an improvement in Germany's auto balance of trade, apparently confirming monetarists' expectations, consequent developments do not. Indeed, the appreciation of the German mark after 1985 (which makes German products more expensive and thus, *ceteris paribus*, less internationally competitive) is not accompanied by a deterioration of the German auto balance of trade, as the monetarist would expect, but by an improvement in the balance of trade. After all, in the long run, exchange rates reflect the relative health of a country's economy.[97]

FIGURE 11

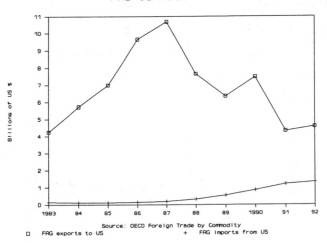

FRG-US Auto Trade

Source: OECD Foreign Trade by Commodity
□   FRG exports to US   +   FRG Imports from US

Next, we examine the auto balance of trade between Germany and the U.S.. Figure 11 charts the dollar value of German auto exports to the U.S. and of American exports to Germany (the much smaller American exports are shown multiplied by an order of 5 in order to assist in the comparison). If the substantial Germany-U.S. difference in their auto balance of trade with the rest of the world reflects the superiority of German auto production, Germany's production superiority should also be reflected in the Germany-U.S. auto balance of trade. Indeed, Germany has had a substantial surplus in auto trade with the U.S., whether we measure the balance of trade in terms of units of trade or in terms of their dollar value.[98] In 1987 German exports of road vehicles to the U.S. amounted to $ 10,687,410,000, while its imports from the U.S. were $ 192,303,000. By 1992 the trade gap decreased markedly: German exports from the U.S. were $ 4,576,461,000, while its imports were 1,326,728,000.[99] Clearly, Jointness in the U.S. was bearing fruit.[100]

Non-Market indicators of industrial performance

We now turn to our other, non-market based indicator of industrial performance, surveys of auto reliability. This is done to provide independent confirmation of the superiority of German production, lest market-based indicators presented above do not reflect the superiority of the German product but the U.S.'s "unfavorable terms of trade" (induced by exchange-rate and trade-policy distortions).

FIGURE 12

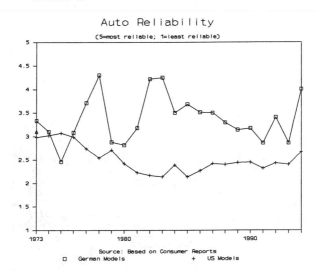

Auto Reliability

(5=most reliable; 1=least reliable)

Source: Based on Consumer Reports
□   German Models   +   US Models

Figure 12 charts the reliability ratings for all German and all American cars sold in the U.S., based on the *Consumer Reports*' frequency-of-repair records, from 1973 to 1994. The average rating, corresponding to the average frequency of repairs for all models is 3. The best possible rating is 5 ("much better than average"), while the worst is 1 ("much worse than average"). For Figure 12 we have added the ratings for each German model sold in the U.S. and divided that sum by the number of models.[101] As could be expected from the ordinal nature of the ratings, for most years the ratings for German and for American autos move in the opposite direction: if German autos improve on a given year relative to all autos sold in the U.S., it is likely that on that year American autos have deteriorated relative to the total.

The more interesting finding that emerges from Figure 12 is that German models rate **consistently and significantly** better than American models. Every year since 1973 (except 1975), German models have been rated as above average in frequency of repairs. It is also noteworthy that while the difference between German and American reliability had been increasing until 1982-84, after that the difference begins to decrease.

FIGURE 13

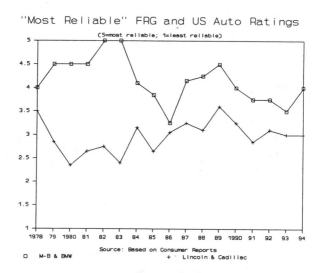

"Most Reliable" FRG and US Auto Ratings
(5=most reliable; 1=least reliable)

Source: Based on Consumer Reports

□   M-B & BMW   + · Lincoln & Cadillac

Figure 13 narrows the focus of comparison to the two most reliable German and three most reliable American nameplates.[102] This narrowing of focus is necessary in order to counter the claim that the results of Figure 9 are biased in favor of German exports to the U.S.; exported products are likely to be better than the average product for domestic consumption. To ensure that we are comparing "like with like," Figure 10 compares the reliability records of the two German makes sold in the U.S. with the best such records, against the two American makes with the best records.

The results in Figure 13 confirm those in Figure 12. German autos have had better reliability records than American autos, with the reliability gap peaking in the early 1980s and declining during the late-1980s and early-1990s.

While the objectivity of the non-profit *Consumer Reports* is beyond reproach, the way in which it we have aggregated its data in Figure 13 may not be. The data charted on Figure 13 are constructed as the aggregate ratings of all the models according to the country of origin of its manufacturer, with no adjustments made for the market share each model represents.[103]

We thus supplement the above data with data from another reliable source of annual surveys of auto reliability, J.D. Power & Associates. Our analysis of published JD Power data is quite revealing.[104] It provides strong support to the hypothesis that German autos are of higher quality than their American counterparts. Specifically, analysis of Vehicle Dependability Study results from the mid-1980s to the mid-1990s confirm (a) the superiority of German auto production compared to the U.S. until the mid-1980s, and (b) the closing of that gap after the late-1980s, since the American regime's transition to Jointness.

Table 3 below lists the German and American auto makers that were among the **top five** most dependable autos sold in the U.S., in JD Power's VDI (see the Appendix).

Table 3: German and US Auto Makers in the Top Five of VDI

Year	Make (Nameplate)	Score	Overall Rank	Origin
1990[105]				
	Mercedes-Benz	149	1	Germany
	Buick	133	4	USA
	Cadillac	121	5	USA
1991[106]				
	Mercedes-Benz	129	4	Germany
1992[107]				
	Mercedes-Benz	176	1	Germany
	Lincoln	137	4	USA
	Porsche	127	5	Germany
1993[108]				
	Mercedes-Benz	163	1	Germany
	Cadillac	151	3	USA
	Porsche	145	4	Germany

Clearly, the JD Power reliability ratings confirm the ratings of Consumer Reports presented above. Top German autos do in fact score higher in reliability on every year since the Vehicle Dependability Survey began. Moreover, top quality American autos, since the American regime moved away from segregation in mid-1980s,[109] have not rated too far behind the best German autos. The narrowing of labor's power gap has been accompanied by a narrowing of the product quality gap.

6. CONCLUSION

Labor's power in the German auto industry is based on an extensive capacity to exit, as well as on a capacity to make its voice heard by capital on a broad range of corporate decisions. We have examined the institutions through which labor's power in redistributive and productivist decisions is exercised in the auto industry, and demonstrated that these claims of labor's power correspond to actual redistributive and productivist outcomes of the production regime for labor. German labor's power, based on parity representation of labor's redistributive and productivist interests in corporate decision making is clearly superior to that of American labor. Both *de jure* and *de facto*, German workers have been able to better defend employment and income security.

Moreover, we have shown that an impressive competitive performance is compatible with labor's integrated inclusion in corporate decision making. While we have not demonstrated the causal nature of the relationship between labor's power and industrial performance, we have made such a hypothesis more plausible by demonstrating that alternative variables affecting productive performance may be in fact dependent on labor's integration in the production regime.

Germany's representative integration will continue to contend with the dangers of (non-) democratic centralism, a danger it shares with "neo-corporatist" modes of interest representation: procedural sclerosis.[110] Recent trends at the level of labor representation (decentralization) as well as at the level of worker involvement in productivist decisions (humanization of work) indicate that the regime is well situated against such challenges.

Labor and capital want to move codetermination in opposite directions. Labor sees the danger of evasion of codetermination requirements through legal and statutory evasion tactics on the part of capital, and of procedures which give advantages to shareholders' representatives in committees with non-parity representation (not in the auto industry). In spite of such problems, however, unions have found codetermination to have gradually modified entrepreneurial goals to include workers' well-being.

Capital, by contrast, sees other problems: the contradiction between ownership in the means of production and control over the means of production, the representation of middle managerial employees below the senior executive level by the same union as production workers, and the wide powers of the labor director in company decision-making. At the same time there is consensus (through successive CDU, SPD, CDU governments and among business and labor federations) that codetermination remains a stabilizing element in industrial relations.

More formidable challenges for the regime may come from the momentous consequences of German reunification, particularly unemployment, transfer of operations, wage and skill differentials between the West and the East—which exacerbate the impact of a globalized economy. But when in 1993 Volkswagen's chairman announced that 30,000 jobs needed to be eliminated, workers offered a daring alternative that was adopted, saving those jobs while addressing the company's undeniable restructuring needs: a four-day week with a proportional pay cut. Furhter, workers responded to the need to shift more operations in plants abroad by establishing a World Works Conference that meets once a year to discuss company strategy. The outcome of the crisis is yet to be determined, and the collapse of representative integration under the pressures of globalization and reunification remains a possibility. The fact that in 1993 the European Union mandated the creation of European Works Councils along the lines of the German works councils at all major companies in its sphere of influence attests to the widening recognition that the regime of representative integration, far from having run its course, remains a dynamic and attractive model of organizing production.

NOTES

1. Wages and working conditions set at the collective bargaining level may be modified by local, supplementary contracts only if the collective agreement expressly authorizes contracts. On some recent developments that seem to blur the distinction between codetermination and collective bargaining rights. See John T. Addison, Kornelius Kraft, and Joachim Wagner, "German Works

Councils and Firm Performance," in Bruce E. Kaufman and Morris M. Kleiner (eds) *Employee Representation: Alternatives and Future Directions* (Madison, WI.: IRRA, 1993), pp. 307-309.

2. On the constructive role of union bureaucracy to combat company, plant, or trade "egoism" see Streeck (1984).

3. Wolfgang Streeck, "Neo-Corporatist Industrial Relations and the Economic Crisis in West Germany," in John H. Goldthorpe (ed.) *Order and Conflict in Contemporary Capitalism: Studies in the Political Economy of Western European Nations* (New York: Oxford University Press, 1984).

4. Piore and Sabel (1984).

5. Kathleen Thelen, *Union of Parts: Labor Politics in Postwar Germany* (Ithaca, NY: Cornell University Press, 1991).

6. Peter J. Katzenstein, (ed), *Industry and Politics in West Germany: Toward the Third Republic* (Ithaca, NY: Cornell University Press, 1989).

7. According to Kathleen Thelen, during the years 1955-1987, 80% percent of works councilors in the steel and metalworking industries were also members of IG Metall. Thelen (1991), p. 80. In firms with more than 12,000 employees, which includes the auto companies, the proportion of non-unionized workers on councils is around 1%. Addison, Kraft, and Wagner, *op. cit.*, p. 310.

8. It is noteworthy that one of labor's representatives on the supervisory board of BMW is also the deputy president of the union: IG Metall's Klaus Zwickel.

9. In 1991 the law applied to about 32 companies with approximately 350,000 employees. US Bureau of International Labor Affairs, Department of Labor, *Foreign Labor Trends: Germany* (Washington, D.C.: G.P.P., 1992), p. 18.

10. Andrei Markovits *The Politics of the West German Trade Unions* (Cambridge: Cambridge University Press, 1986), p. 68.

11. Thelen, *op. cit.*, p. 72.

12. Ibid, p. 72.

13. The Federal Minister of Labor and Social Affairs,*Co-determination in the Federal Republic of Germany* (Bonn: Referat Presse, 1980), p. 10.

14. The supervisory boards of larger companies may consist of fifteen or twenty-one members.

15. Ibid, p. 75.

16. The works council's information rights with respect to the introduction of new technology were expanded in the 1988 amendments to the Works Constitution Act.

17. A "large-scale" impact, according to legal precedent, has been defined as one affecting more than 6% of the plant workforce. The 1985 Employment Promotion Act has amended the definition to connote one affecting more than 10% of the workforce.

18. Press and Information Office of the Federal Republic of Germany, *Employers and Unions* (Bonn: Press and Information Office, 1981); Streeck (1984), Turner (1991 and 1993), Thelen (1991).

19. Ibid; Streeck (1984); Thelen, op. cit; Lowell Turner, *Democracy at Work: Changing World Markets and the Future of Labor Unions* (Ithaca, N.Y.: Cornell University Press, 1991); and idem, "Prospects for Worker Participation in Management in the Single Market" in Lloyd Ulman, Barry Eichengreen and William T. Dickens (eds.), *Labor and an Integrated Europe* (Washington, D.C.: The Brookings Institution, 1993).

20. Arndt Sorge and Wolfgang Streeck, "Industrial Relations and Technical Change: The Case for an Extended Perspective," in Hyman and Streeck (eds), *New Technology and Industrial Relations* (Oxford: Basil Blackwell, 1988), p. 13, n. 4. The significance of the shareholders' selection of the chairman is clearly overstated by Greg J. Bamber and Russel D. Lansbury, "Codetermination and Technological Change in the German Automobile Industry" *New Technology, Work and Employment*, 2 (2), 1987.

21. The Federal Minister of Labor and Social Affairs, *Co-determination in the Federal Republic of Germany* (Bonn: Referat Presse, 1980), pp. 30-31.

22. See, for example, Roy J. Adams, *Industrial Relations Under Liberal Democracy: North America in Comparative Perspective* (Columbia, S.C.: University of South Carolina Press, 1995). p. 78; Otto Jacobi, Brendt Keller, and Walther Muller-Jentsch, "Germany: Codetermining the Future?" in Anthony Ferner and Richard Hyman (eds.) *Industrial Relations in the New Europe* (Cambridge, Mass.: Basil Blackwell, 1992), pp. 231-32. There are no definitive statistics on union density, because of uneven data collection and data reporting. Union membership records are kept by trade unions, but some unions include retired and unemployed individuals as members while others do not. Adding to the collection of meaningful comparative data, union density is reported by government agencies and private organizations as a percent, alternatively, of the total workforce, of the total employed workforce, of the total non-agricultural workforce, of the total non-agricultural private-sector workforce, etc.

23. The figures for IG Metall and DGB are cited in *Foreign Labor Trends: Germany, 1992-1993*, pp. 32-33. IG Metall's membership figures represent a 24% increase from 1990 as a result of incorporation of formerly East German workers.

24. Streeck (1989), p. 125.

25. Streeck (1984), 10.

26. Streeck (1984), p. 9.

27. A major exception is the separate (if quite similar) bargaining and contract signed with Volkswagen, which dates back to the company's distinct status as a state-owned entity.

28. Streeck (1984), p. (13).

29. Ibid, p. 17.

30. Ibid, pp. 14-15.

31. Wolfgang Streeck, "Neo-Corporatist Industrial Relations and the Economic Crisis in West Germany" in John H. Goldthorpe, ed., *Order and Conflict in Contemporary Capitalism* (Oxford: Oxford University Press, 1984), p. 306.

32. Thelen, *op. cit.*, p. 155. See also Harry C. Katz, "The Decentralization of Collective Bargaining: A Literature Review and Comparative Analysis," *Industrial and Labor Relations Review* (October, 1993).

33. Lowel Turner describes, for example, how IG Metall formulated and then promoted specific proposals for "group work. Works councils are granted greater authority in the implementation of group work. Idem (1991), pp. 111-117.

34. Otto Jacobi and Walther Muller-Jentsch, "West Germany: Continuity and Structural Change," in Guido Baglioni and Colin Crouch (eds.), *European Industrial Relations: The Challenge of Flexibility* (London: Sage, 1990).

35. OECD *Yearbook of Labour Statistics, 1988* (Paris: OECD, 1988), p. 198.

36. Union density in manufacturing during the 1980s was around 50%. OECD, *OECD Employment Outlook* (Paris: OECD, July 1991), p. 101.

37. According to most estimates while 39-45% of the German workforce belongs to a union, 90% of it is covered by a union contract. Adams, *op. cit.*, p. 78.

38. David R. Cameron, "Social Democracy, Corporatism, Labour Quiescence and the Representation of Economic Interest in Advanced Capitalist Society," in John H. Goldthorpe (ed) *Order and Conflict in Contemporary Capitalism* (New York: Oxford University Press, 1985). Thelen seems to agree with a 1986 OECD study crediting German unions with "flexible" wage policies, i.e. with responding more to unemployment than to inflation. Thelen, *op. cit.*, p. 57.

39. Motor Vehicle Manufacturers Association of the U.S., *World Motor Vehicle Data, 1990* (Detroit: MMVA, 1993), p. 74. The earnings/compensation ratio in each country has changed over time, but only marginally.

40. On the definition and measurement of total hourly compensation costs see US Department of Labor, Bureau of Labor Statistics, *Hourly Compensation Costs for Production Workers in Manufacturing: 31 Countries or Areas* (May 1994), pp. 110-114.

41. For good analyses of the struggle for the reduction of working time in Germany in the 1980s see Streeck (1988), Rosenberg (1989), pp. 94-99; Thelen (1991) pp. 161-195.

42. In 1992, the third best-paid auto workers in the world were the Swedish, with a total hourly compensation of $24.81. In 1991, German auto workers were again first with an hourly compensation of $28.65, US workers were second with $24.21, while Swedish workers were a close third at $22.61 (the different order reflects the dollar-krona rate change). Motor Vehicles Manufacturers Association, *Motor Vehicles Facts & Figures, 1993* (Detroit: MMVA, 1993), p. 74.

43. Streeck (1987) and (1989), p. 24.

44. Ben Dankbaar, "Sectoral Governance in the Automobile Industries of Germany, Great Britain, and France," in J. Rogers Hollingsworth, Philippe C. Schmitter, and Wolfgang Streeck (eds.) *Governing Capitalist Economies: Performance and Control of Economic Sectors* (New York: Oxford University Press, 1994). For a good list of references to and discussion of "the humanization of work" in German autos dating to the 1970s, see Turner (1991), pp. 103-117. Sweden is probably even more advanced in appreciating the significance of work organization and design for labor-management relations and industrial efficiency. See Christian Berggren, *Alternatives to Lean Production: Work Organization in the Swedish Auto Industry* (Ithaca, N.Y.: ILR Press, 1992).

45. Altshuler et al. (1984), p. 288.

46. Ibid., pp. 287-288.

47. Christoph F. Buechtemann, "Employment Security and Deregulation: The West German Experience," in Buechtemann, (ed.), *op. cit.*, p. 274. See ibid for a good historical and literature review of German dismissal legislation.

48. David, Soskice, "Reconciling Markets and Institutions: The German Apprenticeship System," in Lisa M. Lynch (ed.), *Training and the Private Sector: International Comparisons* (Chicago: The University of Chicago Press, 1994), p. 31. He continues, " . . . although tenure in Japan is even longer than in Germany." See also Walter Galenson, *New Trends in Employment Practices: An International Survey* (New York: Greenwood Press, 1991).

49. See earlier references to the unions' campaign for a reduction in working time.

50. Katherine G. Abraham and Susan N. Houseman, *Job Security in America: Lessons from Germany* (Washington, D.C.: The Brookings Institution, 1993), p. 96.

51. Ibid, pp. 91-99.

52. Christoph F. Buechtemann, *op. cit.*, pp. 282-284.

53. Otto Jacobi, Brendt Keller, and Walther Muller-Jentsch, "Germany: Codetermining the Future?" in Anthony Ferner and Richard Hyman (eds.) *Industrial Relations in the New Europe* (Cambridge, Mass.: Basil Blackwell, 1992).

54. Wolfgang Streeck and Harry Katz were among the first researchers in the English-speaking literature to directly reject the suggestion that German unions were deleterious for the auto industry. See their collaboration in Altshuler et al. (1984), ch. 9. For a more focussed examination of the unions' relationship to the performance of the industry see Streeck (1987 and 1989).

55. Joachim Bergmann and Walter Muller-Jentsch, "The Federal Republic of Germany: Cooperative Unionism and Dual Bargaining System Challenged," in Solomon Barkin (ed), *Worker Militancy and its Consequences: The changing Climate of Western Industrial Relations* (New York: Praeger, 1983). See also Andrei S. Markovits and Christopher S. Allen, "Trade Unions and the Economic Crisis: The West German Case," in Peter Gourevitch, Andrew Martin, George Ross, Chris Allen, Stephen Bornstein and Andrei Markovits, *Unions and Economic Crisis: Britain, West Germany and Sweden* (London: Allen & Unwin, 1984).

56. Turner (1991), p. 105.

57. Kathleen Thelen, *Continuity in Crisis: Labor Politics and Industrial Adjustment in West Germany, 1950-1987*, Ph.D. dissertation, University of California, Berkeley, 1987.

58. See discussion of group work in Turner (1991), pp. 111-117.

59. Ibid, p. 150.

60. Streeck (1988), p. 128.

61. Streeck (1984).

62. Ferdinand Protzman, "Planning an Overhaul of Volkswagen," *New York Times*, March 15, 1993, p. D8.

63. In 1974-75, the company was caught in the gasoline crisis, while it was shifting from the famous Beetle to the new Rabbit (Golf).

64. Protzman, *op. cit.*, p. D8.

65. *Harvard Business Review*, July-August 1991, p. 111.

66. *Sueddeutsche Zeitung*, June 16, 1993, p. 27 (Source: Reuter Textline).

67. Dan Stillman, a UAW spokesman, as quoted by Adrian Bridge and Larry Black, "BMW defies union over American plant," *The Independent*, August 3, 1992, p. 18.

68. Dagmar Opoczynske, an IG Metall spokeswoman, as quoted by Adrian Bridge and Larry Black, "BMW defies union over American plant," *The Independent*, August 3, 1992, p. 18.

69. Ibid.

70. James P. Womack, Daniel T. Jones, and Daniel Roos, *The Machine that Changed the World: The Story of Lean Production* (New York: Harper Perennial, 1990); Alan Altshuler, Martin Anderson, Daniel Jones, Daniel Roos, and James Womack, *The Future of the Automobile: The Report of MIT's International Automobile Program* (Cambridge, Mass.: MIT Press, 1986).

71. Streeck does not explicitly characterize Japanese labor as subjugated. But that is clearly his implication. Streeck (1987), p. 458.

72. Reported by Stephen Kizner, "German's Apprentice System is Seen as Key to Long Boom," *New York Times*, February 6, 1993, p. D1.

73. Typically, over 60% of each cohort group go into apprenticeships, 30% go to higher education, 5% drop out. David Soskice, "Reconciling Markets and Institutions: The German Apprenticeship System," in Lisa M. Lynch (ed.), *Training and the Private Sector: International Comparisons* (Chicago: The University of Chicago Press, 1994), p. 26.

74. See Wolfgang Streeck, Josef Hilbert, Karl-Heinz von Kevelaer, Frederike Maier, and Hajo Weber, *The Role of the Social Partners in Vocational Training in the Federal Republic of Germany* (Berlin: CEDEFOP, 1987). See also C. Hayes and N. Fonda, *Competence and Competition* (London: Insititute for Manpower Studies, 1984). C. Lane, "Vocational training and new production concepts in Germany: Some lessons for Britain," *Industrial Relations Journal* 21 (April 1991). David Soskice, *op. cit.*

75. Reported by Kizner, *op. cit.*, p. D1. Margaret Hilton reports that the corresponding figure for 1984 was almost half as much, $ 4,447. Idem, "Shared Training: Learning from Germany," *Monthly Labor Review* (March 1993), p. 33. See also training cost estimates in Susan N. Houseman, *Job Security Policies in the United States and Japan* (Kalamazoo, Mi.: W.E. Upjohn Institute, 1991).

76. Hilton, *op. cit.*, pp. 33-34. Admittedly, it is very difficult to measure training expenditures with any degree of rigor. Of the firms responding to the German interviews for the O.T.A. study in question, only 42.6% said that they kept separate accounts for even part of their training costs.

77. Hilton, *op. cit.*, p. 33.

78. Kizner, *op. cit.*, p. D5.

79. Thus Germany as well as Japan invest a lot in training, although the German training system is tri-partite (capital, state, labor) while in the Japanese system labor's formal role is minimal.

80. Ibid, p. D5.

81. "The vocational training system is one of the most important sources of the West German "industrial consensus." Streeck (1988).

82. Soskice, *op. cit.*, pp. 33-34. For the role of finance capital's relationship to industry as a determinant of German companies' long-term orientation see Hall (1984 and 1986)

83. Peter A. Hall, "Patterns of Economic Policy: An Organizational Approach," in S. Bornstein, D. Held and J. Krieger (eds), *The State in Capitalist Europe* (London: George Allen & Unwin, 1984); and idem, *Governing the Economy: The Politics of State Intervention in Britain and France* (New York: Oxford University Press, 1986).

84. Hall (1984), p. 24.

85. Alessandro Pizzorno, "Political exchange and collective identity in industrial conflict," in Colin C. Crouch and Alessandro Pizzorno (eds.), *The Resurgence of Class Conflict in Wester Europe since 1968* vol. 2 (New York: Holmes & Meier), pp. 277-297.

86. Hall (1984). Also idem, *Governing the Economy: The Politics of State Intervention in Britain and France* (New York: Oxford University Press, 1986).

87. Banks are barred from exercising such voting power in the U.S. by anti-trust legislation.

88. Melvin A. Fuss and Leonard Waverman, *Costs and Productivity in Automobile Production: The Challenge of Japanese Efficiency* (Cambridge: Cambridge University Press, 1992), p. 39. Fuss and Waverman do not subscribe to the output-per-hour definition of productivity.

89. McKinsey Global Institute, *Manufacturing Productivity* (Washington, D.C.: McKinsey & Co., 1993).

90. Womack et al., *op. cit.*

91. Ibid, pp. 89-95.

92. Their data are collected from a tens of assembly plants around the world, while their characterization of the Japanese production system as "lean production" has been at the center of any debate on industrial performance.

93. German producers such as Mercedes-Benz and Audi are lumped together with the British Rover. Womack et al. (1990), p. 88. See also the lumping together of European producers when they report their analysis of assembly plant performance, in Figures 4.4 through 4.9, in ibid, pp. 86-95. See also the similar analysis of the same study by Krafcik (1988).

94. Womack et al, *op. cit.*, p. 93, Figure 4.8.

95. The first years of the 1990s indicate a certain stabilization of the German auto balance of trade, which loosely coincides with a certain improvement in U.S. autos after the mid-1980s (which we have associated, in turn, with Jointness). However, the number of observations (2) for a German slow-down in the balance-of-trade performance is too small justify any conclusion.

96. I.M. Destler, *Dollar Politics: Exchange Rate Policymaking in the United States* (Washington, D.C.: Institute for International Economics, 1989), p. 24.

97. This is also the conclusion of Destler and Henning (1989), although the authors' focus is on the short-term consequences of the political manipulation of exchange rates.

98. Most frequently, data on auto imports and exports are reported in terms of units of autos. While such data are indeed easier to collect, they are not very reliable of the direction of trade between two countries. This is so particularly when the unit-value of trade is different for each country; the average value of the German car unit exported to the US is much higher than the average value of the US car imported there.

99. OECD *Foreign Trade by Commodity 1992* vol. 1 (Paris: OECD, 1992), p. 454.

100. In 1987, Germany imported 6,532 autos from the US, worth $ 82,474,000, while it exported 377,542 autos to the US, worth $ 8,901,850,000. Motor Vehicle Manufacturers Association of the U.S., *World Motor Vehicle Data, 1988* (Detroit: MMVA, 1990), pp. 32-33. It is also true that the balance of trade between the two auto production regimes remained positive for Germany but shrank, as the 1980s wound down and the 1990s began, reflecting the improvement of US auto production in the late-1980s and early-1990s. In 1991, Germany was importing from the US 38,285 units of autos, worth $ 543,664,000, and exporting to the US 172,446 units of autos, worth $ 4,785,802,000. Motor Vehicle Manufacturers Association of the U.S., *World Motor Vehicle Data, 1992* (Detroit: MMVA, 1990).1992, pp. 42-45.

101. Our method of aggregation does not account for the fact that the number of cars sold from each model is not the same. This may somehow bias the aggregate in favor of less popular (or more expensive) models. However the bias will probably affect German and US autos alike.

102. The "most reliable" German nameplates are Audi, BMW, and Mercedes-Benz. The "most reliable" US nameplates are Lincoln (Crown Victoria for 1978-1983), and Cadillac. Based on Consumer Reports. The choice of these models as the most reliable of each country is corroborated by the ordinal rating of model reliability in *Automotive News* (June 1, 1992).

103. For the distortion this may involve, see the Appendix.

104. On-line research on the *Lexis* database has been crucial for the retrieval of citations of JD Power data, since the Power Report is not readily available to the public. Thus I collected published fragments of JD Power data from auto industry journals and newswires. J.D. Power & Associates permits citation of its data with due credit.

105. Based on JD Power VDS 1990, reported in *Automotive News*, April 10, 1990.

106. Based on JD Power 1991 VDS, reported in *PR Newswire* July 8, 1991.

107. Based on JD Power VDS 1992, reported in *Fortune*, May 18, 1992, p. 105.

108. Based]on JD Power VDS 1993, as reported by *PR Newswire* April 6, 1993.

109. Each year's reported results pertain to 4-5 year-old model. Thus the 1990 results pertain to a 1998-86 model.

110. Claus Offe, "The attribution of public status to interest groups: observations on the West German case," in Suzanne Berger (ed.), *Organizing Interests in Western Europe* (Cambridge: Cambridge University Press, 1981).

CHAPTER 6

Integration through Incorporation in Japanese Auto Production

1. THE PRODUCTION REGIME: LABOR INTEGRATION THROUGH INCORPORATION

The Japanese production regime is characterized by the particular mode of labor inclusion in corporate decision making, **incorporation**. As the etymology of the word suggests, incorporation of labor's interests in the firm refers to the encoding (or the inscription, or the stamping) of labor's fundamental interests into the body of the firm. It refers to the jure or de facto fusion of labor's key interests into the decision making process of the firm. Thus, while labor is not formally represented in the process of strategic decision making of the firm in Japan (its role is consultative only), labor's fundamental productivist interests in employment are protected automatically since layoffs is not a managerial option. Thus while capital-appointed management may appear to decide on corporate policy with the interests of capital in mind, it is in fact not free to promote the interests of capital at the expense of labor's fundamental interests (employment security).

Labor's power over capital in corporate decision making in Japan's incorporation regime consists of two components, **exit** power and **fusion** (or "consolidation") power. Labor's interests are included in corporate decision making through two distinct "points of entry": collective bargaining and lifetime employment. Exit power refers to labor's ability to collectively exit (strike) from any cooperation with capital as a leverage in collective bargaining. Fusion power refers to labor's ability to preclude corporate decisions that entail labor's involuntary separation from the means of production (the firm), through institutionalized lifetime employment guarantees. Labor's fusion power is based on its exit power both historically and logically; however, in daily practices, labor's consolidation power operates autonomously from its exit power. Labor's power secures labor's fundamental interest in job security, creates a pressing need for management to design motivating work and training/reskilling, and gives substance to labor's consultative position in management.

Lifetime Employment in the Japanese Auto Industry

The automobile industry has been a pattern setter for Japanese industrial relations in many respects: from the eradication of revolutionary unions that began in Toyota and Nissan in the early 1950s, to the organization of the first Spring Offensive in 1955 within Sohyo, to the kan-ban ("just-in-time") inventory/work-flow/team method of production, to the kaizen (continuous-improvement) approach to workers' contribution to industrial performance. Auto workers played a central role in the postwar industrial conflicts that led to the adoption of lifetime employment, such as the long and violent strikes at Toyota (1951) and at Nissan (1953)[1].

As Joe Moore's historical research shows, at the end of the Second World War Japanese workers developed radical struggles aimed at **control of production**. The latter is the Japanese "version of workers' control—understood here as the common-sense meaning of control over policy making as well as the process of production."[2] In the early postwar days and months, workers occupied factories, ousted top management, and ran these factories on their own in cooperation with line managers. Contrary to their American counterparts, Japanese unions sought to organize workers and managers in enterprize-wide unions. The consequent counter-offensive by employers, while successful in defeating the unions' political aspirations, brought employers a very expensive victory: the price was the incorporation of key workers' demands into corporate policy.[3] First among these was the demand for excluding employment levels from managerial discretion. As a Harvard Business School Project concludes:

> "Ironically, though labor moved away from its political agenda, one of the basic changes brought about by the strikes was, in fact, **political**: the workers had established their legitimacy as an **integral**

part of the enterprise. Management had been democratized; power would be shared, consultation would be carried out . . . From the lose-lose experience of the strikes, both sides emerged determined to make future transactions win-win."[4]

Indeed, it was militant postwar strikes such as the well-chronicled strike against Nissan Motor Co.[5], or the 193-day strike against Nikko Muroran in 1950, that established lifetime employment. In the latter case, although the union lost, and 662 out of 3,742 employees were discharged,

> "the discharge costs amounted to almost twice the company's capital. This dispute made it clear to management that attempts to discharge would be met with determined worker resistance, even under the most moderate leadership, and would be very costly. [The] dispute contributed to the subsequent establishment of the de facto right of the regular worker to obtain permanent employment.[6]

The terms of the accommodation reached between capital and labor in Japan, centering on employment guarantees are not always explicit, except in the public sector. However, as will be documented, they are as constraining and relevant as the also largely tacit British constitution. Moreover, Japanese labor law makes dismissal justifiable only as a measure of last resort; the provision of bonuses or wage increases after dismissal is considered proof that the dismissals were not warranted.[7]

That Japanese relations of production are institution- rather than culture-bound is most succinctly argued by Charles Sabel.

> "What distinguishes U.S. from Japanese agreements is that the relevant cases are much more the substance of the rules they provide rather than the spirit in which those rules are interpreted. Until the culturalists can explain the extensive presence of rules in Japanese agreements and their content, the claim than the interpretive spirit of the agreement is decisive and its letter irrelevant strikes me as, well, spiritualist."[8]

Lifetime employment is a postwar creation of Japanese labor-management relations. Before the war, lifetime employment existed only for a tiny fraction of the workforce: the foremen and managers of some companies[9]. It was only after the war, and after intense labor-capital confrontations, that lifetime employment guarantees began to include blue-collar, production workers.[10] Thus, what has been too often referred as the "traditional system of lifetime employment in Japan," is in fact rather new.[11] Alongside the dispensability of labor, the postwar union movement also sought to eradicate labor's status inferiority in relation to management. This was also achieved after intense struggles against determined capitalist opposition.

At the end of the postwar struggles, capital had defeated labor's radical aspirations. Labor leaders and their organizations were vanquished. However, these were Pyrrhic victories for capital, as they were achieved at a very high price: adopting labor's most radical demand, the inseparability of the means of production from labor, albeit in a less threatening form. In the production regime that emerged, Japanese auto workers' interests were incorporated in the firm's decision making institutions through regularized collective bargaining but also through the institution of lifetime employment.[12]

Lifetime employment, it must be stressed, does not cover a small minority of employees. In large manufacturing firms, such as the auto firms under consideration, lifetime employment is enjoyed by the large majority of the employees. According to data from the Japanese Ministry of Labor, the proportion of male employees covered by lifetime employment (variously referred to as "permanent" or "standard" or "core" or "regular" employees) varies according to the size of the company, from around 50% for small companies, to 88% for companies with more than one thousand employees such as those in the automobile industry (Table 1). Most female workers, however, reflecting the entrenched sexism of Japanese society, are not covered by lifetime employment. Nevertheless, econometric evidence "strongly suggests that Japanese women, on average, enjoy much greater stability in employment than does the average American worker."[13] Thus, the overall proportion of Japanese workers protected by lifetime employment is much larger than the proportion of workers covered by any type of union contract in the U.S. It must be stressed that lifetime employment fundamentally alters traditional precepts concerning the *raison d'etre* and *modus operandi* of the firm. In a radical departure from neo-classical assumptions about the firm, today's Japanese corporation is not, effectively, the exclusive property of capital (stockholders); it operates under the joint control and for the joint benefit of capital and labor[15]. In the words of Masahiko Aoki,

"[The typical Japanese auto firm] is **a coalition** of the body of quasi-permanent employees and the body of stockholders, and [the] behavioral characteristics of the [typical Japanese auto firm] are understood as the **equilibrium outcome** of the interaction between the two."[16]

Table 1: Proportion of 'Permanent' To All Employees[14]

	(Males, All Industries, %)			
SIZE	All	1000		
YEAR	companies	or more	100-999	10-99
1975	72.4	85.0	69.8	57.8
1980	69.7	84.9	70.1	55.4
1985	71.2	88.1	71.6	54.6

The central position of labor's interests in the Japanese firm is borne out in the sharply different self-perception of management's role vis a vis labor and capital in Japan compared to the U.S. (Table 2). Asked whose interests their companies placed most importance on, American managers responded that consumers' interests (46.8%) and shareholders' interests (44.7%) came first, with employees' interests (8.5%) and society's as a whole (4.3%) trailing far behind. For Japanese managers the order was very different: employees (35.8%) came first, followed by shareholders (22.4%), consumers (20/9%), and society as a whole (19.4%). Asked if they would keep down profits for shareholders if necessary in order to maintain jobs for employees, 94.0% of Japanese managers answered yes, compared to 53.2% of American managers.[17] While the meaning of survey results is often questionable, the dramatic differences in the answers above underscore the substantial U.S.-Japan difference in the position of labor in the company.

Table 2: "Whose Interests Does Your Company Place Most Importance On?"

RESPONDENTS	RESPONSES			
	shareholders	employees	consumers	society
J Managers	22.4%	35.8%	20.9%	19.4%
US Managers	44.7%	8.5%	46.8%	4.3%

Japanese workers also perceive their relationship to the firm very differently than their American counterparts. Reportedly, Japanese workers do not describe their morning commute as "going to my job", but as "going to my company."[18] When an international survey asked Japanese and American workers of large manufacturing companies whether their company's profit making would enhance their own well-being, 85.3% of Japanese workers responded in the affirmative, while the U.S. figure was 56.3%.[19]

The core medium of labor-management communications in Japan is **joint consultation** meetings between representatives of management and of the enterprise union (see below). All auto firms, and about 80% of all union and 40% of non-union firms have such bodies.[20] Joint consultation meetings were formalized in the 1970s, when severe turbulence in the auto markets initiated faster adaptation in production schedules as well as in work design. It is very important to note that the subject matter of these labor-management joint consultations includes "management" issues, such as basic management policy, plans for production and sales, changes in company organization, the introduction of new machinery or equipment base on new technology, rationalization of production administration) as well as wages, bonuses, working hours, leave and absences, layoffs and dismissals, health and safety, and training programs and welfare. There is considerable overlap between the subject matter and the individuals involved in joint consultation and collective bargaining institutions. Joint consultation supplements rather than substitutes collective bargaining, the former being broader in scope but less binding than the latter.

It must be noted, however, that joint consultation meetings, as their name suggests, have the character of consultation rather than of joint decision-making. Management can, in principle, decide a certain issue over labor's opposition; the more an issue is a "management issue" the more likely that it will be decided by management, with labor receiving only an explanation for the policy. As a result, joint consultation meetings often operate as information sharing rather than decision making forums. To be sure, this fact underscores the fundamental inequality in the management-labor relationship, and the regime's fundamentally capitalist formation.

Having said that, we must also keep in mind that managerial decisions in direct opposition to labor's fundamental interests is **not** part of the regime's *modus operandi*, not the least because the critical issue of employment reductions is precluded from the menu of policy options available to management. Given the preclusion of capital's (and management's) ultimate productivist sanction against labor, layoffs, the privileged position of management in decision making does not result in the marginalization of labor's fundamental interests in the decision making process. Management has a genuine interest in reaching an agreement with labor on corporate policy—as opposed to in simply "going through the motions" of consultation— because so much of the firm's performance is predicated on a devoted and cooperative workforce.

Apart from joint consultation, there are company, establishment, and workshop **production committees**, where union stewards and section managers discuss quarterly, monthly and weekly production plans, including workloads, delivery dates, work allocation and overtime. Issues such as how many workers it will take to produce so much product in such and such a time, how much overtime will be needed and whether this is within the overtime agreement, etc, are discussed at production committees.

A more immediate form of participation for individual employees is **workshop meetings** headed by workshop supervisors, at which employees and supervisors discuss workplace issues as in production committees mentioned above. Of the establishments surveyed in 1984, 77% had workshop meetings.[21]

Additionally, there are small-group activities and suggestion schemes, officially registered as **Quality Circles**, introduced in the 1960s. Groups meet once a week or once every two weeks for about one hour. Typically, about three to six months are spent on one issue or theme. Quality improvements, rationalization of work procedures, safety and cost cutting are common issues. Suggestions on company policy are filed both by individual workers and by quality circles as a whole. The average number of suggestions per person per year is 12, of which 7 are reportedly taken up.[22] In general, enterprise unions evaluate small-group activities and suggestion schemes quite highly.[23] These *kaizen*, or continuous-improvement activities, are prevalent in all auto companies, although there is some variation in their form. Thus in Toyota, emphasis is placed in quality circles, while Honda emphasizes individual initiative and innovation.[24]

Collective Bargaining in the Japanese Auto Industry

The right of workers to organize, bargain, and act collectively is constitutionally assured in Japan, as it is in Germany but not in the U.S. In Japan unions are neither craft-based nor industry-based. Instead, unions are organized on the basis of individual firms. Enterprise unions organize blue-collar and white-collar employees of a firm alike. This results in the paradoxical, for Western standards, situation where middle-level managers of a firm are often members of the same union that represents production workers. While all the employees (except top-level management) of a firm usually belong to a single enterprise union, Japanese labor law allows more than one union to represent employees of a firm (union pluralism).[25] Working conditions, including wages, are determined by collective bargaining between these enterprise unions and individual employers.

Enterprise unions are organized into industrial federations, which in turn are affiliated with a centralized national labor organization. Both the national organizations and the industrial federations deal with issues difficult to handle at the level of enterprise unions, such as demands concerning political and institutional reforms. Thus, the 220,000-member Nissan Workers Union, along with 11 other major auto enterprise unions, is a member of the industry-wide confederation Jidosha Soren (Japan Automobile Workers Union), which has a membership of about 728,000.[26] Jidosha Soren holds consultations with industrial management organizations and directs and coordinates the activities of the enterprise unions affiliated with it. It is sectorally associated with the Japan Council of Metalworkers, which belongs to the cross-national International Federation of Metalworkers. Since 1989, all union organizations have affiliated with a single national union organization, Rengo, which has a membership of about 7,850,000.[27]

Actual compensation levels and working conditions within a firm are determined in annual collective bargaining between the enterprise union and the individual firm during the period of "Shunto" (Spring Offensive). However, the mobilization for and the general parameters of these negotiations are directed by the industrial and national union organizations. These annual mobilizations and negotiations involve the vast majority of the rank and file and the union leaders. About 80% of organized workers participate in the Shunto.

Japanese auto workers, in a sharp deviation from their counterparts in other advanced capitalist countries, are not paid hourly wages[28], but monthly salaries and biannual bonuses. The typical monthly earnings of a Japanese auto worker consists of three parts: a person-related payment, a job-related payment, and allowances for such things as housing, family, training, overtime, and commuting costs. The person-related payment is based on the employee's seniority and merit, the latter determined biannually by supervisors on the basis of an elaborate evaluation scheme. Thus the remuneration system complements the right of workers to stay within a company by rewarding them for it (seniority pay), while it introduces an element of conditionality in that reward, by providing for bonuses for enterprise and for individual performance.[29]

The process of employee evaluation, while not immune to unfairness and favoritism, is more shielded from abuse than one might suspect. First, the merit assessment procedure is standardized by the personnel department of the firm and monitored by the union to ensure that arbitrary decisions are not made by individual supervisors. Second, because of job rotation, an employee is assessed by many different supervisors during his/her career. Three, the reputation of a supervisor among his/her subordinates has a direct bearing on the career opportunity of the supervisor; the supervisor is subject to "informal" reciprocal monitoring by his/her subordinates.[30]

While Japanese unions' ultimate leverage in collective bargaining is their exit power (strike), they rarely resort to strikes. Figure 1 charts the annual number of working days lost to strikes as a share of the total number of working days, for non-agricultural industries. Clearly, the level of strike activity in the 1980s has fallen to a trickle. The much higher level of strikes in the 1950s underscores the conflictual origins of Japan's postwar production regime, while the resurgence of strikes in the mid-late-1970s underscores that enterprise unions have not lost their ability to strike since the 1950s, but use strikes only when their consolidation (lifetime employment) power does not suffice to protect their interests: indeed, the oil crisis shook the Japanese economy more severely than its competitors, as Japan was more dependent on oil imports for its energy, and more dependent on exports for its growth. As we will see in the next section, the mid-1970s is the only period when layoffs took place in the auto industry.

FIGURE 1

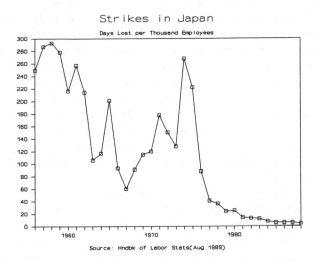

Strikes in Japan

Days Lost per Thousand Employees

Source: Hndbk of Labor Stats(Aug. 1989)

Figure 2 offers a comparison of the level of strikes in Japan and in the U.S. in the 1980s, in the form of working days lost to strikes per thousand employees in non-agricultural industries. Clearly, there is a qualitative difference in the volume of strikes between the two countries.

American observers of Japan's enterprise-based unions may wonder whether these are akin to the American "company" or "yellow" unions of the 1920s. The origin of enterprise unionism is not particularly enlightening in this regard. On the one hand, Japan's enterprise unions were created as such by militant workers themselves, immediately after the end of the Second World War. On the other hand, companies played a central role in decimating these radical unions in the 1950s and encouraging the creation of more moderate, "second" unions. The territorial organization of enterprise-based unions in Japan indicates that their difference from "industrial unions" in the U.S. is smaller than one might surmise: in the U.S. auto industry, collective bargaining agreements are made at the enterprise, not the industrial level,[31] while in the Japanese auto industry, enterprise-level bargaining is coordinated by an industrial federation of enterprise unions.[32]

FIGURE 2

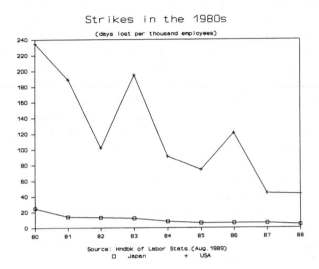

Strikes in the 1980s

(days lost per thousand employees)

Source: Hndbk of Labor Stats.(Aug.1989)
□   Japan   +   USA

One may also wonder whether the membership of foremen and middle-level managers in the enterprise union compromises the interests of the production workers of the same union. After all, in the U.S. labor law, supervisory employees are prohibited to join the union of production employees for fear of thus compromising the latter's independence from company intimidation. Many in the labor movement consider such segregation a useful tool for fostering class consciousness among production workers.[33] Most pertinent here, we believe, are two observations. First, whatever adverse effects this inclusiveness of the enterprise union may have for the formulation and representation of the interests of production workers, these must be considered alongside the possible positive effects of such inclusiveness: contributing to the development among foremen and managers of a union consciousness and a good appreciation of production workers' needs, which would otherwise be lacking. This is particularly significant given that a sizeable portion of the board of directors in Japan are former members of executive committees of their enterprise-based unions.[34]

Secondly, plural unionism in Japan curbs the possibility of management interests dominating the union's leadership by allowing workers who feel "sold out" by their union to be represented by a rival union. It is even possible that a closer relationship exists between the union leadership and the rank-and-file interests in Japan than in the U.S.. Plural unionism in Japan compels the union leadership to rely on consensus building to gain the support of different constituent members; whereas exclusive representation provisions in the U.S. allows the union leadership to rely on the support of the "median" member.[35]

Our analysis so far has only demonstrated that the **formal structure** of the Japanese auto production regime is **consistent with** our hypothesis that labor integration through incorporation represents labor's power in corporate decision making. It is still possible, however, that we have interpreted this formal structure too optimistically. What we have described as institutions of labor integration and incorporation are, in fact, seen by some as institutions of labor cooptation or "super-exploitation". It is suggested, for example, that lifetime employment does not, in reality, offer job security, and that the joint representation of production workers and foremen in the same enterprise union acts as a mechanism of legitimizing low wages and management's goals.[36]

In order to adjudicate between our "optimistic" interpretation of labor's position in the Japanese auto production regime and other, more "pessimistic" interpretations, we shall turn to an analysis of the **substantive outcomes** of the regime for labor: the degree of employment stability which is actually enjoyed by labor, and the actual levels of labor's compensation.

2. LABOR'S POWER AND REDISTRIBUTIVE AND PRODUCTIVIST OUTCOMES

It is widely believed that labor in Japan is paid less than in the U.S.. In fact, Japanese labor's alleged low pay is the basis of the super-exploitation thesis/explanation of Japanese industrial relations and competitive success. Labor in Japan, according to the super-exploitation thesis, is culturally and/or organizationally ill-equipped to stand against management: as a result, workers get low wages, which helps Japanese companies make products of better value (quality/price) than Americans and other competitors. Of course not all approaches to Japanese production center on the super-exploitation of labor. Some analyses consider labor's weakness as symptomatic of rather than causal for the Japanese system of production, which these analyses define through non-labor categories such as the role of the state, the role of the organization of capital, the role of culture, etc. However, none examines Japanese labor's power as a defining parameter of Japan's production regime.

We have hypothesized, contrary to all variants of the super-exploitation thesis, that labor has been more powerful in Japan than in the U.S., at least in the auto industry. We have argued that labor's power in Japan is based in part on exit and in part on fusion. Labor is more powerful in Japan than in the U.S. because in Japan labor's redistributive **and** productivist interests are included in corporate decision making (integration), the former interests mainly through collective bargaining, and the latter through incorporation with the means of production (lifetime employment).

If our hypothesis is correct, and Japanese auto workers exercise significant influence in the firm, as we described, we should find that Japanese workers's interests are well-served by the production regime compared to their American counterparts. In what follows, we examine whether the Japanese auto production regime's outcomes confirm or contradict labor's hypothesized power in redistributive and productivist decisions, by analyzing key redistributive and productivist outcomes: wages and employment stability, respectively.

However, we do not expect to find that both wages and employment security are necessarily higher in Japan than in the U.S.. First, it is possible that Japanese wages are lower, in absolute terms, than American wages, as a result not of Japanese labor's weakness, but of the low point of departure of the Japanese economy after the devastation of the Second World War, especially since there was not even an auto industry to reconstruct (as, for example, was the case in Germany). Accordingly, we expect that Japanese auto workers have been receiving higher wage **increases** than their American counterparts, if not higher **wages**.

Second, it is possible that Japanese wages may be lower than American wages not because of Japanese labor's relative weakness, but as a consequence of its strength: precisely because both redistributive and productivist decisions of the firm are within Japanese labor's legitimate area of influence, Japanese labor can possibly trade-off real wage increases in exchange for no layoffs in a year of severe crisis in the industry. Accordingly, we expect that, if wages are lower in Japan than in the U.S., then employment security will be higher in Japan than in the U.S. by a larger margin than the wage differential.[37]

labor's power and redistributive outcomes

In order to compare the compensation of Japanese auto workers to American compensation we provide hourly compensation data both for Japan and the U.S. (it will be remembered that Japanese workers receive monthly salaries).[38] Moreover, in comparing auto worker compensation in Japan and the U.S. we must keep in mind that often-cited comparisons of "hourly earnings" can be misleading because hourly earnings do not constitute the same proportion of the total hourly compensation received by labor in the two countries. Thus what is reported as "hourly earnings" in Japan is 84% of total hourly compensation, while what is reported as "hourly earnings" in the U.S. is only 63% of total hourly compensation. Table 3 shows how the 1992 total hourly compensation of American and Japanese automobile production workers breaks down into hourly earnings and other monetary benefits.[39]

Table 3

	Hourly Earnings	Additional Monetary Benefits	Total Compensation
JAPAN	2,043.00 Yen	400.00 Yen	2,443.00 Yen
U.S.A.	15.19 US$	9.02 US$	24.21 US$

But let us examine the evolution of labor's compensation in Japanese autos, and compare it to that of American auto workers.

Figure 3 charts the evolution of hourly compensation costs in the Japanese auto industry, in US dollar terms, from 1975 to 1992. The conversion of Japanese costs from yen to US dollars serves to establish a common yardstick in measuring wages in different countries. In 1975, hourly compensation in Japanese autos was **half** of its American equivalent, when measured in US dollar terms. It can also be seen that ever since, the Japan-U.S. gap in this regard has been diminishing. By 1990, Japanese hourly compensation was over 80% of its American equivalent.

While the comparison of hourly compensation costs in dollar terms provides us with a good idea of the comparative evolution of the standard of living of Japanese and American auto workers, it is not sufficient as a demonstration of Japanese labor's redistributive power, for two main reasons. First, changes in the dollar compensation differentials between Japanese and American auto workers may reflect changes in the exchange rate rather than changes between Japanese and American auto workers' redistributive powers. Exchange-rate fluctuations are likely to distort labor's actual redistributive power if they are short-lived. A sustained strengthening of the yen against the dollar, inasmuch as it translates in a sustained improvement in the purchasing power of the Japanese worker, cannot be dismissed as merely an exchange-rate anomaly. A lasting improvement in the dollar value of Japanese wages reflects an improvement in Japanese labor's ability to advance its redistributive interests.

FIGURE 3

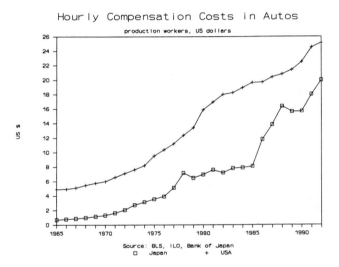

Hourly Compensation Costs in Autos
production workers, US dollars

Source: BLS, ILO, Bank of Japan
□ Japan   + USA

However, there is a second reason why the dollar value of hourly compensation of Japanese and American auto workers may not reflect respective redistributive power. The dollar compensation figures compare **absolute** levels of compensation between the two countries, with no regard to possibly critical differences in the cost of living.

The above problems with the dollar value of compensation can be circumvented by comparing the evolution of Japanese and American labor's compensation in autos in national currency terms, adjusted for inflation. The comparability of yen to dollar wages is facilitated by

comparing per cent **changes** in compensation.[40] Figure 4 charts the
annual changes in **real** hourly compensation costs for production auto
workers in Japan and the U.S..[41] The results are quite startling for the
stereotypical view of wages in Japan. Japanese auto workers have been
receiving a more secure and faster-rising hourly compensation than
their American counterparts. Japanese auto workers's real hourly
compensation fell in only 3 of the 24 years since 1968, while that of
American workers fell in 12 years. It must be also be noted in Figure 4
that Japanese workers have been enjoying higher real wage increases
not only during the decade of Japanese autos' phenomenal global
success, the 1980s, but even before then, during the late-1960s and
early-1970s.

FIGURE 4

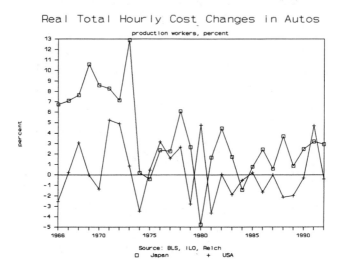

Real Total Hourly Cost Changes in Autos

production workers, percent

Source: BLS, ILO, Reich
□ Japan   + USA

Lastly, comparisons between Japanese and American labor
compensation must be assessed against compensation differentials
between Japanese and American corporate executives. In the U.S. the
total compensation of an average chief executive officer (CEO) was
110 times greater than that of the average worker, but only 17 times
greater in Japan.[42] "Unlike companies in [...] the U.S. where
shareholders reward executives for cutting costs, in Japan, management
is expected to make sacrifices before it imposes restructuring on the rest

of the employees."[43] While these compensation differentials refer to large companies in general, they are quite applicable for the auto industry as well. In 1990, General Motors' president and chief executive officer Robert C. Stempel's compensation was $ 1.44 million,[44] when the average compensation of an auto worker was 40,478.[45]

labor's power and productivist outcomes

Let us now examine whether Japanese auto workers are indeed more influential in corporate decision making than their American counterparts, as hypothesized, by comparing the respective regimes' outcomes for labor's central productivist interest, employment stability. A large econometric analysis by Abraham and Houseman concludes that

> "Japanese workers appear to enjoy, on average, considerably greater
> job security than American workers."[46]

Further, consistent with our hypothesized functional integration of labor and management, the authors find another difference between the Japanese and American employment patterns. In Japan whatever (little) adjustment in employment occurs in response to changes in demand affect production and nonproduction workers similarly, whereas in the U.S. the brunt of employment adjustment falls primarily on production workers.[47]

Figure 5 charts the evolution of annual employment levels for production workers in the auto industries of Japan and the U.S.. It can be seen that, as hypothesized, Japanese auto workers are enjoying significantly higher employment security than their American counterparts.

The results of Figure 5 are brought into sharper relief if we compare annual **changes** in employment levels in the two auto industries. Figure 6 charts annual employment changes expressed as the difference in employment levels in two consecutive years as a percentage of the employment level in the first year.[48] It can be seen that employment reductions in Japan are nearly **half as frequent** as in the U.S.: they occur on 7 occasions in a 20-year period in Japan, compared to 12 occasions in the U.S.. Even more important, employment reductions in Japan are more than **four times smaller** than in the U.S.: employment reductions average 1.7% of total employment in Japan, compared to 7.3% in the U.S..

Figures 5 and 6 make it clear that lifetime employment and labor incorporation are rooted in reality, corresponding to substantive outcomes in employment security. Whether these outcomes are actually attributable to labor's power in the regime, as we have been arguing, or to other fortuitous circumstances for Japanese labor will be addressed in the concluding chapter.

FIGURE 5

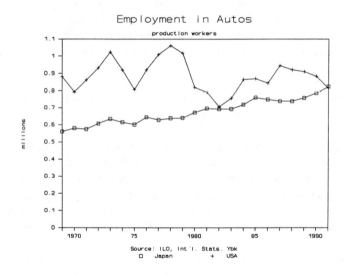

FIGURE 6

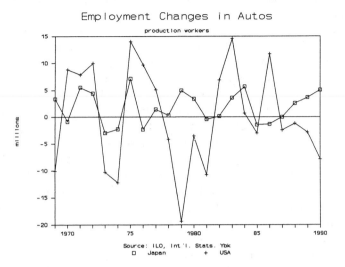

Employment Changes in Autos

3. ILLUSTRATIONS

In 1983, the Japan Automobile Workers' Union agreed with Nissan Motor Company on the basic principles accompanying the introduction of new technologies: prior consultation, employment security (no layoffs due to the introduction of new technology), adequate industrial safety and hygiene, education and training, and securing the adaptability and capacity of each individual affected by transfers through retraining.[49]

The Office of Technology Assessment estimates that auto workers in Japan receive three times as much training each year as workers in American-owned plants in the U.S..[50] New workers are trained in groups for one week immediately after they start employment. During their first year of service, they attend the company's own vocational training school for 640 hours. Training to cope with technical change is organized in each workshop. In body-assembly shops, for example, three courses aim to train workers in the following skills: the operation of automated equipment and machinery, including robots; developing test cars through various welding abilities (such as gas-, arc-, and spot-welding), craft-type skill, such as fitting sheet metal processing and soldering. In the spring of 1981 a "skills inventory" system was introduced which keeps detailed personnel records of each worker on computer files.[51]

By 1985, a total of 730 industrial robots had been introduced in Nissan Motor Company. Theoretically, each robot substitutes 0.7 workers,[52] and, since the robots are worked two shifts a day, each robot substitutes 1.4 workers. However, these robots had been introduced over ten years, with joint consultation with the Nissan Workers Union, and were accompanied with no layoffs. Instead, robots replaced hazardous and monotonous jobs, and resulted only in intra-plant transfers of workers. In the 1980s, the union become more conscious about the possible adverse effects of automation and put forward demands for a formal agreement on new technology to supplement the less formal process of joint consultation. It has asked that prior consultation be applied even at the initial stage of planning the introduction of new technologies. This demand, it should be stressed, merely reflected the strengthening of long-established labor-management practices. The unions' demand was a reaction to the company's new president's attempt to restore management prerogatives in the area of technological change. In March 1983, both parties agreed to sign a new contract on the introduction of new technology, based largely on the union's proposal.[53]

With respect to all rationalization plans and new technologies, enterprise unions have made the preservation of employment security for the core work force at large plants a major focus of their efforts, with considerable success.[54] The automobile manufacturers and major component makers have reported that the overall job employment impact of the microelectronic technology was marginal. Far greater was the influence of these factors: (1) the level of production, (2) the product mix (more manual work was required for production of the higher class vehicles) (3) the design of cars, and (4) work organization, i.e. industrial engineering. All assemblers stressed that minor improvements at the workshop level originating from the quality circles and the suggestion scheme had greater cumulative effect on labor productivity than microelectronic technology. At Toyota, for example, 1.9 million suggestions, or 38.8 per employee, were made in one year. Of this total, 95 per cent were adopted by the company.[55]

There has been no major labor dispute about microelectronic innovation in Japan. According to the Japan Automobile Workers Union, the following reasons were behind the smooth adoption of technological change. First, the industry kept growing, although at a slower rate that before. Second, job security was more or less assured to every existing worker by the unwritten company constitution against the dismissal of workers. Third, consultation with workers took place as a matter of routine procedure whenever innovation was planned, so much so that some firms let workers choose the robots to be installed in their workplace. Fourth, most robots had been installed to reduce dirty and/or strenuous work, and robots often opened up new, more creative types of work. the JAW confirmed the authenticity of company reps statements summarized above.[56]

While in some companies the union has only a de facto and not de jure veto power on innovation plans, in most automobile companies its veto power is de jure as well. In 1983 an unnamed automobile company concluded an agreement with the union on the introduction of new technology, according to which management would have to consult with union before the introduction of new technology, and could not introduce new technology without the consent of the union. Indeed, on the basis of this agreement, the union has sometimes demanded successfully to change the introduction plan of new machines because of the estimated negative influences of these machines on workers.[57]

What the labor union usually demands with respect to the introduction of robots is that resulting personnel transfers are confined to the boundaries of the establishment, that wages and working conditions should not deteriorate as a result of personnel transfers, and that proper training should be given to the workers concerned beforehand and afterwards.[58]

Despite a deep recession that hit the Japanese economy in the 1990s, lifetime employment is still "entrenched, and firms are making most of their cutbacks by reducing the hiring of new graduates."[59] In fact, every time Japan's economy slows down, influential foreign observers can be counted on to write the system's obituary. Such reports reached a crescendo when influential news publications, led by the Wall Street Journal and the Economist, vied with one another in printing comments from anonymous sources suggesting that lifetime employment was doomed. But according to *Fortune* magazine, Japan is not about to give up lifetime employment, and the system is "stronger than ever."[60] This is a key reason why Japan, with an unemployment rate of just 3% at its peak during the last recession, has bucked the trend toward downsizing and mass layoffs.

There is a profound self-reinforcing effect of the Japanese production regime, in the way that lifetime employment helps stabilize the economy in times of recession. To an individual employer, the no-firing rule may seem undesirable but, from the regime's or the whole nation's point of view, the rule pays off in damping the downswing in the business cycle. In other regimes, by contrast, workers fired in a recession necessarily cut back their consumption, which throws other workers out of a job and thus further burdens the national welfare system. In Japan it is believed, not unreasonably, that workers contribute more to national output if they are in jobs rather than in dole queues. Thus the emerging picture is one of a highly organized and quite self-sustaining employment system—a system that is the antithesis of the cultural hangover it has long been portrayed as in the West.

4. IN SEARCH OF EFFICIENCY

We have hypothesized that Japan's auto production regime (a) expresses the extensive incorporation of Japanese auto workers's fundamental interests in corporate policy relative to their American counterparts; and (b) that the Japanese auto production regime is more efficient than the American one. Having already addressed (a), we now turn to address the efficiency of the Japanese regime.

Besides providing labor with employment stability, lifetime employment plays a crucial role in fostering another characteristic of Japanese production politics that is critical for its efficiency: the functional integration, as opposed to segregation, of labor and management in the organization of and coordination of work. Related expressions of such integration are the broad, as opposed to narrow skills of the workforce, the team system of task coordination, and the close interaction, as opposed to isolation, between company divisions (marketing, design, engineering, manufacturing). There are three reasons why we expect the Japanese regime to utilize its resources more efficiently than the American regime.

First, the Japanese regime is likely to be more efficient because it is likely to be less wasteful of human capital. In the American regime, a company can lay off a worker during a period of slow product demand, rehire the worker six months later, and consider this adjustment practically cost-free and therefore quite efficient. Examining this process from the vantage point of the regime as a whole, however, would discern other costs involved in this process of adjustment—costs which are called "externalities" because they are dumped elsewhere: the costs (to the worker and/or the community) of depression, alienation, crime, and others associated with unemployment. According to the latter approach, a hire-fire method of adjustment is wasteful and therefore inefficient for the regime as a whole because it idles labor power and the spirit of the worker.

Second, the Japanese regime is likely to be more efficient than the American regime because the integration of labor and management functions in the labor process facilitates the much-touted need for flexibility in production or continuous adjustment of production to product market signals. Integration of labor and management functions results in a smaller conception-execution divide in the production process than under the American taylorism identified by Braverman and others. Job rotation, teamwork, and discretion over the quality of production gives workers the skills necessary to help minimize adaptation of the organization of work to changes in product design. Indeed, in Japanese auto companies model changeover is achieved several times faster than in American companies.

Third, the Japanese regime is likely to be more efficient than the American regime because, to the extent to which Japanese management is more restricted than American management in adjusting employment to changes in demand, it is **forced** to discover efficiency improvements to compensate for the added costs it may bear due to over-employment. In other words, because Japanese management cannot externalize the cost of layoffs to the workers and the community, it is compelled to find new sources of improving productivity. Thus, for example, while American managers may be willing to forego the benefit of incorporating the "hands-on knowledge of the worker" to the production process for the sake of greater control over the worker, Japanese managers may not be afforded such luxury. Moreover, given the cooperative relationship between labor and management that results from lifetime employment, Japanese management is in less need of giving priority to control over efficiency. The Japanese regime is likely to be more efficient because labor inputs are more skilled as a result of management's need to invest in worker training given its inability to simply discharge workers as their original skills become obsolete.

The linchpin of Japan's system of integrating labor and management functions in the production process is *kanban* or just-in-time delivery. This is a method of organizing the timing of component inputs and outputs of a production unit. In the U.S. and other auto industries, until very recent changes, the production schedule of a production unit is determined centrally by top management, according to its analysis and forecasts of demand and supply conditions. Unforeseen changes in component supply or product demand are addressed by a system of buffer stocks. By contrast, in Japan, central planning provides only the broad parameters within which each team/workshop/plant adjusts its contribution to the chain of production in direct response to changes in the supply of (quality) components to it and in the demand for its product.

While the just-in-time provides for savings in inventory costs and responsiveness to market conditions, it is also a very "fragile" system of production— a disruption in one part of the production chain brings the whole chain to a standstill. The system cannot function properly in the context of workers willing to subvert production.[61] It must be stressed that the kanban is not only a method of inventory organization and production pacing, but also a method of quality control. The same unit of workers of working assembling a component is also responsible for the quality of that component; defects must be checked for and fixed as they are made. The kanban method of production requires that workers have the skills and authority needed to improve production. The most famous symbol of the Japanese auto workers' skill and discretion in the production process is their ability to stop the assembly line when they detect a defect, without having to consult a supervisor.[62]

Functional integration in Japanese production is widely recognized in the literature, as are the broad skills of Japanese workers. Various, although largely synonymous, terms have been used to conceptualize Japan's functional integration in contrast to the U.S.'s functional segregation: "horizontal-vertical information structure"[63], "organizational integration-segmentation"[64], "lean-mass production"[65], "lean-bufferred production"[66], or "fragile-robust management systems[67].

It is widely agreed that the way in which work is organized and coordinated is intimately related to the level and quality of skills possessed by the workforce: they are mutually reinforcing. Indeed, "blue-collar workers in large Japanese firms share important skill and work characteristics with white-collar workers in Western countries . . . The system under which Japanese workers gain their skills enables them to perform a wide range of jobs, and is a cornerstone of both internal markets and industrial relations in Japan."[68] The team system is also related to the two other constituents of functional integration; it is in fact the synthesis/embodiment of the other two. Not surprisingly, the extensiveness of coverage of the team system in a plant often serves as a key criterion for classifying the plant as "traditional" or "modern." It is also noted that not only labor has certain management skills, but that management also has labor skills. As already mentioned, top-level management is recruited internally from lower managerial ranks, while the latter often rise from the ranks of workers.[69]

There is less consensus on the relationship between Japan's lifetime employment and functional integration. While no one denies that lifetime employment is **compatible with** functional integration (and its broadly-skilled workforce, organized in teams), no one has made the argument that the functional integration of management and labor in Japan is **predicated on** lifetime employment, or its functional equivalent). A few authors, however, do come close to making such an argument. Kenney and Florida, for example, note that lifetime employment, by discouraging employee turnover, encourages a firm to invest in training, given the low risk of losing trained employees to a "poaching" firm[70]. Lazonick points out that lifetime employment elicits more employee motivation and cooperation in work, which are requisites for a well-functioning team system.[71] Further, Lazonick alludes to a point which we stipulate, that lifetime employment in effect **forces** management to invest generously in worker training. Since management is "stuck" with a given workforce, it has a strong stake in preparing them to handle changing work requirements and be eager and willing to cooperate with management in daily problem-solving functions[72].

Functional integration becomes possible if, and only if, (a) management is assured that labor will not use the discretion it is allowed under functional integration to undermine efficiency, and (b) labor is assured that its willing cooperation with management in directing work will not affect its interests adversely by, for example, being discharged as a consequence of productivity improvements it helped achieve. Under more "traditional" production systems, such as the prewar American auto production system described by Gartman, management's imposition of a hierarchical, centralized control system aimed at minimizing worker initiative was a "rational" complement to labor's equally "rational" attempts to subvert the process of production.[73] The adversarial relationship of labor and capital in production, according to Gartman, is the direct consequence of the adversarial relationship between the interests of these classes, as this relationship was structured in the U.S.. Japan's regime of labor incorporation through lifetime employment can thus be seen as alleviating the adversarial positioning of class interests in the firm, and thus enabling the functional integration of capital and labor in the process of production.

5. LABOR'S POWER AND INDUSTRIAL PERFORMANCE

There is little dispute that Japan is a very competitive economy. There is also little dispute that Japan's industrial performance is best exemplified in the case of the auto industry. Important disagreements arise, however, as soon as the sources of the Japanese auto industry's success are sought. A first line of division in the vast literature on Japan's economic success is between "state-policy" and "economic" explanations. The former group locates Japan's economic success in the dedication of the Japanese state to the promotion of the auto industry[74]. The latter group is further divided between those who emphasize the dynamism of the private sector: active business investment demand, high private saving, and industrious and skilled labor operating in a market-oriented environment; and those who emphasize the dynamism of Japan's organization of production and industrial relations as the source of its success.

There is a further division of opinion in several important ways. Some see the success of Japan's production system to be rooted not in its relative efficiency but to its "super-exploitation" of labor. Others see the success of Japan's production system as rooted in its relative efficiency. In the latter group, most authors locate the efficiency of the production regime in the way in which capital is organized (networks), and the cooperative relationship it has developed with labor. The net result is high degree of flexibility in the allocation of resources, an attribute all the more synonymous with efficiency in a context of continuously changing product markets.

But what accounts for such cooperative and flexible industrial relations? Most accounts point to Japan's cooperative "culture" and traditions, and/or to its managerial philosophy and structure. Authors in the latter group attribute the system's flexibility to Japanese capital's long-term profit maximizing strategies, interdependence, and sensitivity to industrial disputes, all of which encourage capital to commit to the strategic choice of investing in the functional integration of the workforce with management—reskilling and authority for labor, rather than to deskilling and controlling labor, the strategic choice in many Western production systems.[75] Labor's cooperation is elicited through more meaningful work, and, inasmuch as flexibility brings in profits for the firm, employment security.

My approach explores the opposite line of causation. I argue that the success of Japan's production system is rooted in the lifetime employment security which capital was forced to concede to labor in the 1950s, and through which (and collective bargaining) the relative integration of labor's and capital's interests was accomplished. **Functional integration is predicated on interest integration**, as are the constituent elements of functional integration, flexibility and cooperation (training and diffuse authority lines). While a virtuous circle between training and employment security obviously exists, I stress that the dynamic of the circle originates in employment security.

Measuring efficiency

We have already pointed out the shortcomings of certain popular measures of industrial efficiency. The output-per-hour or output-per-employee measures result in the paradoxical finding that in the mid-1980s, amid Japanese autos' spectacular strides in world markets, the productivity of Japan's auto industry was 36% lower than that of the U.S. and 14% lower than Canada's.[76] Based on the similar value-added-per-employee definition of productivity, even after adjusting for differences in capacity utilization, cost of materials and other factors, a large study by McKinsey Global Institute found that in 1990 Japan's auto industry was 16% more productive than the U.S. auto industry.[77] While this finding is more plausible, the definition of productivity on which it is based leads McKinsey to a paradoxical conclusion: the venerable German auto industry is found to be only 57% as productive as Japan's.[78]

A different approach in measuring industrial efficiency is taken by M.I.T.'s International Motor Vehicle Program. These studies adopt two measures of efficiency. The first measure, hours-per-vehicle, is simply the inverse of the output-per-hour measure. The second measure focuses on product quality, under the assumption that the more efficient the process, the fewer the deviations from the manufacturing plan, the fewer the resulting defects-per-car. Accordingly, Womack et al. find that, in 1989, auto assembly plants in Japan were 47% more productive than in the U.S. in terms of hours worked per car, and 37% more productive in terms of defects per car.[79]

However, the measure of defects-per-car, while correctly looking at product quality as a dimension of industrial efficiency is not entirely satisfactory. Most importantly, it measures defects at the time the car ready to be shipped to car dealers, which may or may not reflect actual manufacturing quality. Indeed, a car with zero defects at the time of manufacturing, considered of high quality by the M.I.T. study, may well be proven to have been of lesser quality if defects appear after a few months or years of use.

We now turn to an examination of the efficiency of Japanese auto production on the basis of more appropriate measures, discussed in Chapter 2, the auto balance of trade and auto reliability surveys.

Market-based indicators of industrial performance

We can gauge the evolutionary trend of the efficiency of Japanese auto production through the purchasing choices and evaluations of consumers in the two countries. The balance of trade of a given country in autos reflect the extent to which the consumers in that country prefer domestic brands to autos that can be imported. While factors independent of industrial efficiency, such as changes in exchange rates and tariffs may have an impact of their own on the relative desirability of imported autos, they are of only minor significance when we compare trends, as opposed to absolute magnitudes, in the balance of trade.[80]

Figure 7 below charts Japan's and the U.S.'s annual balance of trade in autos, from 1952 until 1992. It can be seen that Japan's auto balance of trade has been positive and increasing. It can also be noted that this trend is not inherent to Japan, but that it exists since the late-1960s.

Many would disagree with our contention that differences between Japan's and U.S.'s auto balance of trade is indicative of the two auto industries' relative efficiency and manufacutring quality, arguing instead that it is a reflection of Japanese protectionism. This point cannot be countered directly, particularly since the alleged protectionism is acknowledge to be not in the form of tariff barriers, but in the form of more subtle, often concealed inconveniences levied against imported autos.

FIGURE 7

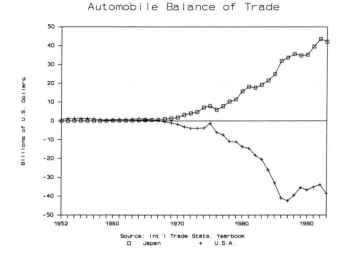

Automobile Balance of Trade

Source: Int'l Trade Stats. Yearbook
□   Japan   +   U.S.A.

The protectionism objection above can be countered with a rhetorical question: If Japan's auto trade surplus results from its protectionism rather than undistorted patterns of consumer preferences, why do Japanese consumers show a clear preference for German (and Swedish) autos over American imports? Indeed, in 1990, Japan imported 221,706 autos, of which 58.1% were German brands (Volkswagen/Audi, Mercedes-Benz, BMW), and only 6.5% were American brands (General Motors, Ford). Also attesting to the inadequacy of claims of Japanese protectionism in explaining the auto trade deficit with the U.S. is another evidence of the relative inability of American auto producers to adapt production to diverse market demands: until 1993, American auto producers did not offer any autos with steering wheels on the right side, as autos are built and driven in Japan!

Another objection to our interpretation of the auto trade surplus stems from monetarist quarters. Accordingly, the balance of auto trade does not reflect relative manufacturing efficiency but changes in exchange rates we compare the evolution of Japan's balance of auto trade to the evolution of the Yen/Dollar exchange rate. Figure 8 charts Japan's balance of auto trade in billions of dollars, and the Yen/Dollar rate, multiplied by 100 to facilitate visual comparability, during the 1980s.

FIGURE 8

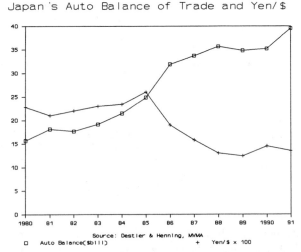

Japan 's Auto Balance of Trade and Yen/ $

Source: Destler & Henning, MVMA

□   Auto Balance($bill)   +   Yen/$ x 100

From 1982 to 1985 Japan's balance of trade in autos improves at the same rate as the Yen/Dollar ratio, apparently confirming the importance of the monetarist influence in the determination of the balance of trade. Maybe it was the weaker Yen rather than the higher Japanese auto production efficiency that made Japanese autos so attractive to Japan's export markets. However, the 1985-1989 period presents the opposite relationship between the balance of trade and the exchange rate. During this period, the Yen/Dollar rate was falling, i.e. the Yen was strengthening. According to the monetarist hypothesis, this would render Japanese products more expensive abroad, and thus result in a deteriorating trade balance. In fact, however, Japan's balance of trade continued to improve. The evidence suggests that fluctuations in Japan's exchange rate do not suffice to explain its balance of trade except, perhaps, in the short run.

FIGURE 9

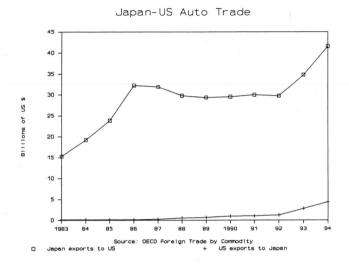

Next, we examine the auto balance of trade between Japan and the U.S. more closely by focussing on the 1980s and rearly 1990s (Figure 9). What is impressive in Figure 9 is not the magnitude of the difference in the balance of U.S.-Japan auto trade during the last decade or so, but the fact that this gap, during the early 1980s was increasing at such a fast rate. It is also significant that since the mid-1980s the trade gap stopped to expand, remaining constant and, by 1990 even beginning to slowly decline. The sustained levelling-off of the Japan-U.S. auto trade gap is a reflection of the levelling-off the Japan-U.S. auto efficiency gap, as we hypothesized.[81]

Non-Market indicators of industrial performance

We now turn our other, non-market based indicator of industrial performance, surveys of auto reliability.

FIGURE 10

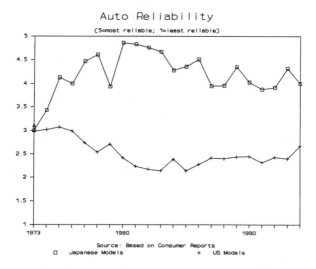

Auto Reliability
(5=most reliable; 1=least reliable)

Source: Based on Consumer Reports
□   Japanese Models   +   US Models

Figure 10 charts the reliability ratings for all Japanese and all American cars and minivans sold in the U.S. from 1973 to 1994, based on the *Consumer Reports'* frequency-of-repair records. The average rating, corresponding to the average frequency of repairs reported for all models is 3. The best possible rating is 5 ("much better than average"), while the worst is 1 ("much worse than average"). The results lend strong support both to our hypothesis that Japanese auto production is more efficient than the American auto production, that this performance gap was increasing until the early-1980s, that the performance gap has stopped growing after the mid-1980s when reforms in industrial relations took root in the U.S.. Moreover, the results of Figure 10 corroborate our methodological hypothesis, that changes in the trade gap reflect, primarily, changes in manufacturing efficiency (rather than exchange rates, protectionist policies, fashion): the surge in the Japan-U.S. trade gap that lasted until the early 1980s (Figure 9), coincides with a parallel surge in the reliability gap (Figure 10).

The above conclusion, however, may be challenged on the grounds that the above figures overstate the reliability of Japanese autos, by comparing American autos with Japanese autos sold in the U.S.. The latter category, the objection goes, by virtue of the fact that it consists of Japanese exports, is likely to be of better quality than the average Japanese car.

The above objection is addressed by narrowing the focus of comparison to the two most reliable models from each country. Thus Figure 11 compares the average reliability of two most reliable nameplates from each country.[82] It can be seen that the pattern of improvement and then levelling-off of the overall Japan-U.S. auto reliability gap (traced in Figure 10), is mirrored quite closely when we narrow our comparison to the top two performers from each country (in Figure 11).

FIGURE 11

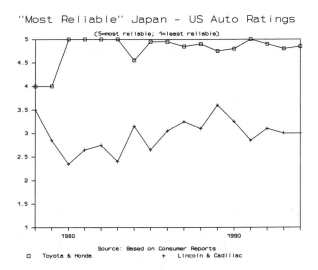

Lastly, lest our conclusions are too much reliant on a single source of data, the Consumer Reports, we furnish data from another source of auto survey data, J.D. Power & Associates's Vehicle Dependability Index (VDI),[83] which measures the number of problems after five years of ownership.[84]

Table 4 below lists the German and American auto makers that were among the **top five** most dependable autos sold in the U.S., in JD Power's VDI.

Table 4: Japanese and US Auto Makers in the Top Five of VDI

Year	Make	Origin	Score	Rank
1990[85]				
	Toyota	Japan	149	2
	Honda	Japan	137	3
	Buick	USA	133	4
	Cadillac	USA	121	5
1991[86]				
	Lexus	Japan	144	1
	Infiniti	Japan	142	2
	Honda	Japan	132	4
	Acura	Japan	150	5
1992[87]				
	Honda	Japan	157	2
	Acura	Japan	150	3
	Lincoln	USA	137	4
1993[88]				
	Acura	Japan	160	2
	Cadillac	USA	151	3
	Toyota	Japan	139	5

Our analysis of published JD Power data is quite revealing.[89] It provides strong support to the hypothesis that Japanese autos are of higher quality than their American counterparts. Specifically, analysis of the Vehicle Dependability Study results from the mid-1980s to the mid-1990s confirm (a) the superiority of Japanese auto production compared to the U.S. until the mid-1980s, and (b) the closing of that gap after the late-1980s, since the American regime's transition to Jointness.

Clearly, the JD Power data confirm the Consumer Reports data. Japanese autos are more reliable than American autos, placing above American models every year since the VDI survey began. The JD Power data also indicate that American models showed an improvement after the mid-1980s.[90-]

6. CONCLUSION

As in the pre-Jointness American regime of segregated inclusion, Japanese labor is not represented in the board of directors. Despite labor's formal exclusion, however, in both cases there is a substantive inclusion of labor's redistributive interests in decision making, as collective bargaining deprives capital from the right to decide redistributive issues unilaterally. Moreover, while under segregated inclusion labor's productivist interests are not included in corporate decision making, either formally or substantively, in the Japanese production regime labor's productivist interests are included in a substantive manner, through lifetime employment.

The structure of labor's integration in the Japanese auto production regime ("incorporative integration") can be seen, in a way, as the inverse of the German case ("representative integration"). In Japan, labor's representatives are not involved in corporate decision-making in a formal way or as directly as they are in Germany, while Japanese rank-and-file workers are more involved than their German counterparts in daily decisions pertaining to production. Japanese management solicits workers' advice on the shop floor even on issues of product design. By contrast, in Germany the functions of design, engineering, scheduling, work organization, assembly, and quality control are more strictly differentiated.

Not surprisingly, the Japanese regime is likely to continue to contend with different kinds of challenges in the future than its German counterpart. While Germany's representative integration must guard against (non-)democratic centralism, Japan's incorporative integration must guard against atomization (of individual enterprise unions and of individual workers) and the associated tendency for self-exploitation.

Japanese labor's power, based on exit and on the incorporation of its interests in corporate decision making, has been in important respects superior to that of American labor, at least until the introduction of Jointness. We have supported this argument with a description of the institutions on which Japanese labor's power rests, which we found consistent with the hypothesized characteristics of a production regime of incorporative integration. Additionally, we have furnished compensation and employment data showing how Japanese labor's hypothesized superior power embedded in the institutions described does correspond to more favorable substantive results for Japanese labor than its American counterparts. Both de jure and de facto, Japanese workers have been better able to defend their income and employment security.

As hypothesized, Japanese labor's superior power is associated with superior production performance, compared to the American case.

We have argued that this association is not spurious; labor's ability to integrate its interests with capital's, through collective bargaining and lifetime employment (exit and fusion) fosters the integration of functions traditionally divided strictly between labor and capital/management. Such integration, we have argued, results in production practices that are less wasteful of human capital (seasonal and cyclical unemployment, deskilling) and more capable of nurturing the skills and motivation necessary to meet the demands of a global market.

The question remains whether it has been labor's power in corporate decision making that eventuated these outcomes—the good fortunes of labor and the high efficiency of Japanese auto production—or some other, unexplored factor—state policy, societal corporatism, corporate-supplier networks, marketing strategies, car design etc. We will address the question of causality in the final chapter. Here suffice it to conclude that a high level of labor's power (as it is institutionalized in the production regime, and as reflected in wages and employment) is not antithetical to a strong industrial performance, and may in fact constitute a key element of Japan's industrial success.

NOTES

1. For a good account of the Nissan strike, albeit one that focuses perhaps too much on personalities see David Halberstam, *The Reckoning* (New York: Morrow, 1986), pt. 3.

2. Joe Moore, *Japanese Workers and the Struggle for Power, 1945-1947* (Madison: University of Wisconsin Press, 1983), p. 100. Similar conclusions, tracing lifetime employment but also teamwork to Japanese workers' militant efforts to wrest control of production from capital are reached by Andrew Gordon, *The Evolution of Labor Relations in Japan: Heavy Industry, 1853-1955* (Cambridge, MA.: Harvard University Press, 1985).

3. The roots of lifetime employment are also traced to workers' postwar demands and struggles by Martin Kenney and Richard Florida, "Beyond Mass Production: Production and the Labor Process in Japan," *Politics and Society* (March 1988). The authors add, however, that these worker demands were "later integrated into the logic of capitalist accumulation" (p. 127), remaining thus ambiguous as to whether lifetime employment today represents labor's power against or capitulation to capital.

4. Davis Dyer, Malcolm Salter and Alan Weber, *Changing Alliances* (Boston: Harvard Business School Press, 1987), p.109, emphasis added.

5. Halberstam, *op. cit.*, pt. 3.

6. Masahiko Aoki, *Information, Incentives, and Bargaining in the Japanese Economy* (New York: Cambridge University Press, 1988), p. 189.

7. For a US-Japan comparison of dismissals in labor law see William B. Gould, *The Japanese Reshaping of American Labor Law* (Cambridge, Mass: MIT Press, 1984).

8. Charles F. Sabel, "Learning by Monitoring: The Institutions of Economic Development," (Cambridge, Mass.: MIT, 1993), pp. 17-18.

9. H. Hazama, *Undercurrents of Co-operative Labor-Management Relations in Japan* (Tokyo: Waseda Daigaku Shuppankai, 1978).

10. K. Odaka, *The Analysis of Labour Market* (Tokyo: Iwanami Shoten, 1984).

11. Takeshi Inagami, *Japanese Workplace Industrial Relations* (Tokyo: Japan Institute of Labor, 1988), p. 5.

12. Lifetime employment is not unique to Japan. What is uniquely Japanese is its broad application to workers in manufacturing.

13. Katherine G. Abraham, and Susan N. Houseman, "Job Security and Work Force Adjustment: How Different Are U.S. and Japanese Practices?" in Christoph F. Buechtemann (ed.), *Employment Security and Labor Market Behavior: Interdisciplinary Approaches and International Evidence* (Ithaca, N.Y.: ILR Press, 1993), p. 199.

14. Source: Ministry of Labor, *Basic Survey on Wage Structure*, 1986. Cited by Takeshi Inagami, *Japanese Workplace Industrial Relations* (Tokyo: Japan Institute of Labor, 1988), p. 9.

15. Masahiko Aoki, *The Co-operative Game Theory of the Firm* (Oxford: Clarendon Press, 1984).

16. Masahiko Aoki (1988), p. 154. In a related formulation, management in Japan plays the role of referee between the employees and the stockholders rather than acting as servants of the latter. Masahiko Aoki (1984), p. 116.

17. Takeshi Inagami et al., *A Research Survey on the Advanced Nations' Syndrome and the Changing Work Ethic* (Tokyo: Japan Productivity Centre, 1985).

18. Haruo Shimada, "Japan's Postwar Industrial Growth and Labor-Management Relations," in Lloyd G. Reynolds, Stanley H. Masters, Coletta H. Moser (eds), *Readings in Labor Economics and Labor Relations* (Englewood Cliffs, NJ: Prentice-Hall, 1986), p. 470.

19. Takeshi Inagami et al. (1985).

20. The Japan Institute of Labor, *op. cit.*, p. 28.

21. Policy Planning and Research Department, Minister's Secretariat, Ministry of Labour (ed.) *A Research Survey on Labour-Management Communication* (Tokyo: Okurasho Insatsu-kyoku, 1985).

22. Susumu Watanabe (ed), *Microelectronics, Automation and Employment in the Automobile Industry* (New York: John Wiley & Sons, 1987).

23. Takeshi Inagami (1988), pp. 26-27.

24. Kenney and Florida, *op. cit.*, pp. 106-107.

25. For a perceptive comparison of legal frameworks between Japanese unionism and Western unionism see Masahiko Aoki (1984), chapters 9-11.

26. *Japan Economic Newswire*, December 26, 1990.

27. The Japan Institute of Labor, *op. cit.*.

28. Only the peripheral, part-time workers are paid hourly wage.

29. Michael Cusumano, *The Japanese Automobile Industry: Technology and Management at Nissan and Toyota* (Cambridge, Mass.: Harvard University Press, 1985).

30. Masahiko Aoki (1988), p. 56.

31. This is not to deny the close coordination of the separate collective agreements signed with different firms by the UAW. The point is that in terms of territorial organization, the UAW is not as "industrial" some would like to believe. In fact, US "business" unionism is more akin to Japanese "enterprise" unionism than to Germany's genuinely industrial unionism.

32. Masahiko Aoki, *Information, Incentives, and Bargaining in the Japanese Economy* (New York: Cambridge University Press, 1988), p. 91.

33. For the vicissitudes and dilemmas of the inclusiveness and "purity" of working class parties in Western Europe see Adam Przeworski, "Social Democracy as a Historical Phenomenon," *New left Review*, no. 122 (August 1980). See also Ernesto Laclau and Chantal Mouffe, *Hegemony and Socialist Strategy: Towards a Radical Democratic Politics* (London: Verso, 1985).

34. Aoki cites a 1978 study by Nikkeiren (the Japan Management Association) which puts that portion to 15.7%. Masahiko Aoki (1988), p. 92.

35. This point is made by Masahiko Aoki (1988), p. 92.

36. Knuth Dohse, Ulrich Jurgens, and Thomas Malsch, "From 'Fordism' to 'Toyotism'? *Politics & Society* 14, no. 2 (1985). The authors have modified their position in their more recent work, *Breaking from Taylorism: Changing Forms of Work in the Automobile Industry* (Cambridge: Cambridge University Press, 1993). They put less emphasis on super-exploitation and more on the mutual benefits for labor and for management, suggesting a post-Taylorist organization of production. For a view of Japanese production as "despotic" regime see Michael Burawoy, *The Politics of Production* (London: Verso, 1985). For a critical review of the super-exploitation thesis see Martin Kenney

and Richard Florida, "Beyond Mass Production: Production and the Labor Process in Japan," *Politics and Society* (March 1988), and idem (1993).

37. Schematically we expect that Wj/Wu > Eu/Ej, where Wj is wages in Japan, Wu is wages in the US, Eu is employment stability in the US, Ej is employment stability in Japan.

38. Department of Commerce, United Nations and industry-association data convert Japanese monthly salaries to hourly figures by dividing annual figures by the total number of employee-hours.

39. Motor Vehicle Manufacturers Association of the U.S., *World Motor Vehicle Data, 1990* (Detroit: MMVA, 1993), p. 74.

40. If compensation in a given year is A yen and in the next year it rises to B yen, the per cent change in compensation is ([B yen - A yen] x 100)/A yen. By dividing the numerator and denominator by 1 yen, we get an equivalent, yen-free value,

$$([A-B]x100)/B.$$

41. Figures are in 1982 US dollars.

42. Figures are for 1990, from the international comparison of executive pay is conducted by Towers, Perrin, Forster & Crosby, cited in Linda L. Carr and Moosa Valinezhad, "The role of ethics in executive compensation: Toward a contractarian interpretation of the neoclassical theory of managerial remuneration," *Journal of Business Ethics*, February 1994. Total compensation included cash, benefits, perks, and long term incentives for the CEOs of organizations with $ 250 million annual sales (same size companies).

43. *Financial Times*, "Survey of Japanese Industry," September 25, 1995, p. 31.

44. *The New York Times*, April 14, 1992, p. D1.

45. OECD, *The OECD STAN Database for Industrial Analysis* (Paris: OECD, 1995), p. 317.

46. This is the conclusion of a major econometric study of employment patterns in the manufacturing sectors of Japan and the US by Katherine G. Abraham and Susan N. Houseman, "Job Security and Work Force Adjustment: How Different Are U.S. and Japanese Practices?" in Buechtemann (ed.), *op. cit.*, p. 197.

47. Ibid, p. 198.

48. The percent change in employment in Figure 4 is given by _e=100x[E2-E1]/E1, where _e is percent change in employment, E1 is employment in a given year, E2 is employment in the next year.

49. Kazutoshi Koshiro, "The Organization of Work and Internal Labour Market Flexibility in Japanese Industrial Relations", in *New Directions in Work Organization* (Paris: OECD, 1992), pp. 116-117.

50. John Hoerr, "Sharpening Minds for a Competitive Edge," *BusinessWeek* (December 17, 1990).

51. Koshiro, *op. cit.*, pp. 124-125.

52. Watanabe (ed), *op. cit.*, p. 65.

53. Koshiro, *op. cit.*, p. 125.

54. Koji Taira and Lolomin B. Levine, "Japan's Industrial Relations: A Social Compact Emerges," in Harvey Juris, Mark Thompson, and Wilbur Daniels (eds) *Industrial Relations in a Decade of Economic Change* (Madison, WI., Industrial Relations Research Association, 1985), pp. 277-282.

55. Watanabe (ed), *op. cit.*, p. 66.

56. Reported in ibid, p. 68.

57. Nomura Masami, "Model Japan? Characteristics of Industrial Relations in the Japanese Automobile Industry" (Berlin: Wissenschaftszentrum, 1985).

58. Watanabe, (ed), *op. cit.*, pp. 68-69.

59. Peter Langan, "Why lifetime jobs will stay" *Asian Business* (July 1994), p. 69.

60. *Fortune*, March 20, 1995, p. 119.

61. For the conceptualization of the just-in-time system as "fragile", compared to the American inventory-buffer system as "robust," see John Paul MacDuffie and John Krafcik, "Flexible Production Systems and Manufacturing Performance: The Role of Human Resources and Technology," (Sloan School of Management and International Motor Vehicle Program, MIT, 1989). The "fragile-robust" distinction corresponds to the "lean-rigid" distinction developed by Womack et. al. (1990).

62. In the US, workers have this discretion only in Saturn, which is advertised as a sign of the novelty of the company's production philosophy in Saturn commercials.

63. Aoki (1988).

64. William Lazonick, "Value Creation on the Shop Floor: Skill, Effort, and Technology in U.S. and Japanese Manufacturing," Department of Economics, Barnard College, Columbia University, October 1988.

65. James P. Womack, Daniel T. Jones, and Daniel Roos, *The Machine that Changed the World: The Story of Lean Production* (New York: Harper Perennial, 1990).

66. John F. Krafcik, "Triumph of the Lean Production System," *Sloan Management Review* (Fall 1988).

67. John F. Krafcik and John Paul MacDuffie, "Explaining High Performance Manufacturing: The International Automotive Assembly Plant Study," (Cambridge, Mass.: MIT Press, 1989).

68. Kazuo Koike, "Internal Labor Markets: Workers in Large Firms," in T. Shirai (ed) *Contemporary Industrial Relations in Japan* (Madison, Wi.: University of Madison Press, 1983), p. 29.

69. Aoki (1988), p. 92.

70. Kenney and Florida (1988), p. 131.

71. William Lazonick, "Business Organization and Competitive Advantage: Capitalist Transformations in the Twentieth Century," Department of Economics, Barnard College, Columbia University (September 1988).

72. William Lazonick, *Business Organization and the Myth of the Market Economy* (New York: Cambridge University Press, 1991).

73. David Gartman, *Auto Slavery: The Labor Process in the American Automobile Industry, 1897-1950* (New Brunswick: Rutgers University Press, 1986), esp. p. 72.

74. Some see this as the result of a Gerschrenkon-like late-comer's "developmental state," such as Chalmers Johnson, *The MITI and the Japanese Miracle: the Growth of Industrial Policy* (Stanford, CA: Stanford University Press, 1982), and Chalmers Johnson, *Japan, Who Governs? The Rise of the Developmental State* (New York: W.W. Norton, 1995); others to Japan's economic and political backwardness, such as Michael Burawoy, *The Politics of Production* (London: Verso, 1985).

75. Thomas Kochan, Harry C. Katz and Robert B. McKersie (eds), *The Transformation of American Industrial Relations* (New York: Basic Books, 1986).

76. Melvin A. Fuss and Leonard Waverman, *Costs and Productivity in Automobile Production: The Challenge of Japanese Efficiency* (Cambridge: Cambridge University Press, 1992), p. 39.

77. McKinsey Global Institute, *Manufacturing Productivity* (Washington, D.C.: McKinsey & Co., 1993).

78. The McKinsey study reports that the value-added-per employee of the US, Japanese, and German auto industries compares as 100:116:66, respectively.

79. Womack et al. (1990), p. 92. Similar results are reported by Krafcik (1988).

80. We assume that alleged Japanese protectionism, whatever its actual extent, has a uniform impact on the preferences of US consumers over time. Thus, even if allegations of Japan's covert protectionism are true, we believe that these practices are not new and thus not central to Japan's impressive balance of auto trade in the 1980s.

81. The rise of Japanese "transplants" in the mid-1980s has certainly affected the trade gap, but not in a major way. The volume of transplant production remained small until well into the 1990s.

82. The "most reliable" Japanese nameplates were Toyota (includes Lexus) and Honda (includes Acura). The "most reliable" US nameplates were Lincoln (Crown Victoria for 1978-1983), and Cadillac. Based on Consumer Reports. The choice of these models as the most reliable of each country is corroborated by the ordinal rating of model reliability in *Automotive News* (June 1, 1992).

83. J.D. Power & Associates is an Agoura Hills-based international marketing information firm, specializing in consumer opinion and customer satisfaction studies. Its annual surveys of auto customer satisfaction are the most highly regarded in the industry. See Appendix.

84. Thus, the "1990" VDI refers to the reliability of 1985 models, the "1991" VDI to the 1986 models, and so on.

85. Based on JD Power 1991 VDS, reported in *Automotive News*, April 10, 1990.

86. Based on JD Power 1991 VDS, reported in *PR Newswire* July 8, 1991.

87. Based on JD Power VDS 1992, reported in *Fortune,* May 18, 1992, p. 105.

88. Based on JD Power VDS 1993, as reported by *PR Newswire* April 6, 1993.

89. On-line research on the *Lexis* database has been crucial for the retrieval of disparate citations of JD Power data, since its complete publications are not readily available to the public.

90. Note that the 1992 and 1993 data pertain to 4-5 year-old 1987 and 1988 models, respectively.

CHAPTER 7

Conclusion: The Normative and the Pragmatic in Production Politics

This has been an attempt to bridge normative concerns for workers' rights in the workplace with pragmatic concerns for a competitive organization of production, by reconceptualizing political contestation in the realm of advanced capitalist production.[1] We have examined how the type of labor inclusion in a production regime affects labor's interests as well as the production regime's industrial performance.

Our analysis of the automobile production regimes of the US, Germany and Japan substantiates the pertinence of the analytic framework of production politics. The distinct mode of inclusion of labor's interests in corporate decision making in each country can in fact explain (a) the decline in labor's fortunes but also in industrial performance of the US auto industry's segregation regime, during the 1970s and early-1980s; (b) the steady improvement in labor's fortunes and in industrial performance of the representative integration regime of Germany and incorporative integration regime of Japan during the same period; (c) the transformation of the US production regime in the direction of integration with the establishment of Jointness, since the mid-1980s.

The postwar institutionalization of collective bargaining gave US auto workers a false sense of security. With the Treaty of Detroit, corporate decisions would include labor's fundamental redistributive interests, but not its fundamental productivist interests.[2] In a rapidly expanding postwar economy, the seasonal and cyclical stints of retractions and accompanying layoffs, the low levels of training provided for workers, the increasing gap between conception and execution, and the loss of skills and pride associated with the job—were all rendered tolerable, given the rising wages that accompanied them and the continuously expanding market that kept layoffs limited in number and duration.

"Job control" unionism, however, soon proved to be an ironic misnomer. Narrow job specifications provided a certain protection to a negotiated effort/reward ratio against arbitrary managerial intensification of the work effort or its reward, but not the job itself. This became ever more apparent in the 1970s, when US auto capitalists responded to a combination of technological and market developments with massive layoffs. Once a *de jure* disposable labor became also *de facto* disposed, the crumbling of its much-touted redistributive power was not far behind.

The widespread attribution of US labor's declining fortunes in the 1970s and early-1980s to technological change and to competition from low-wage, high-managerial-discretion foreign producers is belied by the actual dynamics of the integration regimes of Germany and Japan. Their differences aside, the German and Japanese production regimes share a corporate decision making process that, rather than segregating, integrates labor's redistributive and productivist interests therein. Far from being less constrained than US management, German and Japanese managers are not afforded the luxury of adjusting their production schedules according to monthly or annual variations in demand for autos, nor can they use technology as a labor-shedding device. Unable to thus dispose of "redundant" labor, investing in its training, reskilling, but also in its motivation for actively contributing to a continuously changing labor process become a rational *modus operandi* for German and Japanese employers. Thus, while the cultural lenses of US observers have been focussing on the "military discipline" of German labor and the "paternalistic docility" of the Japanese, German and Japanese workers have been enjoying considerable levels of influence over the creation as well as the distribution of wealth.

The mid-1980s transformation of the US production regime into Jointness, a hybrid regime combining elements from its segregationist past and from the integration regimes of Germany and Japan, has been the result, above all, of the inability of the old US regime to compete with its more efficient foreign counterparts, as well as the pressures of US auto workers for deeper labor participation in decision making.

US capital's initial attempts at what it considered an "easy Japanization," or the introduction of "flexibility" in the deployment of labor by simply breaking union resistance and changing work rules, soon proved problematic. Shop floor flexibility, as a closer look into the Japanese (and the German) regime showed, was predicated on a restructuring of the relations in production and of production. If workers were to contribute to quick changeovers in production layout, quality control and problem-solving, heavy investments in broad worker skills and shop floor discretion had to be made. And if workers' requisite allegiance to an otherwise fragile labor process with supple lines of demarcation between operative and administrative functions was to be secured, a "new deal" with labor, involving a new level of employment security had to be made.

Indeed, under Jointness, US labor's redistributive interests in corporate decision making were included along with its newly recognized productivist interests, granting labor an unprecedented (for US standards) level of influence over the utilization of the means of production. A variety labor-management joint committees involved labor in increasingly higher levels of decision making. An altogether new kind of company created by General Motors, Saturn, inlvolved the union most thouroughly, inlcuding in strategic-level decision making. Interestingly, the result was not only the reduction of the ominous performance gap between US and German or Japanese autos, but also the reconstitution of US labor's place in production on a more solid foundation than ever before. While this reconstitution was accompanied by an erosion of traditional pillars of labor strength (arms-length relationship with capital, regularly rising real wages irrespective of company performance), this should not obscure the concurrent construction of deeper labor beachheads against capitalist autocracy. If uninterrupted real wage increases came to an end, so did the dehumanizing hire-and-fire method of production; if work rules were diluted, so were capitalist management's "sole prerogatives."

QUANTITATIVE INDICATORS OF LABOR'S POWER AND INDUSTRIAL PERFORMANCE

Quantitative indicators of labor's power provide independent support for our institutional analysis. A problem of institutional analysis is that the facts it analyzes are often open to competing interpretations with no easy way of adjudicating between them. Quantitative analysis of employment data is useful in showing that, for example, Japan's lifetime employment guarantees are not simply empty promises but have the hypothesized substantive impact on workers' employment security. Similarly, our contentions about the significance of GENs,

JOBs, and other joint committees under the US regime of Jointness, and of parity codetermination on investment and employment decisions under Germany's regime of representative integration, need to be reinforced with independent evidence of substantive outcomes for labor's fortunes.

To corroborate Hypothesis I, that in regimes of integrated inclusion (integration) labor has more (productivist) power than in regimes of segregated inclusion, we present quantitative indicators of labor's redistributive and productivist power in the U.S., German, and Japanese auto industries.

FIGURE 1

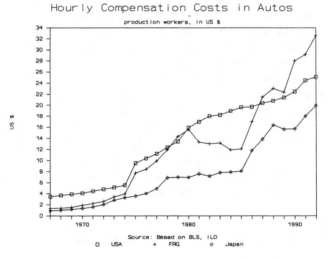

Hourly Compensation Costs in Autos
production workers, in US $

Source: Based on BLS, ILO
□ USA   + FRG   ◊ Japan

First, we look at a key indicator of labor's redistributive power, total hourly labor compensation. Figure 1 charts the U.S. dollar equivalents of total hourly labor costs, as annual averages in the auto industries of the U.S., Germany, and Japan, from the late-1960s to the early-1990s.[3] It is evident that, in dollar terms, Japanese labor's total compensation has been substantially lower than American or Germany levels. Note, however, that German compensation surpasses American compensation by a larger margin than the American case leads Japan. Moreover, Japan's lower compensation level may not attest to Japanese labor's lower redistributive power per se, but to the lower starting point of Japanese compensation after the Second World War—a plausible assumption given the lateness of industrialization in Japan.[4]

FIGURE 2

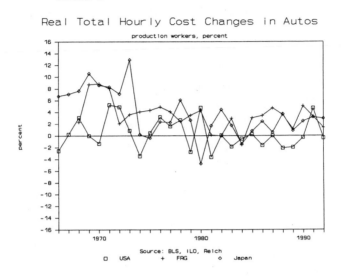

Real Total Hourly Cost Changes in Autos

production workers, percent

Source: BLS, ILO, Reich

□ USA   + FRG   ◊ Japan

Indeed, we get a better sense of labor's redistributive power in each regime if we compare the rates of increase of hourly compensation, as opposed to absolute levels of hourly compensation. As Figure 2 shows, the annual rate of increase of Japanese auto workers' compensation, in real terms, has been comparable to that of the U.S. and of Germany. In fact, looked at from this more accurate indicator of labor's redistributive power, it becomes clear that even before the crisis of the 1980s, American labor has not been as capable as German and Japanese labor in keeping its compensation in line with the cost of living. From the late-1960s until 1980, American auto workers experienced negative annual changes of their real wages on four occasions, Japanese auto workers on only one, and German workers never.

Finally, labor's redistributive power in each regime is further illuminated if we also consider labor's compensation in relation to the compensation of chief executive officers. Indeed, worker-CEO compensation differentials in large companies in the three countries corroborate our hypothesis: while the pay of an average CEO of a similarly large company in 1990 was 110 times greater than the average worker's compensation in the United States, it was only 17 and 23 times greater in Japan and Germany, respectively.[5] These executive-worker pay differentials indicate that Japanese and German labor's redistributive power is higher than either absolute compensation levels of rates of change of compensation indicate.

FIGURE 3

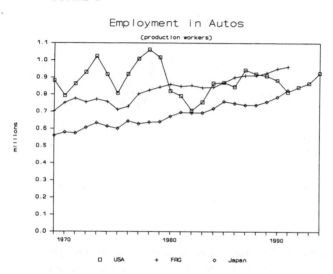

Turning to a key indicator of labor's productivist power, we look at annual employment levels in the auto industry, from the end of the 1960s to the early-1990s.[6] Figure 3 charts the annual employment levels in the auto industries of the U.S., Germany, and Japan. As hypothesized, labor enjoys a qualitatively higher employment stability in the integration regimes of Germany and Japan than in the U.S. Moreover, the employment stability enjoyed by American auto workers after the consolidation of Jointness in the mid-1980s improves qualitatively, as evidenced by the significant reduction in the wide oscillations in employment which were a characteristic of the pre-Jointness regime. This reinforces our contention that under Jointness labor's participation in productivist decision making has not been just "window dressing," as critics of Jointness suggest. The institutional innovations through which American labor's productivist interests have been included in corporate decision making have had positive substantive outcomes for labor's fundamental interest in employment security (Hypothesis III-a).

It is important to emphasize that the above assessments of labor's power in auto production regimes are relative to a capitalist "ideal" where labor's power approaches zero, where capital maintains unilateral decision making over the utilization of the means of production: what to produce, how to produce it, how to redistribute the wealth produced, what kinds of technologies to invest in, etc. Thus, our references to labor's power to steer many such decisions in a direction that serves (to an extent) its own interests is not meant to obfuscate that these are still essentially capitalist regimes, where labor's place in production still leaves a lot to be desired.

My personal observations from the U.S. and other case studies concur on that the life of the auto worker, while it has improved vastly from earlier years, is still quite bleak. Even Japanese lifetime employment comes at a cost to auto workers, who are thereby tied to one company for the course of their careers,[7] while younger workers find it increasingly difficult to join the ranks of tenured workers. On the other hand, grim accounts of "dehumanizing" working conditions in Japanese auto plants make a stronger impression in the West than they should, given the comparably grim working conditions in the US. After all, the description of an auto plant as a "metallic ant farm," of an auto worker's job as "repetition as strangulation," and of the prospects of working-class teenagers as "the jail, the morgue or the auto plant," are by a former assembly worker of a General Motors plant in the U.S..[8] Lastly, while German codetermination seems the most attractive of the three regimes (from the standpoint of American labor), it is not without its problems, particularly as a model for the whole country. German auto workers enjoy high levels of job security but German workers as a whole experience high levels of unemployment.

Next, we compare the production performance of the three auto industries, in order to confirm Hypothesis II, that integration regimes display a higher level of industrial performance than segregation regimes, and Hypothesis III, that a regime that moves away from segregation and towards integration will improve its performance and labor's fortunes. We have already suggested how labor's power might be a critical determinant of the regime's efficiency, and how labor's productivist power, in particular, is consequential for the regime's industrial performance. Flexibility and functional integration in the labor process, we have argued, are important ingredients for a strong industrial performance, but are predicated on interest integration in decision making.

Here, we review our quantitative substantiation of the hypothesized relationship among the industrial performance of these regimes, through our two indirect yet telling indicators of regime performance for the three auto industries, the auto balance of trade and auto reliability surveys.[9]

FIGURE 4

Automobile Balance of Trade

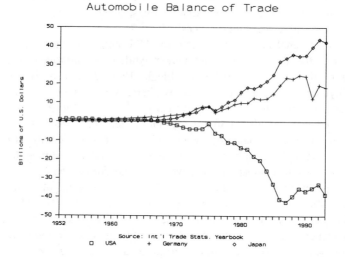

Source: Int 'l Trade Stats. Yearbook
□   USA   +   Germany   ◇   Japan

Figure 4 charts the auto balance of trade for the U.S., Germany and Japan from the early-1950s to the early-1990s. U.S. auto trade deficits, as well as German and Japanese surpluses are not primordial, inherent fixtures of the respective countries, but arise in the late-1960s, after Germany and Japan have completed their postwar reconstruction on the basis of distinctive production regimes. The U.S. auto trade balance deteriorates steadily from the late-1960s until the mid-1980s. This deterioration comes to an end when the hybrid production regime of Jointness replaces the traditional American segregation regime.

It should be added that the auto balance of trade figures above do not include offshore production, a possible source of such distortion. That is, had we counted as the U.S. exports the autos produced abroad by American-owned companies, we would get a more favorable (for the

U.S.) picture of customer preferences reflected in the auto balance of trade. Such distortion would be all the more significant, the larger the differences between the US, Germany, and Japan in the level of offshore production. Data for 1993 indicate that 45.9% of American-owned auto production was done overseas, while the corresponding figures for German- and Japanese-owned production was 13.22% and 10.7%, respectively.[10]

Two considerations, however, limit the amount of distortion involved in our calculation of auto balance of trade. First, the differences in the auto balance of trade between the US, on the one hand, and Germany and Japan on the other, are so large, as charted in Figure 1, that adjustments for offshore production would alter only the magnitude of the said differences: even if we add all offshore US-owned production to US exports, the US would still have a negative balance of trade while Germany and Japan would have large surpluses. Second, it is not always plausible to consider all US-owned auto companies abroad as working under the same production regime as at home. For example, Adam Opel AG (a General Motors subsidiary) and Ford-Werke AG (a Ford subsidiary) share most of the features of the representative integration regime of German-owned companies. On the other hand, Japanese-owned "transplants" in the US operate more like other Japanese companies than US companies. Thus it would be very difficult to make precise adjustments to the auto balance of trade on the basis of overseas production.

What is particularly important is that the noted patterns in the auto balance of trade persist over a long period of time, which strengthens our contention that they reflect underlying efficiency differentials in auto production among the three regimes—as opposed to temporal or exogenous distortions in the product market. And, fundamental regime changes, such as that of the US regime in 1982-84, coincide with fundamental changes in the level/direction of the balance of trade. However, our contention would be further strengthened if it is corroborated by an indicator of industrial performance that is less susceptible to fluctuations in labor costs, tariffs, and exchange rates—such as the auto reliability ratings.

Figure 5 charts consumer ratings of auto reliability, based on Consumer Reports' annual frequency-of-repair records.[11] The ratings reflect how frequently a car needed repairs compared to the average number of repairs for all cars. As anticipated, relative consumer ratings of American autos are consistently lower than for German and Japanese models sold in the U.S. Moreover, while ratings for American autos deteriorate (as ratings for competing German and Japanese models improve) from the 1970s to the mid-1980s, there is a small yet steady improvement in the reliability of American autos that corresponds with the transformation of the American regime in the direction of integration.

FIGURE 5

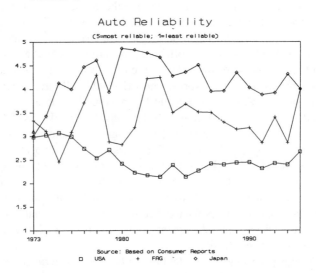

Auto Reliability

(5=most reliable; 1=least reliable)

Source: Based on Consumer Reports
□ USA   + FRG   ◇ Japan

One may plausibly object that the above comparison underemphasizes the reliability of American autos, since it compares the latter with the reliability of German and Japanese imports which, precisely because they are imports are likely to represent only the best products of those regimes. In order to address this objection, we compare the reliability ratings of the two best brands of each regime (Figure 6).[12] It can be seen that the three regimes' relative auto reliability as shown in Figure 5 (all models) does not change fundamentally in Figure 6 (best models).

FIGURE 6

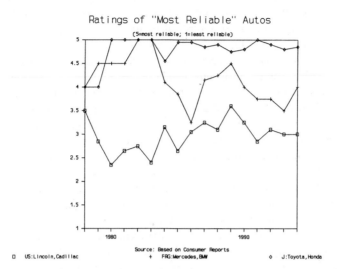

Ratings of "Most Reliable" Autos

(5=most reliable; 1=least reliable)

Source: Based on Consumer Reports

□   US:Lincoln,Cadillac   +   FRG:Mercedes,BMW   ◇   J:Toyota,Honda

COINCIDENCE, COVARIATION, CAUSALITY: LABOR'S POWER AND INDUSTRIAL PERFORMANCE

Our institutional analysis of labor-management relations and our quantitative analysis of regime outcomes for labor's fundamental interests confirm the hypothesized correlation between modes of labor inclusion on the one hand and labor's fortunes and industrial performance on the other. What is more difficult, of course, is to demonstrate the causal nature of these relationships. Even if causality is impossible to establish, we should at least address the possibility that the modes of labor inclusion we identified in each regime are only coincidentally related with labor's fortunes and industrial performance therein. We maintain that the relationship between the two sets of variables is not likely to be coincidental for four major reasons.

First, the correspondence between the mode of labor's inclusion and industrial performance hold over too long a period of time—from the early-1950s to the early-1990s—for a purely coincidental relationship between the two sets of variables to be likely.

Second, the large, persistent, and qualitative character of the differences documented between the production regimes of Germany and Japan, on the one hand, and of the U.S., on the other (in terms of labor's power as well as of industrial performance) make it unlikely that such regime differences are the result of measurement error or temporal exogenous disturbances. By the same reasoning, however, the much smaller differences documented between Germany's and Japan's integration regimes in labor's power and industrial performance prevent us from drawing but the most tentative conclusions about the efficiency and equity differences between a regime of representative integration (Germany) and a regime of incorporated integration (Japan).

Third, the timing and hypothesized direction of changes in the mode of labor inclusion (in the case of the U.S. in 1982-84) corresponds with the timing and actual direction of changes in labor's fortunes and in industrial performance. In other words, not only are modes of labor inclusion are closely related to labor's fortunes and industrial performance, but changes in the former are closely related to changes in the latter. Thus even if the causal relationship between the two sets of variables remains unproven, a too-remote relationship between modes of labor inclusion and labor's fortunes/industrial performance is further discounted.

Fourth, alternative explanations of labor's fortunes in the three countries are not supported by the data—a point to which we now turn.

ALTERNATIVE EXPLANATIONS OF LABOR'S FORTUNES AND REGIME PERFORMANCE

While, undeniably, factors besides the mode of labor inclusion in corporate decision making also contribute to labor's fortunes, no single such other factor can explain labor's fortunes in the three auto industries under consideration.

- "Labor-friendly" state policy/legislation, for example, can explain labor's relatively good fortunes in Germany compared to the US, but not labor's relatively good fortunes in Japan compared to the US—unless, quite implausibly, we consider the Japanese state, long beyond the reach of pro-labor political parties and unions, as more labor-friendly than the US state (frequently controlled by a Democratic Party supported by—but often disloyal to—trade unions).[13]

- Union density, while certainly an important indicator of labor's power, is also overrated because it pertains to only one dimension of labor's power, its capacity to exit (strike). In fact, union density cannot explain the ordinal position of the three countries with respect to labor's fortunes. Union density cannot explain differences in labor's power across the three regimes, whether union density is measured on an auto-industry basis (where it is at similarly high levels of more than 70 percent in all cases), or on a national-economy basis (where the US:Germany:Japan unionization rates are on a 1:3:2 ratio). The same can be said of another possible explanation of variations in labor's fortunes across production regimes, the national level of unemployment. As with union density, the level of unemployment certainly affects labor's power, but only its exit-based dimension. Thus a full-employment national economic policy is in labor's interests, but not all of labor's woes are attributable to unemployment: German auto workers have been doing better than their US brethren despite considerably higher levels of unemployment in Germany throughout the 1980s.

- Union centralization, or neo-corporatism, or social-democratic organization is also unable to account for the differentials in labor's fortunes among the three auto industries. It may account for German labor's prosperity but certainly not for Japanese auto workers' comparably good fortunes. In fact, from the social-democratic/democratic-centralist perspective, the ability of the highly decentralized, enterprise unionism of Japan to secure impressively rising wages and employment security, in a context of rapid technological change and global competition, is nearly unintelligible.

- Another possible explanation for the differentials in labor's fortunes we documented is industrial performance itself. German and Japanese auto workers, it may be argued, do better than their US counterparts because German and Japanese auto industries do better than the US one and thus can afford better conditions for their workers. The problem with this explanation is two-fold. First, it begs the question why German and Japanese auto industries perform better than the US auto industry, if not for the mode of labor inclusion. Second, even if we assume a non-labor reason behind German and Japanese industrial success, it is still far from obvious why German and Japanese employers are willing to share the fruits of their success with their workers, unless the latter have the power to mandate such sharing.[14] In particular, even if industrial success can explain the employment security enjoyed by German and Japanese auto workers, it cannot explain why such employment security does not disintegrate during business downturns. Conversely, if we attribute the employment fluctuations of the US auto regime in the 1970s and early-1980s to the "crisis in US auto production," how can we explain the similarly wide fluctuations in US auto employment during the industry's period of ascendancy, in the 1950s and 1960s?

- The U.S. performance deficit, especially until the mid-1980s, cannot be explained by fashion trends in the American market, or the effect of German or Japanese consumer nationalism. In fact,

> "U.S. buyers exhibit the strongest national-industry bias in the world, with about 50 percent of U.S. buyers naming U.S. vehicles as best. This is at odds with world opinion, with U.S.-made vehicles ranking well below Germany's and Japan's outside North America."[15]

- Technological sophistication cannot explain the performance differentials among regimes, or even among plants in the same regime. Germany has the lowest robot-to-worker ratios among the three cases analyzed yet its performance is very strong; technologically less advanced plants often surpass more advanced ones in a variety on performance indicators.[16] Relatedly, the investment-in-research explanation of the performance gap is contradicted by R&D spending data: all auto companies under consideration have similar levels of R&D expenditures, around 5% of sales.[17]

- Given the recently displayed preference by many American firms for downsizing and/or subcontracting as a means of improving their efficiency, one might be tempted to attribute relative U.S. inefficiency to the high degree of vertical integration of U.S. auto companies. The facts, however, contradict this explanation. Japanese auto companies differ among themselves significantly in the degree of vertical integration, with no discernible differences in performance. Toyota and Honda, both among the most efficient auto companies, are at the antipodes of vertical integration.[18] The degree of vertical integration is not regime-specific, but differs from country to country and from firm to firm: GM is 70% vertically integrated, Chrysler and most Japanese firms are 30% integrated, while German assembly firms average 50%.[19]

- Industrial policy or state involvement in export industries is not as decisive a factor in industrial performance as it is often assumed, at least in the case of the auto industry. State guidance levels correspond with the performance ranking of the three countries, only if we consider the role of Japan's MITI as much larger than its actual size indicates.[20] But even then, the state-involvement theory cannot explain the significant changes in the US auto balance of trade after the late-1980s (was the state's involvement really higher then?), or the improvement in the reliability ratings of U.S. autos after the mid-1980s. Nor can industrial policy explain the remarkably strong performance of Japanese transplants in the US.

- Trade policy, another type of state involvement, is also unsatisfactory as an explanation of industrial success differentials among the three auto industries. Even if protectionism can account for Japan's impressive auto trade balance, it cannot account for the Japanese autos' equally impressive reliability evaluations. Moreover, even if Japan's success can be attributed to its protectionism, the latter can certainly not explain Germany's also impressive balance of trade or product quality evaluations. Lastly, Japan's trade policy, as with its industrial policy, cannot account for the impressive performance of Japanese transplants in the US (and elsewhere).

BRINGING LABOR BACK IN

The 1980s began with severe blows to American auto workers' interests, but ended with the consolidation of Jointness— a production regime that departs significantly from its segregationist past and moves significantly in the direction of integration. After experiencing dramatic decimation of their ranks, especially between 1979 and 1982, by the second half of the decade American auto workers began to enjoy higher job security than ever before, while their wages stopped increasing at the brisk pace of the past decades. As the history of their German and Japanese counterparts indicates, however, moderating redistributive demands in exchange for more influence in productivist decisions is a good trade-off for labor and for the regime as a whole.

The transformation of the U.S. auto regime in the direction of integration was, in effect, forced onto capital but also on elements of labor by competitive pressures from more efficient producers abroad. By 1982-84, US labor was rudely awakened to the precariousness of the type of power (exit-over-wages) it had enjoyed since the 1950s. US capitalists were also rudely awakened to their inability to compete against production regimes that elicited labor's active cooperation. While the changes undertaken were too timid to be proven adequate to the task, they did prove to be in the right direction. The recovery of the US auto industry under Jointness, and the continuing success of its conceptual outpost, Saturn, portend a strong future for labor's integration in the US auto production regime.

We have been careful to restrict the domain of our analysis to the automobile industries of the US, Germany, and Japan in order to control for the type of labor process involved, the degree of labor's exit-based power, the maturity of industrial relations, and the type of national economy involved. Further research and considerable analytic adjustment is needed before the implications of our analysis are extended beyond the auto industry and beyond the three countries examined. While our analysis is highly suggestive of its relevance for the dynamics of the auto industries of other countries, we must caution against reaching more than tentative conclusions for those cases. Issues of comparability make it far from evident that the hypothesized relationships between labor' inclusion and its fortunes/industrial performance will hold to the same extent in counties beyond the US, Germany, and Japan, or even beyond the auto industry in those countries.

The very small population of Sweden, for example, may render that case too dissimilar with the other three in resource endowments and domestic market size to make a comparison of its industrial performance meaningful enough. France, on the other hand, is very dissimilar from the other three in the level of unionization in the auto industry, which may help explain the disappointing effects of the legally mandated inclusion of certain productivist interests of labor in corporate decision making there. Moreover, the French state's considerable regulation of mass layoffs might suggest that French labor's productivist interests are in effect included in corporate decision making through the state. It seems, however, that the state's intervention is aimed at facilitating labor's orderly exodus from employment, rather than injecting labor's interests in the formulation of corporate decisions affecting employment.[21] The lower levels of performance of the British and Italian auto industries under regimes of segregated inclusion seem to validate our analysis, but without further research this remains an impressionistic evaluation.

Whether Jointness will spread from the auto industry to the rest of the U.S. economy is also difficult to ascertain from the evidence, because we cannot readily control for possibly important independent variables as we have done in this book: union density, size of company, capital intensity, etc. Union density, for example, is very low in the US economy as a whole, but very high in the US auto industry. Jointness, as well as the German and Japanese regimes it approximates, is predicated on labor's ability/will to use its exit-based power (the strike) in order establish a new basis of power, the inclusion of its interests in productivist decision making. In this sense, the very low level of unionization outside the auto industry bodes ill for the prospects of expanding the coverage of Jointness beyond the auto industry.

The demonstration effect of the successes of Jointness in the auto industry and the pressures of foreign competition may not suffice to convince other capitalists of the need to integrate labor's interests into corporate decision making. In the absence of effective labor pressures, individual capitalists may continue to seek profits through their more familiar if socially ever more wasteful production regime: one which allows them to externalize costs of production, such as wasted human labor power and creative potential, to labor and to society at large.

It remains possible, however, that labor's advances in the auto industry will have a strong "demonstration effect" on other workers, as they have done in the past. The rising number of ESOPs and of "employee-owners" (especially in the airlines industry) corroborates such expectation.

A central aim of this book has been to restore the notion that the working class is not only an object but also a subject of history. The evidence presented in this book goes a long way in affirming that workers' control over the utilization of the means of production, properly construed, far from being antithetical to industrial performance, is at least consonant with it—at least in the case of the top three automobile industries of the world. Moreover, the evidence undermines the notion of a functional equivalence in competitive performance between a strong-labor method and a weak-labor method of organizing production. Rather, we have found that in the three leading auto industries of the world, labor's power is strongly and positively related to productive performance. A functional equivalence is to be found, rather, between different institutional arrangements that secure labor's interests, namely between arrangements whereby labor's interests are formally represented in decision making (codetermination, Germany) and those whereby labor's interests are incorporated in the very framework of decision making (lifetime employment, Japan).

Access to the levers of the state will remain an important tactical goal for labor, but (labor) should not mistake it for its strategic goal, control over the means of production. Whether by the state's explicit sanctioning or sufferance, labor's task, as it pushes the limits of capitalism, is to establish that business is not only capital's but also labor's business. Only then will it be widely accepted that "what is good for labor is good for America," and labor's hegemonic position in a less wasteful society will be at hand.

NOTES

1. For a lucid discussion of normative and pragmatic concerns, and of the compartmentalization of the political and the economic realms in the best of political economy research see Mark Kesselman, "How Should One Study Economic Policy-Making? Four Characters in Search of an Object," *World Politics* (July 1992).

2. Labor's redistributive interests denote wages and benefits (as well as disciplinary procedures that affect compensation); its productivist interests denote employment (as well as the less measurable skilled and meaningful work). See chapters 1 and 2.

3. Total hourly labor costs include wages as well as benefits.

4. Moreover, Japanese auto workers' wages are understated in Figure 1, inasmuch as the data, in the case of Japan, include the compensation of (lower-paid) motorcycle and breaks workers. It should be noted that Japan did not have an auto industry at all before World War II.

5. The international comparison of executive pay is reported by Towers, Perrin, Forster & Crosby; cited in Linda L. Carr and Moosa Valinezhad, "The role of ethics in executive compensation: Toward a contractarian interpretation

Bibliography

Abernathy, William J., Kim B. Clark, and Alan M. Kantrow, *Industrial Renaissance: Producing an Competitive Future for America* (New York: Basic Books, 1983).

Abraham, Katherine G. and Susan N. Houseman, *Job Security in America: Lessons from Germany* (Washington, D.C.: The Brookings Institution, 1993).

Abraham, Katherine G. and Susan N. Houseman, "Job Security and Work Force Adjustment: How Different Are U.S. and Japanese Practices?" in Christoph F. Buechtemann (ed.), *Employment Security and Labor Market Behavior: Interdisciplinary Approaches and International Evidence* (Ithaca, N.Y.: ILR Press, 1993).

Adams, Roy J. and C.H. Rummel, "Workers' Participation in Management in West Germany," *Industrial Relations Journal*, no. 8 (Spring 1977).

Adams, Roy J., *Industrial Relations Under Liberal Democracy: North America in Comparative Perspective* (Columbia, S.C.: University of South Carolina Press, 1995).

Addison, John T. and Barry T. Hirsch, "Union Effects on Productivity, Profits and Growth: Has the Long Run Arrived?" *Journal of Labor Economics*, vol. 7, no. 1 (1989).

Addison, John T., Kornelius Kraft, and Joachim Wagner, "German Works Councils and Firm Performance," in Bruce E. Kaufman and Morris M. Kleiner (eds) *Employee Representation: Alternatives and Future Directions* (Madison, WI.: IRRA, 1993).

Aglietta, Michel, *A Theory of Capitalist Regulation: The U.S. Experience* (London: Verso 1979).

Altshuler, Alan, Martin Anderson, Daniel Jones, Daniel Roos, and James Womack, *The Future of the Automobile: The Report of MIT's International Automobile Program* (Cambridge, Mass.: MIT Press, 1986).

Anderson, Perry, *Lineages of the Absolutist State*, (London: Verso Editions, 1979).

Aoki, Masahiko, *The Cooperative Game Theory of the Firm* (Oxford: Clarendon Press, 1984).

Aoki, Masahiko, *Information, Incentives, and Bargaining in the Japanese Economy* (New York: Cambridge University Press, 1988).

Aranowitz, Stanley, *False Promises: The Shaping of American Working Class Consciousness* (New York: McGraw Hill, 1973).

Aranowitz, Stanley, "The End of Political Economy," *The Crisis in Historical Materialism: Class, Politics and Cutlure in Marxist Theory* (New York: Praeger, 1981).

Aranowitz, Stanley, "The decline of American liberalism," *New Politics* (Summer 1986).

Automotive Industries, various issues.

Bain, George S. and Robert Price, *Profiles of Union Growth: A Comparative Portrait of Eight Countries* (Oxford: Basil Blackwell, 1980).

Baldwin, Carliss Y. and Kim B. Clark, "Capital-Budgeting Systems and Capabilities Investments in U.S. Companies After the Second World War," *Business History Review* (March 22, 1994).

Bamber, Greg J. and Russel D. Lansbury, "Studying Internationnal and Comparative Industrial Relations," in idem (eds.), *International and Comparative Industrial Relations: A Study of Developed Market Economies* (London: Allen & Unwin, 1987).

Bamber, Greg J. and Russel D. Lansbury, "Codetermination and Technological Change in the German Automobile Industry" *New Technology, Work and Employment*, 2 (2), 1987.

Barnett, George, "American Trade Unionism and Social Insurance," *American Economic Review* (March 1933).

Batstone, Eric and Stephen Gourlay, *Unions, Unemployment and Innovation* (Oxford: Basil Blackwell, 1986).

Belman, Dale, "Unions, the Quality of Labor Relations, and Firm Performance," in Larry Mishel and Paula Voos (eds), *Unions and Economic Competitiveness* (Armonk, N.Y.: M.E. Sharpe, Inc., 1991).

Bergmann, Joachim and Walter Muller-Jentsch, "The Federal Republic of Germany: Cooperative Unionism and Dual Bargaining System Challenged," in Solomon Barkin (ed), *Worker Militancy and its*

Consequences: The changing Climate of Western Industrial Relations (New York: Praeger, 1983).

Berger, Suzanne, "Politics and antipolitics in Western Europe in the seventies," *Daedalus* (108:1 1979).

Berger, Suzanne (ed.), *Organizing Interests in Western Europe* (Cambridge: Cambridge University Press, 1981).

Berggren, Christian, *Alternatives to Lean Production: Work Organization in the Swedish Auto Industry* (Ithaca, N.Y.: ILR Press, 1992).

Berggren, Christian, "NUMMI vs. Uddevalla," *Sloan Management Review* (January 1994).

Blackwood, George Douglas, *The United Automobile Workers of America 1935-1951*, Ph.D. Dissertation (Chicago: University of Chicago, 1951).

Blauner, Robert, *Alienation and Freedom* (Chicago: University of Chicago Press, 1964).

Bluestone, Irving, "How Quality-of-Worklife Projects Work for the United Auto Workers," *Monthly Labor Review*, v. 103 no. 7 (July 1980).

Bluestone, Barry and Bennett Harrison, *The Deindustrialization of America* (New York: Basic Books, 1982).

Bluestone, Barry and Irving Bluestone, *Negotiating the future: a labor perspective on American business* (New York: Basic Books, 1992).

Bornstein, Stephen, "States and unions: from postwar settlement to contemporary stalemate", in S. Bornstein, D. Held and J. Krieger (eds), *The State in Capitalist Europe* (London: George Allen & Unwin, 1984).

Bornstein, Stephen, David Held, and Joel Krieger (eds), *The State in Capitalist Europe* (London: George Allen & Unwin, 1984).

Borzeix, Anni, "Trade union positions on the organziation of production", in Mark Kesselman (ed) *The French Workers' Movement: Economic Crisis and Political Change* (London: George Allen & Unwin, 1984).

Bowles, Samuel, "Post-Marxian economics: labour, learning and history," *Social Science Information* (September 1985).

Bowles, Samuel and Herbert Gintis, "The crisis of liberal democratic capitalism," *Politics and Society* (January 1982).

Bowles, Samuel, David M. Gordon and Thomas Weiskopf, *Beyond the Wasteland* (New York: Anchor, 1984).

Bowles, Samuel, David M. Gordon and Thomas Weiskopf, "Power and Profits: The Social Structure of Accumulation and the Profitability of the Postwar U.S. Economy," *Review of Radical Political Economics* (Spring-Summer 1986).

Boyer, Robert, *The Search for Labour Market Flexibility: The European Economies in Transition* (Oxford: Clarendon Press, 1988).

Boyer, Robert, "The Economics of Job Protection and Emerging New Capital-Labor Relations" in Christoph F. Buechtemann (ed.), *Employment Security and Labor Market Behavior: Interdisciplinary Approaches and International Evidence* (Ithaca, N.Y.: ILR Press, 1993).

Braverman, Harry, *Labor and Monopoly Capital: The Degradation of Work in the Twentieth Century* (New York: Monthly Review Press, 1974).

Brenner, Robert, "The Origins of Capitalist Development: A Critique of Neo-Smithean Marxism," *New Left Review* (July-August 1977).

Brodner, Peter, *Skill Based Automation: Proceedings of the IFAC Workshop, Karlsruhe, FRG, 3-5 September, 1986* (New York: Pergamon Press, 1987).

Brody, David, *Workers in Industrial America: Essays on the 20th Century Struggle* (New York: Oxford University Press, 1980).

Buchele, Robert and Jens Christiansen, "Worker Rights Promote Productivity Growth," *Challenge*, September-October 1995.

Buechtemann, Christoph F. (ed.), *Employment Security and Labor Market Behavior: Interdisciplinary Approaches and International Evidence* (Ithaca, N.Y.: ILR Press, 1993).

Buechtemann, Christoph F., "Employment Security and Deregulation: The West German Experience," in Christoph F. Buechtemann, (ed.), *Employment Security and Labor Market Behavior: Interdisciplinary Approaches and International Evidence* (Ithaca, N.Y.: ILR Press, 1993).

Burawoy, Michael, "Between the Labor Process and the State: The Changing Face of Factory Regimes Under Advanced Capitalism," *American Sociological Review* 48 (October 1983).

Burawoy, Michael, *The Politics of Production: Factory Regimes under Capitalism and Socialism* (London: Verso, 1985).

Burawoy, Michael, "Marxism without Micro-Foundations," *Socialist Review* No. 2, 1989.

Bureau of Economic Affairs, *National Income and Product Accounts* (Washington, D.C.: Department of Commerce, various years).

Bureau of National Affairs, Inc., *Basic Patterns in Union Contracts* (Washington, D.C.: BNA Books, 1986).

Bureau of National Affairs, Inc., *Collective Bargaining Negotiations and Contracts. Basic Patterns in Union Contracts. Vol. 2: Management and Union Rights* (Washington, D.C.: BNA, Inc., 1986).

Bureau of National Affairs, Inc., *Collective Bargaining Negotiations and Contracts* (Washington, D.C.: BNA, Inc., 1990, 1993).

BusinessWeek, various issues.

Cameron, David R., "Social Democracy, Corporatism, Labour Quiescence and the Representation of Economic Interest in Advanced Capitalist Society," in John H. Goldthorpe (ed) *Order and Conflict in Contemporary Capitalism* (New York: Oxford University Press, 1985).

Carr, Linda L. and Moosa Valinezhad, "The role of ethics in executive compensation: Toward a contractarian interpretation of the neoclassical theory of managerial remuneration," *Journal of Business Ethics*, February 1994.

Chamberlain, Neil W., *Sourcebook on Labor* (New York: McGraw-Hill Book Co., 1964).

Chandler, Alfred D., Jr., *Strategy and Structure: Chapters in the History of American Industrial Enterprise* (Cambridge, MA: MIT Press, 1962).

Chandler, Lester, *America's Greatest Depression* (New York: Harper & Row, 1970).

Chandler, Alfred D., Jr., "The Competitive Performance of U.S. Industrial Enterprises since the Second World War," *Business History Review* 68 (Spring 1994).

Child J., "Managerial Strategies, New Technology and the Labour Process", in David Knights, Hugh Willmott, and David Collinson (eds), *Job Redesign: Critical Perspectives on the Labour Process* (Aldershot: Gower, 1985).

C.I.O. Committee on Economic Policy, *The Challenge of Automation* (Washington, DC: Public Affairs Press, 1955).

Clark, Kim, "The Impact of Unionization of Producitivy: A Case Study," *Industrial and Labor Relations Review*, vol. 33, no. 4 (July 1980).

Clark, Kim B., Robert H. Hayes, and Christopher Lorenz (eds), *The Uneasy Alliance: Managing the Productivity-Technoogy Dilemma* (Cambridge: Harvard Business School Press, 1985).

Clark, Kim B. and Takahiro Fujimoto, *Product Development Performance: Strategy, Organization, and Management in the World Auto Industry* (Boston, Mass.: Harvard Business School Press, 1991).

Cohen, Stephen S. and John Zysman, *Manufacturing Matters* (New York: Basic Books, 1987).

Cohen, Jean, *Class and Civil Society* (Amherst, Mass.: 1982).

Cole, Robert E., *Japanese Blue Collar* (Berkeley: University of California Press, 1979).

Cole, Robert E., *Work, Mobility and Participation* (Berkeley: University of California Press, 1979).

Cole, Robert E. and Taizo Yakushiji, *American and Japaneese Auto Industries in Transition* (Ann Arbor: University of Michigan, 1984).

Commons, John, *Institutional Economics* (New York: Macmillan, 1934).

Coombs, Rod, "Automation, Management Strategies, and Labour-Process Change", in David Knights, Hugh Willmott, and David Collinson (eds), *Job Redesign: Critical Perspectives on the Labour Process* (Aldershot: Gower, 1985).

Cooper, Laura, "Authorization cards and union representation outcome: An empirical assessment of the assumption underlying the Supreme Court's 'Gissel' Decision," *North-western University Law Review* 79 (March 1984).

Coriat, Benjamin *L'Atelier et le Chronometre: Essai sur la Production de Masse* (Paris: Editions Bourgeois, 1979).

Coriat, Benjamin, "The restructuring of the assembly line: a new economy of time and control", *Capital and Class* 11 (Summer 1980).

Coriat, Benjamin, "L'atelier fordien automatise, micro-electronique et travail ouvrier dans les industries de chaine", *Non!* (November-December 1981).

Coriat, Benjamin, *Penser a l'envers: travail et organization dans l'enterprise japonaise* (Paris: Christian Bourgeois Editeur, 1991).

Cornfield, Daniel B., "Labor-Management Cooperation or Managerial Control: Emerging Patterns of Labor Relations in the United States", in Daniel B. Corfield (ed), *Workers, Managers, and Technological Change: Emerging Patterns of Labor Relations* (New York: Plenum Press, 1987).

Cornfield, Daniel B. (ed), *Workers, Managers, and Technological Change: Emerging Patterns of Labor Relations* (New York: Plenum Press, 1987).

Cornfield, Daniel B., "Workers, Managers, and Technological Change", in Daniel B. Corfield (ed), *Workers, Managers, and Technological Change: Emerging Patterns of Labor Relations* (New York: Plenum Press, 1987). Review of literature.

Cormier, Frank and William J. Eaton, *Reuther* (Englewood Cliffs, N.J.: Prentice-Hall, 1970).

Cusumano, Michael, *The Japanese Automobile Industry: Technology and Management at Nissan and Toyota* (Cambridge: Harvard University Press, 1985).

Cutcher-Gershenfeld, Joel, Robert B. McKersie, and Richard Walton, "Negotiating Transformation: Negotiations Lessons from Current Developments in Industrial Relations." In Lawrence R. Janch and Jerry L. Walls (eds.), *Academy of Management Best Papers Proceedings* (Washington, D.C.: Academy of Management, 1989).

Cyert, Richrd M. and David C. Mowery (eds), *Technolgoy and Employment: Innovation and Growth in the US Economy* (Washington, DC: National Academy Press, 1987). (Panel on Tech. and Employment—National

Academy of Sciences/National Academy of Engineering/Institute of Medicine).

Dahl, Robert A., *A Preface to Economic Democracy* (Berkeley: University of California Press, 1985).

Dalton, Russel J., Scott C. Flanagan and Paul Allen Beck (eds), *Electorla Change in Advanced Industrial Democracies* (Princeton: Princeton University Press, 1984).

Dankbaar, Ben, "Sectoral Governance in the Automobile Industries of Germany, Great Britain, and France," in J. Rogers Hollingsworth, Philippe C. Schmitter, and Wolfgang Streeck (eds.) *Governing Capitalist Economies: Performance and Control of Economic Sectors* (New York: Oxford University Press, 1994).

Dassbach, Carl H.A., "Industrial Robots in the American Automobile Industry," *The Insurgent Sociologist*, (Summer 1986).

Davis, Mike, "The Stop-Watch and the Wooden Shoe: Scientific Management and the Industrial Workers of the World," *Radical America*, 1975.

Davis, Mike, "The Barren Marriage of American Labour and the Democratic Party," *New Left Review*, 124 (November-December 1980).

Davis, Mike, *Prisoners of the American Dream: Politics and Economy in the History of the U.S. Working Class* (London: Verso, 1986).

Destler, I.M., *Dollar Politics: Exchange Rate Policymaking in the United States* (Washington, D.C.: Institute for International Economics, 1989).

Doeringer, Peter and Michael Piore, *Internal Labor Markets and Manpower Analysis* (Lexington, MA.: D.C. Heath and Co., 1971).

Doyle, Kevin, "Can Saturn save GM?" *Incentive* (December 1992).

Dunlop, John T., *Industrial Relations Systems* (New York: Holt Rinehart, and Winston, 1958).

Dunlop, John T., "Have the 1980s changed U.S. industrial relations?" *Monthly Labor Review* (May 1988).

Dyer, Davis, Malcolm Salter and Alan Weber, *Changing Alliances* (Boston: Harvard Business School Press, 1987).

Edwards, Richard, *Contested Terrain: The Transformation of the Workplace in the Twentieth Century* (New York: Basic Books, 1979).

Elger, Tony, "Braverman, capital accumulationa and deskilling," in Stephen Wood (ed), *The Degradation of Work?* (London: Hutchinson & Co., 1982).

Esping-Andersen, Gosta et. al., "Modes of Class Struggle and the Capitalist State," *Kapitalstate*, 4/5 (1980).

Esping-Andersen, Gosta, *Politics against Markets: The Social Democratic Road to Power* (Princeton: Princeton University Press, 1985).

Esping-Andersen, Gosta, *The Three Worlds of Welfare Capitalism* (Princeton: Princeton University Press, 1990).

Evans, Peter B., Dietrich Rueschemeyer, Theda Skocpol (eds.) *Bringing the State Back In* (New York : Cambridge University Press, 1985).

The Federal Minister of Labor and Social Affairs, *Co-determination in the Federal Republic of Germany* (Bonn: Referat Presse, 1980).

Feldacker, Bruce S., *Labor Guide to Labor Law*, 3rd ed. (Englewood Cliffs, N.J.: Prentice Hall, 1990).

Filemon, Elisabeth, "Robots: their present-day use and prospects for the future," in *IMPACT of Science on Society* (# 146, 1987).

Fischer, Lydia "Auto Crisis and Union Response," in D. Kennedy, C. Craypo and M. Lehman (eds), *Labor and Technology: Union Response to Changing Environments* (Pennsylvania State University, 1982).

Flanagan, R.J., "Unemployment as a Hiring Problem," *OECD Economic Studies* 11 (Autumn 1988).

Fogel, Robert William, *Time on the Cross: The Economics of American Negro Slavery* (New York: W.W. Norton, 1979 and 1989).

Fox, Alan, *Beyond Contract: Work, Power and Trust Relations* (London: Faber & Faber, 1974).

Francis, Arthur, *New Technology at Work* (Oxford: Clarendon Press, 1986).

Freedman, Audrey, "How the 1980s have changed industrial relations," *Monthly Labor Review* (May 1988).

Freeman, Richard B. and James L. Medoff, *What Do Unions Do?* (New York: Basic Books, 1984).

Freeman, Richard B. (ed.), *Working Under Different Rules* (New York: Russel Sage Foundation, 1994).

Friedman, Andrew, *Industry and Labour* (London: Macmillan, 1977). Seminal work on 'responsible autonomy'.

Friedman, David, *The Misunderstood Miracle: Industrial Development and Political Change in Japan* (Ithaca, N.Y.: Cornell University Press, 1988).

Fuss, Melvin A. and Leonard Waverman, *Costs and Productivity in Automobile Production: The Challenge of Japanese Efficiency* (Cambridge: Cambridge University Press, 1992).

Galbraith, John Kenneth, *The New Industrial State* (Boston: Houghton Mifflin, 3rd rev. ed., 1978).

Galenson, Walter, *New Trends in Employment Practices: An International Survey* (New York: Greenwood Press, 1991).

Gallie, Duncan *In Search of the New Working Class: Automation and Social Integration Within The Capitalist Enterprise* (Cambridge: Cambridge University Press, 1978).

Garbarino, Joseph, "Unionism without Unions: The New Industrial Relations?" *Industrial Relations* 23 (Winter 1984).

Garson, Barbara, *The Electronic Sweatshop* (New York: Penguin Books, 1988).

Gartman, David, *Auto Slavery: The Labor Process in the American Automobile Industy, 1897-1950* (New Brunswick: Rutgers University Press, 1986).

Goldfield, Michael, *The Decline of Organized Labor in the United States* (Chicago: The University of Chicago Press, 1987).

Goldthorpe, John H. (ed.) *Order and Conflict in Contemporary Capitalism: Studies in the Political Economy of Western European Nations* (New York: Oxford University Press, 1984).

Goldthorpe, John H. "The end of convergence: corporatism and dualism in modern western societies", in John H. Goldthorpe (ed), *Order and Conflict in Contemporary Capitalism: Studies in the Political Economy of Western European Nations* (Oxford: Clarendon Press, 1984).

Gordon, Andrew, *The Evolution of Labor Relations in Japan: Heavy Industry, 1853-1955* (Cambridge, MA.: Harvard University Press, 1985).

Gordon, David, "Stages of Accumulation and Long Economic Cycles," in T. Hopkins and I. Wallerstein (eds), *Processes of the World System* (Bevelry Hills: Sage Publications, 1980).

Gordon, David M., Richard Edwards, and Michael Reich, *Segmented Work, Divided Workers: The Historical Transformation of Labor in the United States* (New York: Cambridge University Press, 1982).

Gorz, Andre, *Farewell to the Working Class* (London: Pluto, 1982).

Gould, William B., *The Japanese Reshaping of American Labor Law* (Cambridge, Mass: MIT Press, 1984).

Gourevitch, Peter A., Andrew Martin, George Ross, and Stephen Bornstein, *Unions and Economic Crisis: Britain, West Germany, and Sweden* (London: George Allen & Unwin, 1984).

Gourevitch, Peter A., *Politics in Hard Times: Comparative Responses to International Economic Crises* (Ithaca, N.Y.: Cornell University Press, 1986).

Green, James R., *The World of the Worker: Labor in Twentieth Century America* (New York: Hill and Wag, 1980).

Groehn, Kathy, *The Bargain: The Story Behind the Thirty Year Honeymoon of GM and the UAW* (New York: Nellen Publishing Co., Inc., 1980).

Groux, Guy "Trade Unionism and Technology," in Mark Kesselman (ed) *The French Workers' Movement: Economic Crisis and Political Change* (London: George Allen & Unwin, 1984).

Groux, Guy "De l'interventionnisme etatique au 'Nouvel echange politique'" paper delevered for the Conference "A France of Pluralism and

Consensus?" in Columbia University and New York University (October 9-11 1987).

Gustavsen, Bjorn, Peter Grootings, Lajor Hethy (eds), *New Forms of Work Organization in Europe* (New Brunswick, N.J.: Transaction Books, 1989).

Halberstam, David, *The Reckoning* (New York: Morrow, 1986).

Hall, Peter A., "Economic planning and the state: the evolution of economic challenge and politial response in Frane," in Esping-Anderson and Friedland (eds), *Political Power and Social Theory* vol. 3 (Greenwich, Conn.: Jai Press, 1981).

Hall, Peter A. "Patterns of Economic Policy: An Organizational Approach," in S. Bornstein, D. Held and J. Krieger (eds), *The State in Capitalist Europe* (London: George Allen & Unwin, 1984).

Hall, Peter A., *Governing the Economy: The Politics of State Intervention in Britain and France* (New York: Oxford University Press, 1986).

Hashimoto, Masanori, *The Japanese Labor Market in a Comparative Perspective with the United States* (Kalamazoo, Mi.: Upjohn Institute for Employment Research, 1990).

Hayes, Robert H. and William A. Abernathy, "Managing Our Way to Economic Decline," *Harvard Business Review* 58 (July-August 1980).

Howell, Chris, *Regulating Labor: The State and Industrial Relations Reform in Postwar France* (Princeton: Princeton University Press, 1992).

Hamper, Ben, *Rivethead: Tales from the Assembly Line* (New York: Warner Books, 1991).

Harris, Howell, *The Right to Manage: Industrial Relations Policies of American Business in the 1940s* (Madison, WI: University of Wisconsin Press, 1982)

Hart, Jeffrey A., *Rival Capitalists: International Competitiveness in the United States, Japan, and Western Europe* (Ithaca, N.Y.: Cornell University Press, 1992).

Hatsopoulos, George N. and Stephen H. Brooks, "The Gap in the Cost of Capital: Causes, Effects, and Remedies," in Ralph Landau and Dale W. Jorgenson (eds.) *Technology and Economic Policy* (Cambridge, Mass., 1986).

Hayes C. and N. Fonda, *Competence and Competition* (London: Insititute for Manpower Studies, 1984).

Hayward, Jack, "Institutional inertia and political impetus in France and Britain," *European Journal of Political Research* (December 1976)

Heckscher, Charles and Ronnie Straw, *QWL Focus* (Montral: Ontario Ministry of Labour, Spring 1984.

Heilbroner, Robert L. and James K. Galbraith, *The Economic Problem* (Englewood Cliffs, N.J.: Prentice-Hall, 1987).

Heshizer, Brian "Union Officials Assess the Labor Movement and Labor-Management Relations," *Labor Studies Journal* (Spring 1987).

Hibbs, Douglas A. Jr., "Industrial conflict in advanced industial societies", *American Political Science Review* (December 1976).

Hill, Stephen *Competition and Control at Work: New Industrial Sociology* (Cambridge: MIT Press, 1981).

Hilton, Margaret, "Shared Training: Learning from Germany," *Monthly Labor Review* (March 1993).

Hirschhorn, Larry *Beyond Mechanization* (Cambridge, Mass: MIT Press, 1984).

Hirschman, Albert O., *Exit, Voice, and Loyalty* (Cambridge, Mass.: Harvard University Press, 1970).

Hoerr, John, "Sharpening Minds for a Competitive Edge," *BusinessWeek* (December 17, 1990).

Horner, William T., "Tarrytown: A Union Perspective," *National Productivity Review* (Winter 1981-82).

Houseman, Susan H., *Job Security Policies in the United States and Japan* (Kalamazoo, Mi.: W.E. Upjohn Institute, 1991)

Howe, Irving and B.J. Widick, *The UAW and Walter Reuther* (New York: Random House, 1949).

Hunt, Allan H. and Timothy L. Hunt, *Human Resource Implications of Robotics* (Kalamazoo, MI: W.E. Upjohn Institute for /Employment Research, 1983).

Huntington, Samuel, "The United States," in Michel, Crozier (ed.), *The Crisis of Democracy: Report on the Governability of Democracies to the Trilateral Commission* (New York: NYU Press, 1975).

Hyman, Richard and Tony Elger, "Job controls, the employers' offensive, and alternative strategies", *Capital and Class* 15 (Autumn 1981).

Hyman, Richard and Wolfgang Streeck, *New Technology and Industrial Relations* (New York: Blackwell, 1988).

Inagami, Takeshi, *Japanese Workplace Industrial Relations* (Tokyo: Japan Institute of Labor, 1988).

Inagami Takeshi et al., *A Research Survey on the Advanced Nations' Syndrome and the Changing Work Ethic* (Tokyo: Japan Productivity Centre, 1985).

Indegaard, Michael and Michael Cushion, "Conflict, Cooperation, and the Global Auto Factory," in Daniel B. Cornfield (ed), *Workers, Managers, and Technological Change: Emerging Patterns of Labor Relations* (New York: Plenum, 1987).

Inglehart, Ronald, *The Silent Revolution* (Princeton: Princeton University Press, 1977).

Jacobi, Otto and Walther Muller-Jentsch, "West Germany: Continuity and Structural Change," in Guido Baglioni and Colin Crouch (eds.), *European Industrial Relations: The Challenge of Flexibility* (London: Sage, 1990).

Jacobi, Otto, Brendt Keller, and Walther Muller-Jentsch, "Germany: Codetermining the Future?" in Anthony Ferner and Richard Hyman (eds.) *Industrial Relations in the New Europe* (Cambridge, Mass.: Basil Blackwell, 1992).

Japan Economic Newswire, December 26, 1990.

The Japan Institute of Labor, *Labor-Management Relations in Japan* (Tokyo: Ministry of Labor, 1994).

Jensen, Michael, "The Modern Industrial Revolution: Exit and the Failure of Internal Control Systems," *Journal of Finance* 48 (July 1993).

Johnson, Chalmers, *The MITI and the Japanese Miracle: the Growth of Industrial Policy* (Stanford, CA: Stanford University Press, 1982).

Johnson, Chalmers, *Japan, Who Governs? The Rise of the Developmental State* (New York: W.W. Norton, 1995).

Jurgens, Urlich, Thomas Malsch and Knuth Dohse, *Breaking from Taylorism: Changing Forms of Work in the Automobile Industry* (Cambridge: Cambridge University Press, 1993).

Kanter, Rosabeth Moss, *The Change Masters* (New York: Simon and Schuster, 1983).

Kapsa, Michael J., *A Structural Model of Strike Determination in U.S. Manufacturing, 1971-1980*, Ph.D. Dissertation (New York: New School for Social Research, 1994).

Katz, Harry C., *Shifting Gears: Changing Labor Relations in the U.S. Automobile Industry* (Cambridge: MIT Press, 1985).

Katz, Harry C., "Automobiles," in David B. Lipsky and Clifford B. Donn (eds), *Collective Bargaining in American Industry* (New York: Lexington Books, 1987).

Katz, Harry C., "The Decentralization of Collective Bargaining: A Literature Review and Comparative Analysis," *Industrial and Labor Relations Review* (October, 1993).

Katz, Harry C., Thomas A. Kochan and Kenneth R. Gobeille, "Industrial Relations Performance, Economic Performance, and QWL Programs: An Interplant Analysis," *Industrial and Labor Relations Review*, (October 1983).

Katz, Harry C. and Charles F. Sabel, "Industrial Relations and Industrial Adjustment in the Car Industry." *Industrial Relations*, Vol.24, No.3 (Fall 1985).

Katzenstein, Peter J. (ed), *Industry and Politics in West Germany: Toward the Third Republic* (Ithaca, NY: Cornell University Press, 1989).

Keefe, Jeffrey H., "Do Unions Influence the Diffusion of Technology?" *Industrial and Labor Relations Review*, vol. 44, no. 2 (January 1991).

Keeran, Roger, *The Communist Party and the Auto Workers Unions*, (Bloomington, IN: Indiana University Press, 1980).

Kelley, Maryellen R. and Bennett Harrison, "Unions, Technology, and Labor-Management Cooperation," in Larry Mishel and Paula Voos (eds), *Unions and Economic Competitiveness* (Armonk, N.Y.: M.E. Sharpe, Inc., 1991).

Kennedy, Donald, Charles Craypo, and Mary Lehman (eds), *Labor and Technology: Union Response to Changing Environments* (Department of Labor Studies, The Pennsylvania State University, 1982).

Kenney, Martin and Richard Florida, "Beyond Mass Production: Production and the Labor Process in Japan," *Politics and Society* (March 1988).

Kenney, Martin and Richard Florida, *Beyond Mass Production: the Japanese system and its transfer to the U.S.* (New York: Oxford University Press, 1993).

Kesselman, Mark, "Socialism without the Workers: The Case of France" *Kapitalstate*, 10/11, 1983.

Kesselman, Mark, "How Should One Study Economic Policy-Making? Four Characters in Search of an Object," *World Politics* (July 1992).

Kesselman, Mark (ed) *The French Workers' Movement: Economic Crisis and Political Change* (London: George Allen & Unwin, 1984).

Knights, David, Hugh Willmott, and David Collinson (eds), *Job Redesign: Critical Perspectives on the Labour Process* (Aldershot: Gower, 1985).

Kochan, Thomas A., Harry C. Katz, and Nancy R. Mower, *Worker Participation and American Unions* (Kalamazoo, MI: W.E. Upjohn Institute for Employment Research, 1984).

Kochan, Thomas A., Harry C. Katz and Robert B. McKersie (eds), *The Trasformation of American Industrial Relations* (New York: Basic Books, 1986).

Kochan, Thomas, and Michael Piore, "U.S. Industrial Relations in Transition", in Thomas Kochan (ed), *Challenges and Choices Facing American Labor* (Cambridge: MIT Press, 1985).

Koike, Kazuo, "Internal Labor Markets: Workers in Large Firms," in T. Shirai (ed), *Contemporary Industrial Relations in Japan* (Madison, Wi.: University of Madison Press, 1983).

Korpi, Walter, *The Working Class in Welfare Capitalism: Work, Unions and Politics in Sweden* (London: Routlege, 1978).

Korpi, Walter and Michael Shalev, "Strikes, Industrial Relations and Class Conflict in Capitalist Societies," *British Journal of Sociology*, 30, 1979.

Koshiro, Kazutoshi, "The Organization of Work and Internal Labour Market Flexibility in Japanese Industrial Relations", in *New Directions in Work Organization* (Paris: OECD, 1992).

Krafcik, John F., "Triumph of the Lean Production System," *Sloan Management Review* (Fall 1988).

Krafcik, John F. and John Paul MacDuffie, "Explaining High Performance Manufacturing: The International Automotive Assembly Plant Study," (Cambridge, Mass.: MIT Press, 1989).

Krieger, Joel and Teresa Amott, "Thatcher and Reagan: state theory and the 'hyper-capitalist' regime," *New Political Science* (Spring 1982).

Laclau, Ernesto, and Chantal Mouffe, *Hegemony and Socialist Strategy: Towards a Radical Democratic Politics* (London: Verso, 1985).

Lange, Peter, George Ross, and Maurizio Vannicelli, "Unions as Objects of History and Unions as Actors," in Lange, Ross, and Vannicelli (eds.), *Unions, Change and Crisis: French and Italian Union Strategy and the Political Economy, 1945-1980* (New York: Allen & Unwin, 1982).

Lane, C., "Vocational training and new production concepts in Germany: Some lessons for Britain," *Industrial Relations Journal* 21 (April 1991).

Layard R. and L. Calmfors (eds.) *The Fight Against Unemployment* (Cambridge, Mass.: MIT Press, 1987).

Lazonick, William, "Business Organization and Competitive Advanctage: Capitalist Transformations in the Twentieth Century," Department of Economics, Barnard College, Columbia University (September 1988).

Lazonick, William, "Value Creation on the Shop Floor: Skill, Effort, and Technology in U.S. and Japanese Manufacturing," Department of Economics, Barnard College, Columbia University, October 1988.

Lazonick, William, *Competitive Advantage on the Shop Floor* (Cambridge, MA.: Harvard University Press, 1990).

Lazonick, William, *Business Organization and the Myth of the Market Economy* (New York: Cambridge University Press, 1991).

Leary, Elly and Marybeth Menaker, *Jointness at General Motors: Company Unions in the 21st Century* (New Directions, Internet access, 1995).

Leontief, Wassily and Fay Duchin, *The Future Impact of Automation on Workers* (Oxford: Oxford University Press, 1986).

Levitan, Sar A. and Clifford M. Johnson, "Labor and Mangement: The Illusion of Coopertion," *Harvard Business Review* (September-October 1983).

Lewin, David, and Peter Feuille, "Behavioral Research in Industrtial Relations", *Industrial and Labor Relations Review* 36 (April 1983). Review of behavioral labor relations research.

Lichtenstein, Nelson, *Labor's War at Home: the CIO in World War II* (Cambridge, MA.: Cambridge University Press, 1982).

Lichtenstein, Nelson, "Reutherism on the Shop Floor: Union Strategy and Shop-Floor Conflict in the USA 1946-70," in Steven Tolliday and Jonathan Zeitlin (eds) *The Automobile Industry and its Workers: Between Fordism and Flexibility* (Cambridge: Polity Press, 1986).

Lijphart, Arend, "The comparable-cases strategy in comparative research", *Comparative Political Studies* (July 1975).

Linz, Juan, *The Breakdown of Democratic Regimes: Crisis, Breakdown, and Reequilibration* (Baltimore: The Johns Hopkins University Press, 1978).

Lipietz, Alain, "Behind the Crisis: The Exhaustion of a Regime of Accumulation. A 'Regulation School' Perspective," *Review of Radical Political Economics*, (Spring and Summer 1986).

Lipietz, Alain, *Mirages and Miracles* (London: Verso, 1987).

Lipset, Seymour M. (ed), *Unions in Transition: Entering the Second Century* (San Francisco: Insitute for Contemporary Studies, 1986).

Lipsky, David B. and Clifford B. Donn (eds), *Collective Bargaining in American Industry* (New York: Lexington Books, 1987).

Littler, Craig, *The Development of the Labor Process in Capitalist Societies* (London: Heinemann, 1982).

Lojkine, Jean, "The decomposition and recomposition of the working class," in Mark Kesselman (ed.) *The French Workers' Movement: Economic Crisis and Political Change* (London: George Allen & Unwin, 1984).

Lukes, Steven (ed.), *Power* (New York: New York University Press, 1986).

Mann, Eric, *Taking on General Motors: A Case Study of the UAW Campaign to Keep GM Van Nuys Open* (Los Angeles: Institute of Industrial Relations, 1987).

Marglin, Stephen A. "What Do Bosses Do? The Origins and Functions of Hierarchy in Capitalist Production," *Review of Radical Political Economy* (Summer 1974).

Marglin, Stephen A., "Catching Flies with Honey: An Inquiry into Management Initiatives to Humanize Work," *Economic Analysis and Workers' Management*, 11, 1979.

Markovits, Andrei S. and Christopher S. Allen, "Trade Unions and the Economic Crisis: The West German Case," in Peter Gourevitch, Andrew Martin, George Ross, Chris Allen, Stephen Bornstein and Andrei

Markovits, *Unions and Economic Crisis: Britain, West Germany and Sweden* (London: Allen & Unwin, 1984).

Markovits, Andrei S., *The Politics of the West German Trade Unions* (Cambridge: Cambridge University Press, 1986).

Marx, Karl *Capital: A Critique of Political Economy*, vol. I (New York: International Publishers, 1967).

Marx, Karl, *The Poverty of Philosophy* (New York: International Publishers, 1967).

Marx, Karl, and Frederick Engels, *The German Ideology* (New York: International Publishers, 1972).

Masami, Nomura, "Model Japan? Characteristics of Industrial Relations in the Japanese Automobile Industry" (Berlin: Wissenschaftszentrum, 1985).

McKinsey Global Institute, *Manufacturing Productivity* (Washington, D.C.: McKinsey & Co., 1993).

McLaughlin, Doris, *The Impact of Labor Unions on the Rate and Direction of Technological Innovation* (Washington DC: National Technical Information Service, 1979).

Meiksins, Peter, "'Labor and Monopoly Capital' for the 1990s: A Review and Critique of the Labor Process Debate" *Monthly Labor Review*, Special Issue: Commemorating Harry Braverman's 'Labor and Monopoly Capital,' (November 1994).

Melman, Seymour, *Decision-Making and Productivity* (Oxford: Blackwell, 1958).

Melman, Seymour, *Profits Witout Production* (Philadelhpia: University of Pennsylvania Press, 1987).

Merleau-Ponty, Maurice, *Adventures of the Dialectic* (Evanston: Northwestern University Press, 1964).

Milkman R. and D. Stevens, "The Anti-concessions Movement in the UAW," *Socialist Review*, no. 65, 1982.

Miscimarra, Philip A., *The NLRB and Managerial Discretion: Plant Closings, Relocations, Subcontracting, and Automation* (Philadelphia: University of Pennsylvania Press, 1983)

Mishel, Larry and Paula Voos (eds), *Unions and Economic Competitiveness* (Armonk, N.Y.: M.E. Sharpe, Inc., 1991).

Mithcell, Brian R., *International Historical Statistics: the Americas 1750-1988* (New York: Stockton Press, 2nd. ed., 1993).

Moberg, David, "Prudent Militancy", *In these Times* (10-16 October, 1984).

Montgomery, David, *Workers' Control in America* (New York: Cambridge University Press, 1979).

Motor Vehicle Manufacturers Association of the U.S., *World Motor Vehicle Data, 1990* (Detroit: MMVA, 1990).

Motor Vehicle Manufacturers Association of the U.S., *Motor Vehicle Facts & Figures* (Detroit: MMVA, various years).

Murphy Kevin, *Technological Change Clauses in Collective Bargaining Agreements* no. 81-82 (Washington, DC: Department for Professional Employees, AFL-CIO 1981).

Naples, Michelle I., "Industrial conflict and its implications for productivity growth", *American Economic Review* (February 1981).

National Research Council, *The Competitive Status of the U.S. Auto Industry*, National Academy Press, 1982.

Neimark, Marilyn Kleinberg, *The Hidden Dimensions of Annual Reports: Sixty Years of Social Conflict at General Motors* (New York: Marcus Wiener Publishing, Inc., 1992).

Noble, David F., *Forces of Production: A Social History of Industrial Automation* (New York: Knopf, 1984).

O'Connor, James, *The Fiscal Crisis of the State* (New York: St. Martin's Press, 1973).

OECD, *OECD Employment Outlook* (Paris: OECD, July 1991).

OECD *Foreign Trade by Commodity 1992* vol. 1 (Paris: OECD, 1992)

OECD, *The OECD STAN Database for Industrial Analysis* (Paris: OECD, 1995).

Offe, Claus and Helmuth Wiesenthal, *Two Logics of Collective Action Theoretical Notes on Social Class and Organizational Forms.* In Maurice Zeitlin (ed.), *Political Power and Social Theory* (Greenwich, CT.: JAI Press, 1980).

Offe, Claus, "The attribution of public sttus to interest groups: observations on the West German case," in Suzanne Berger (ed.), *Organizing Interests in Western Europe* (Cambridge: Cambridge University Press, 1981).

Offe, Claus *Contradictions of the Welfare State*, ed. John Keane (Cambridge, Mass.: MIT Press, 1984).

Oshima, Keichi, "The High Technology Gap: A View from Japan," *Europe/America* (6: 1987).

Panitch, Leo *Working Class Politics in Crisis: Essays on Labour and the State* (London: Verso, 1986).

Pappi, Franz Urban, "The West German party system," *West European Politics* (October 1984).

Parker, Mike *Inside the Circle: A Union Guide to QWL* (Boston: Labor Notes Book, 1986).

Parker, Mike and Jane Slaughter, *Choosing Sides: Unions and the Team Concept* (Boston: South End Press, 1988).

Pascoe, T.J. and R.J. Collins, "UAW-Ford Employee Development and Training Program: Overview of Operation and Structure," *Labor Law Journal* 36: 519-526, 1985.

Piore, Michael J., "The technological foundations of dualism and discontinuity", in Suzanne Berger and Michael J. Piore (eds), *Dualism and Discountinuity in Industrial Societies* (Cambridge: Cambridge University Press, 1980).

Piore, Michael J. and Charles F. Sabel, *The Second Industrial Divide: Possibilities for Prosperity* (New York: Basic Books, 1984).

Pizzorno, Alessandro, "Political exchange and collective identity in industrial conflict," in Colin C. Crouch and Alessandro Pizzorno (eds.), *The Resurgence of Class Conflict in Western Europe since 1968* vol. 2 (New York: Holmes & Meier).

Polanyi, Karl, *The Great Transformation: The Political and Economic Origins of Our Time* (Boston: Beacon Press, 1944.

Poulantzas, Nicos, *State, Power, Socialism* (London: Verso, 1978).

Press and Information Office of the Federal Republic of Germany, *Employers and Unions* (Bonn: Press and Information Office, 1981).

Przeworski, Adam, "Social Democracy as a Historical Phenomenon," *New left Review*, no. 122 (August 1980).

Przeworski, Adam, *Capitalism and Social Democracy* (Cambridge: Cambridge University Press, 1986).

Przeworski, Adam, "Class, Production and Politics: A Reply to Burawoy," *Socialist Review* No. 2, 1989.

Quinn, Dennis Patrick Jr., *Restructuring the Automobile Industry: A Study of Firms and States in Modern Capitalism* (New York: Columbia University Press, 1988).

Rehder, Robert R., "Is Saturn Competitive?" *Business Horizons* (March/April 1994).

Reuther, Victor, *The Brothers Reuther and the Story of the UAW* (Boston: Houghton Mifflin, 1976).

Robson, Janet and Jean-Louis Barsoux, "Executive power pay," *International Management* (May, 1993).

Ross, G., Lange, P. and M. Vannicelli, *Unions, Change and Crisis: French and Italian Union Strategy and the Political Economy, 1945-1980* (London: George Allen & Unwin, 1984).

Roth, Guenther and Claus Wittich, *Max Weber: Economy and Society* (Berkeley: University of California Press, 1978).

Ruback, Robert and Maurice Zimmerman, "Unionization and Profitability: Evidence from the Capital Market," *Journal of Political Economy*, vol. 92, no. 6 (December 1984).

Sabel, Charles F. and Jonathan Zeitlin, "Stories, Strategies, Structures: Rethinking Historical Alternatives to Mass Production," in idem (eds.), *Worlds of Possibility: Flexibility and Mass Production in Western Industrialization* (Cambridge, Mass.: Cambridge University Press, forthcoming).

Sabel, Charles F., "The internal politics of trade unions," in Berger (ed) *Organizing Interests in Western Europe* (Cambridge, Mass.: Cambridge University Press, 1981).

Sabel, Charles F., *Work and Politics: The Division of Labor in Industry* (Cambridge, Mass.: Cambridge University Press, 1982).

Sabel, Charles F., "A Fighting Chance: Stuctural Change and New Labor Strategies," *International Journal of Political Economy* (Fall 1987).

Sabel, Charles F., "Learning by Monitoring: The Institutions of Economic Development," (Cambridge, Mass.: MIT, 1993).

Samuelson, Paul A., *Economics* (New York: McGraw-Hill, 1973)

Saporito, B. "The Revolt Against 'Working Smarter,'" *Fortune* magazine, July 2, 1987, pp. 58-65.

Sartori, Giovanni, "From the Sociology of Politics to Political Sociology," in Seymour Martin Lipset (ed.), *Politics and the Social Sciences* (London: Oxford University Press, 1969).

Savoie, Ernest J. "The New Ford-UAW Agreement: Its Worklife Aspects," *Work Life Review* Issue 1, 1982.

Schmitter, Philippe C., "Still the century of corporatism?" *Review of Politics* (January 1974).

Schmitter, Philippe C. and Gerhard Lehmbruch, *Trends Toward Corporatist Intermediation* (New York: Sage, 1979).

Shaiken, Harley, *Work Transformed: Automation and Labor in the Computer Age* (New York: Holt, Rinehart and Winston, 1984).

Shimada, Haruo, "Japan's Postwar Industrial Growth and Labor-Management Relations," in Lloyd G. Reynolds, Stanley H. Masters, Coletta H. Moser (eds), *Readings in Labor Economics and Labor Relations* (Englewood Cliffs, NJ: Prentice-Hall, 1986).

Slichter, Sumner, *The Turnover of Factory Labor* (Appleton: 1919).

Slichter, Sumner, *Union Policies and Industrial Management* (Washington, D.C.: The Brookings Insitution, 1941).

Slichter Sumner, James Healy, and Robert E. Livernash, *The Impact of Collective Bargaining on Management* (Washington, DC: The Brookings Institution, 1960).

Sloan, Alfred P., *My Years With General Motors* (Garden City, N.Y.: Doubleday, 1964).

Smith, Rand W., "Paradoxes of plural unionism: CGT-CFDT relations in France", *West European Politics* (January 1981).

Smith, W. Rand, "State, Labor, and Corporatism in France: Lessons of Industrial Restructuring," paper presented at the conference "A Century of Organized Labor in France: A Union Movement for the Twenty-First Century," Columbia University and New York University, February 9-10, 1996.

Solomon, Janet Stern, "Union Responses to Technological Change: Protecting the Past or Looking to the Future?" *Labor Studies Journal* (Fall 1987).

Sorge, Arndt and Wolfgang Streeck, "Industrial Relations and Technical Change: The Case for an Extended Perspective," in Hyman and Streeck (eds), *New Technology and Industrial Relations* (Oxford: Basil Blackwell, 1988).

Soskice, David, "Reconciling Markets and Institutions: The German Apprenticeship System," in Lisa M. Lynch (ed.), *Training and the Private Sector: International Comparisons* (Chicago: The University of Chicago Press, 1994).

Stone, Katherine Van Wezel, "The Post-War Paradigm in American Labor Law," *Yale Law Journal*, 90, 7, 1981.

Streeck, Wolfgang, "Neo-Corporatist Industrial Relations and the Economic Crisis in West Germany," in John H. Goldthorpe (ed.) *Order and Conflict in Contemporary Capitalism: Studies in the Political Economy of Western European Nations* (New York: Oxford University Press, 1984).

Streeck, Wolfgang, *Industrial Relations in West Germany: A Case Study of the Car Industry* (New York: St. Martin's Press, 1984).

Streeck, Wolfgang, "Industrial Relations and Industrial Change: the Restructuring of the World Automobile Industry in the 1970s and 1980s," *Economic and Industrial Democracy*, vol. 8, 1987.

Streeck, Wolfgang, Josef Hilbert, Karl-Heinz von Kevelaer, Frederike Maier, and Hajo Weber, *The Role of the Social Partners in Vocational Training in the Federal Republic of Germany* (Berlin: CEDEFOP, 1987).

Streeck, Wolfgang, "Successful Adjustment to Turbulent Markets: the Automobile Industry" in Peter J. Katzenstein (ed), *Industry and Politics in West Germany: Toward the Third Republic* (Ithaca, NY: Cornell University Press, 1989).

Taira, Koji and Solomin B. Levine, "Japan's Industrial Relations: A Social Compact Emerges," in Harvey Juris, Mark Thompson, and Wilbur Daniels (eds) *Industrial Relations in a Decade of Economic Change* (Madison, WI., Industrial Relations Research Association, 1985).

Thelen, Kathleen, "Union Structure and Strategic Choice: The Politics of Flexibility in the German Metalworking Industries" presented at the 1988 Meetings of the A.P.S.A., Washington DC, September 1-4, 1988. Also in Michael Golden, Peter Lange and Jonas Pontusson (eds) *Unions and Economic Change in the 1980s.*

Thelen, Kathleen, *Union of Parts: Labor Politics in Postwar Germany* (Ithaca, NY: Cornell University Press, 1991).

Tolliday, Steven and Jonathan Zeitlin (eds) *The Automobile Industry and its Workers: Between Fordism and Flexibility* (Cambridge: Polity Press, 1986).

Troy, Leo, "The rise and fall of American trade unions: the labor movement from FDR to RR," in S.M. Lipset (ed.), *Unions in Transition: Entering the Second Century* (San Franciso: ICS Press, 1986).

Turner, Lowell, *Democracy at Work: Changing World Markets and the Future of Labor Unions* (Ithaca, N.Y.: Cornell University Press, 1991).

Turner, Lowell, "Prospects for Worker Participation in Management in the Single Market" in Lloyd Ulman, Barry Eichengreen and William T. Dickens (eds.), *Labor and an Integrated Europe* (Washington, D.C.: The Brookings Institution, 1993).

"UAW", *Socialist Review* 65 (1982).

U.S. Bureau of the Census, *Statistical Abstracts of the United States* (Washington, DC: GPO, various years).

U.S. Bureau of Economic Analysis, *National Income and Product Accounts, 1929-1958* (Washington, DC: US Bureau of Commerce, GOP, 1959).

U.S. Bureau of Economic Analysis, *National Income and Product Accounts, 1959-1988* (Washington, DC: US Bureau of Commerce, GOP, 1989).

U.S. Bureau of Industrial Economics, Department of Commerce, *U.S. Industrial Outlook, 1995*, (Washington, D.C.: G.P.O., 1995).

U.S. Bureau of International Labor Affairs, Deparment of Labor, *Foreign Labor Trends: Germany* (Washington, D.C.: G.P.P., 1992).

U.S. Bureau of Labor Statistics, "Collective Bargaining in the Motor Vehicle and Equipment Industry," *BLS Reports, No. 574* (September 1979) (Washington, D.C.: GPO, 1979).

U.S. Bureau of Labor Statistics, *Major Collective Bargaining Agreements: Plant Movement, Interplant Transfer, and Relocation Allowances*, Bulletin no. 1425-20 (Washington, DC: GPO, 1981).

U.S. Bureau of Labor Statistics, *A BLS Reader on Productivity*, Bulletin 2171 (June 1983) (Washington, D.C.: GPO, 1983).

U.S. Bureau of Labor Statistics, *Employment, Hours, and Earnings: United States, 1909-1990, v. I*, Bulletin no. 2370 (Washington, DC: GPO, 1991).

U.S. Bureau of Labor Statistics, *Employment, Hours, and Earnings: United States, 1909-1994, v. I*, Bulletin no. 2445 (Washington, DC: GPO, 1994).

U.S. General Accounting Office, *Dislocated Workers: Local Programs and Outcomes Under the Job Training Partnership Act*, (GAO/HRD-87-41) (Washington, D.C.: U.S. Government Printing Office, 1987.

Voos, Paula B., "The Influence of Cooperative Programs on Union-Management Relations, Flexibility, and Other Labor Relations Outcomes," *Journal of Labor Research* (Winter 1989).

Wall Street Journal, "Many Officers at UAW Locals Voted Out, Portending Problems in GM Labor Talks", (30 May, 1984).

Walton, Richard E., "From control to commitment in the workplace," *Harvard Business Review* (March-April 1985).

Walton, Richard E., "From Control to Commitment: Transforming Work Force Mangement in the United States," in Kim B. Clark, Robert H. Hayes, and Christopher Lorenz (eds), *The Uneasy Alliance: Managing the Productivity-Technoogy Dilemma* (Cambridge: Harvard Business School Press, 1985).

Ward's Auto World, 1995 (Nexis: Ward's Communications Inc., 1995).

Ward's Automotive Yearbook, 1994 (Southfield, MI.: Ward's Communications, 1994).

Watanabe, Susumu (ed), *Microelectronics, Automation and Employment in the Automobile Industry* (New York: John Wiley & Sons, 1987).

Weisskopf, Thomas, David M. Gordon, and Samuel Bowles, "Hearts and Minds: A Social Model of U.S. Productivity Growth," *Brookings Papers on Economic Activity*, 2, 1983.

Weitzman, Martin, *The Share Economy* (Cambridge, Mass.: Harvard University Press, 1984).

Wells, Donald, *Empty Promises: QWL Programs and the Labor Movement* (New York: Monthly Review Press, 1987).

Williams, Karel, Colin Haslam, John Williams, Tony Cutler, Andy Adcroft, Johal Sukhdev, "Against Lean Production," *Economy and Society* (August 1992).

Williamson, Oliver E., *The Economic Institutions of Capitalism* (Detroit: Free Press, 1985).

Wilson D.C, R.J. Butler, D. Cray, D.J. Hickson and G.R. Mallory, "The limits of trade union power in organizational decision making", *British Journal of Industrial Relations* 20 (March[?] 1982).

Womack, James P., Daniel T. Jones, and Daniel Roos, *The Machine that Changed the World: The Story of Lean Production* (New York: Harper Perennial, 1990).

Wood, Stephen and John Kelly, "Taylorism, responsible autonomy and management strategy", in Stephen Wood (ed), *The Degradation of Work?* (London: Hutchinson & Co., 1982).

Wood, Stephen (ed), *The Degradation of Work? Skill, Deskilling and the Labour Process* (London: Hutchinson & Co., 1982).

Woodruff, David, "Saturn: GM finally has a real winner," *BusinessWeek* (August 17, 1992).

Zimbalist, Andrew (ed), *Case Studies on the Labor Process* (New York: Monthly Review Press, 1979).

Index